# The Complete Idiot's Reference Card

*cut here*

## Be Message-Based SM

1. Identify the context.

   In one sentence, why are you making this presentation? What situation exists or has occurred that brings everyone to this presentation today?
2. Identify the message.

   In one sentence, what must the listeners know, think, or do when you have completed your presentation?
3. Create the roadmap.

   What topics and facts must you present to make sure the listeners can know, think, or do what you want them to know, think, or do?
4. Write a message statement for each "chunk" in the roadmap.

   Add just enough data to support the message.

   Stop adding facts once your point is clear.

   Sequence facts so that the most important ones are first.

   Sequence facts so that the bigger concepts are presented before the smaller ones.

   Present the facts chronologically only if chronology is important.
5. Support your Message-based SM presentation with visual aids that have message titles.

   Use visual aids to help listeners remember and understand content or to recognize that you're speaking about a new topic.

## Persuade with an Alternative Structure

1. Why should I listen to you?
2. What is going on?
3. What should we do?
4. How do we do that?
5. What will doing this cost us?
6. What resources must we provide for this?
7. What benefits will we receive?
8. How do I know we'll receive those benefits?
9. What could go wrong?
10. What do you want me to do? Why?
11. What do you want from me right now?

## Your Delivery Says You're Professional and Credible

| | |
|---|---|
| Use Focus: | Stand "centered" |
| | Use sincere eye contact |
| Use Energy: | Use your full voice |
| | Pronounce vowels completely and clearly |
| | Let gestures be spontaneous and "in the window" |

### Remember the one rule of presenters:

Do not talk unless you have eye contact!

alpha
books

## Establish Your Message Plan

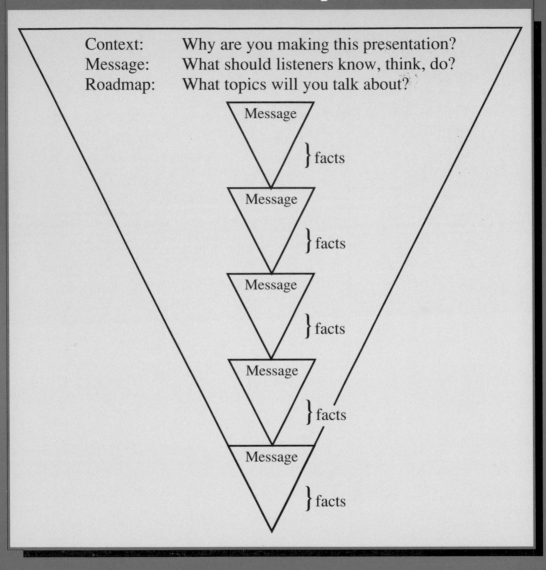

Context:   Why are you making this presentation?
Message:   What should listeners know, think, do?
Roadmap:   What topics will you talk about?

Message
} facts

Message
} facts

Message
} facts

Message
} facts

Message
} facts

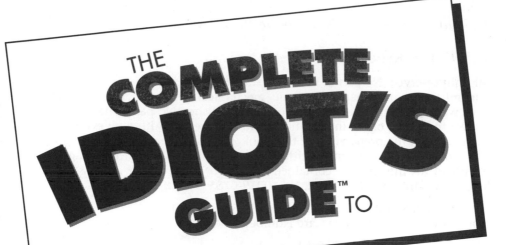

# THE COMPLETE IDIOT'S GUIDE™ TO

# Successful Business
# Presentations

*by Lin Kroeger*

## alpha
## books

A Division of Macmillan General Reference
A Simon & Schuster Macmillan Company
1633 Broadway, New York, NY 10019

*To Alan and Janice Olivia. You're the ones!*

## ©1997 Lin Kroeger

International Standard Book Number: 93-56761-168-0
Library of Congress Catalog Card Number: 97-07118

99  98  97      8  7  6  5  4  3  2  1

Interpretation of the printing code: the rightmost number of the first series of numbers is the year of the book's printing; the rightmost number of the second series of numbers is the number of the book's printing. For example, a printing code of 97-1 shows that the first printing occurred in 1997.

*Printed in the United States of America*

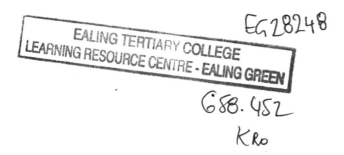

**Publisher**
*Theresa Murtha*

**Editorial Manager**
*Gretchen Henderson*

**Development Editor**
*Faithe Wempen*

**Production Editor**
*Beth Mayland*

**Cover Designer**
*Mike Freeland*

**Illustrator**
*Judd Winick*

**Designer**
*Glenn Larsen*

**Indexer**
*Eric Brinkman*

**Production Team**
*Angela Calvert*
*Cynthia Fields*
*Daniela Raderstorf*
*Rowena Rappaport*

# Contents at a Glance

# Contents

## Part 3: Support—Space and Visual Aids      103

## 10   Be Sure the Room is Presentation-Friendly     105

## 11   Visual Support Helps Deliver the Message     117

## Part 4: Getting Ready

# Foreword

Does the prospect of standing up in front of a group of people to make a presentation excite you, or does it scare you to death? I've seen frequent reference made to an opinion survey showing that many people are more frightened of public speaking than of death itself. I'm not sure I buy that, but the universal nightmare of being in front of a group of people with no slides, no notes, and no clothes suggests that if it's not on par with dying, it's at least up there with snakes and spiders.

Anyone who does a lot of speaking can tell the story of their most profound learning experience (a.k.a. disaster at the podium). Mine was after a simple luncheon talk for several hundred Rotarians. Over lunch, the person who was to introduce me warned me that other elements of the program might run long, and I should be prepared to cut back 10 minutes if necessary, since the group always ended precisely at 1:00. While pretending to enjoy my lunch, I mentally traced read lines through dispensable sentences, and visualized myself delivering what survived in double time.

I was introduced at 12:35, but I was so tense I didn't check the time. I raced through my newly abbreviated presentation, forgetting a cardinal rule of public speaking—slow down and breathe. As I neared the conclusion, I looked at my watch and realized with horror that it was not yet 12:45, and I was expected to captivate the Rotarians until 1:00. Not having had the benefit of Lin Kroeger's wonderful book, I did what, for a speaker, is worse than sleeping with snakes and spiders; I froze at the microphone. "I'm sorry," I said, "I don't have anything else to say. Are there any questions?"

Silence. It seemed to last forever. Finally, from the back of the room someone hollered the words, "Never fear, never quit!" It's only time in my life I regretted having written a book by that title.

Fortunately, the gaffe was not fatal. I've since given hundreds of presentations for thousands of people, including quite a few Rotary meetings. The more I speak, however, the more I appreciate this paradox: Anyone who has something important to say can learn the skills and tools of effective presentation, but no matter how good you get you can always learn more from reading a book like this one.

*The Complete Idiot's Guide to Successful Business Presentations* is an indispensable resource for anyone who ever presents information or ideas in a business setting.

Are you in sales? Actually, that's a trick question. There are only two kinds of people in this world: Those who know they're in sales, take it seriously, and learn how to sell effectively; and those who don't think they're in sales, don't take the effort to learn how to sell their ideas and dreams effectively, and then wonder why nothing in their lives ever seems to work out. Anybody who is in sales will benefit from learning how to conceptualize, research, and prepare an effective question.

Are you a leader? Another trick question! Of course you are. Whether it's at work, in the family, or in a community group, we're all leaders. The ideas and information included in this book can help you do a better job of selling your ideas to a committee at work, asking the boss for a promotion, or kicking off a family meeting.

*The Complete Idiot's Guide to Business Presentations* is an indispensable resource. Read it through from cover to cover, then refer back to pertinent chapters as needed. After all, you never know when the Rotary might call.

—Joe Tye

*Joe Tye is a frequent speaker on organizational effectiveness and personal success, and is the author of* Never Fear, Never Quit: A Story of Courage and Perseverance.

# Introduction

Making business presentations is a challenge for each of us at some point. You might be an excellent presenter, but the day isn't the best of your career. You might be brand new in business and don't really know what to do to succeed. You might be nervous every time you speak to groups. Or you might not be prepared for the presentation, but you have to make it anyway.

Remember, though, that you can always be an effective presenter if you decide to be successful. You should practice, but you can always follow the one rule of presentations (Chapter 20) and look professional and prepared. You can choose to behave nervously, or you can choose to appear confident (Chapters 4, 15, 20, 21). You have to decide whether the most important person in the room is you or the listener.

If you use the Message-based$^{SM}$ approach to organizing your material to be strategically focused, and if you use the guidelines for how to deliver the presentation, you'll appear confident, prepared, and professional. Chapter 19 will help you understand why behaving confidently can make you look professional, even if you're dying inside.

This book will give you the information and guidelines you need to be effective; all the advice comes from the experience of a business presenter who forgot her name at her very first business presentation! You see, nervousness is something we all have to manage, and some of us learn the hard way that it is better to manage it than to let it win. This book is the easy way.

## How This Book Is Organized

This book's chapters are broken down into six parts that correspond to the phases that a new presenter goes through in planning and executing a presentation:

Part 1 of the book will help you understand the role of presentations in business and the many kinds of presentations business people make. They're a great way to get people thinking about important ideas.

Part 2 will show you how to get control over all the information you want to present and organize it to support a key strategic message. It will also give you an alternative structure for organizing persuasive presentations.

Part 3 reviews how to set up the room to use space and visual aids to your advantage. It will show you how to prepare visual aids and when to use handouts.

Part 4 will help you get ready, from what to wear to how to manage your nervousness. And if you'll be attending a pre-presentation social get-together, you'll find some advice on what to eat and drink, or what not to eat and drink, before you have to speak.

Part 5 talks through the challenges that most people think of as "presenting." You do have to show up, and you do need to use effective skills so that the listeners can hear and understand you. This section will describe what's expected of you and how to meet those expectations. This is the part that helps you look great even if you'd rather swim with sharks than present.

If you're using slides, or if you're presenting to multiple conference sites, you'll find some suggestions on how to manage machinery and technology, too. This section will also give you reliable guidelines on how to use humor and manage hecklers.

Part 6 will show you how to manage question and answer sessions and how to learn from each presentation. You have to follow up on all the commitments you make during the presentation. You also have to let the listeners ask you questions so you'll have to know what to do with questions to continue to behave confidently. You'll also need to review what you did well and what you can do better. Each time you present, you can learn how to increase your effectiveness for the next public conversation.

Your value in business is having excellent and relevant ideas, but no one will know you've got them unless you present them. So look at every presentation as a chance to make a contribution to the business. Consider every presentation an important conversation with other people who want to make a difference.

Focus on the listeners and help them understand the message and you'll be the presenter that everyone describes as "clear, interesting, and always making important and difficult ideas easy to understand and implement."

## Special Helps

There are a number of special elements in this book that can help you pick up on the material presented more easily.

> **Consider This**
>
> If you want a discussion or example, review the information in these boxes. There's a lot to learn from other people, and these real stories and discussions will help you appreciate how easy it is to be an effective presenter and how to avoid making common mistakes.

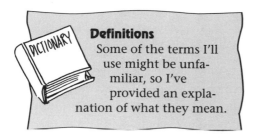

**Definitions**
Some of the terms I'll use might be unfamiliar, so I've provided an explanation of what they mean.

**Handy Hint**
When there's a great idea that can really help you, you'll find it in this sidebar.

**Beware**
This sidebar will show you how to avoid making a mistake.

# Getting More Help

If you want to find answers to many presenters' commonly asked questions, you can order *A Pragmatist Answers Questions on How to Prepare and Deliver Effective Presentations,* available for $10 by calling (212) 397-0166 during normal business hours.

# Acknowledgments

A lot of clients have helped me grow by asking me to help them excel as leaders and presenters. We've learned together that communicating the strategic value of an idea is more important than showcasing it, that connecting with each listener is more powerful than having a gorgeous speaking voice, that caring whether the message is clear and relevant is more important than having lots of facts.

Special thanks to all my clients, especially Ted Doyle, for asking tough questions and expecting great answers; to Louis Catron for teaching me how integral ideas are to communication and that a pretty package of communication skills is worthless if there's no substance in the thought being communicated; to my family for their endless willingness to let me keep changing and growing; to Faithe Wempen (my editor) for her advice; and to Beth Mayland, my copy/production editor, for taking care of all the details so graciously and supportively.

## Special Thanks from the Publisher

The publisher wishes to thank the Technical Reviewer, Helio Fred Garcia.

Helio Fred Garcia is a managing director at Clark & Weinstock, a management and public affairs consulting firm. He is also a seasoned executive coach on presentations, press interviews, and television interview skills. Through Clark & Weinstock and on his own he has trained hundreds of senior executives, including chief executive officers of major corporations, investment bankers, lawyers, doctors, academics, and senior officers in the U.S. armed forces. He is an adjunct associate professor of Management and Communications in the Management Institute and Undergraduate Degree Studies Program, School of Continuing Education, New York University, where he received the school's award for teaching excellence. At NYU, Fred teaches executive seminars on crisis management and business ethics and an undergraduate seminar on the intersection of politics, philosophy, and economics in business and public policy. He also trains the Management Institute faculty on classroom teaching skills. Fred received an MA in Philosophy from Columbia University, studied Classical Greek languages and literature in the Latin/Greek Institute of the City University of New York, and received a BA with honors in Politics and Philosophy from New York University.

## Servicemarks

Message-based[SM] is a servicemark of Lin Kroeger.

# Part 1
# Thinking Ahead

*Presentations are a fact of life in business. We make presentations all the time, any time anyone can see us or hear us! If you understand how common presentations are and what all the different types and styles of presentations are that you'll make during your career, you'll be able to manage each one effectively. Remember, you're not an actor, you're a business professional.*

# So You Have to Make a Presentation!

A business presentation can be a terrifying challenge for many. You have to decide what to say and how to say it, and worse, you have to stand up and say it in front of real people—often a lot of people. Real people ask questions, and many times, they just don't cooperate. They refuse to recognize that you're trying hard to be credible, they don't give you a chance to finish, and they don't consider how difficult it is to give a presentation.

What possible benefit can a presentation provide if so many people find it difficult to make an effective business presentation? And why should you have to worry about performance anxiety, especially if you specialize in an analytical field? You didn't choose business because you could make presentations!

So, you have to make a presentation, a business presentation.

But how will you get ready? When will you get ready? What will you say? What will you include? What will you leave out? How much do the listeners already know or want to hear? What kinds of visual aids will you need? How many visual aids will be needed?

Most of all, why do you have to make the presentation? Why can't you send everyone a memo or report so that you don't have to stand up in front of everyone?

# They Want an Update!

The new vice president has just arrived and wants to know about your progress on your special project. You have two hours to find out how everyone's doing, gather information on what needs to be done to complete the project on time, and create a presentation for the new vice president and the rest of her executive staff.

Or perhaps it's the end of the quarter, and the marketing group needs to know how their forecasts fared. You have a week to prepare, but the marketing group is very demanding and they've been having trouble meeting expectations. They'll want to know lots of details, all in charts, and they'll want everything in full color, with hand-outs. They're always a tough group, too, with questions, challenges, and an unwillingness to listen. They read the hand-outs ahead of time and during the presentation. You never know what issues they'll bring up next.

## Consider This

You are making a presentation anytime anyone can hear you. When you meet your supervisor at lunch and make a comment, you're presenting. When you interrupt a discussion to make a comment, you're presenting.

Or perhaps you talked about an idea last week at lunch, and the department head wants to hear more. You hadn't really thought too much more about the idea, and you were really just thinking out loud, and suddenly, she wants to hear what you've done with the idea. What profitability is possible? How much lead time will be needed? How many people will be required? How much investment is necessary?

Use the checklist that follows to help you think through how often you make presentations in your job.

How many of these situations have you encountered?

➤ You have to give a presentation you've never seen because the person who prepared it is out ill.

➤ You are at a meeting and suddenly realize, based on the discussion, that you must explain your team's project. But you hadn't planned on making a presentation, and you have no material about the project with you.

➤ You have a new boss who wants everyone to make a presentation about their job. The presentations are scheduled to begin in two days.

➤ Another department needs to know what your department does, and you're going to develop and deliver the presentation.

# What Is a Presentation?

A presentation is telling someone else something they need to hear or want to hear. Usually, presentations take place in a formal setting, but often they can take place in informal or semiformal settings. Most of the time, you make business presentations to groups of people, and you stand up while you talk to the group. Often, you use visual aids to make certain points clear and to help the listeners remember key points. Complete the worksheet on the next page to determine how formal or informal your presentation will be.

Sometimes, you'll make a presentation during a meeting when everyone is sitting. You might have slides or transparencies or be using a flipchart, but you won't have the power that comes from standing and communicating that you have some level of authority. Standing tends to convey power, and you might want to stand, but "all seated" is not an unusual presentation set-up.

You're making a presentation when you sit in a meeting and say something to the rest of the group. And you make a presentation when you're chatting informally with your business associates, maybe over lunch. In these settings, you're not usually aware that you're making a presentation, but people are evaluating you and your comments, so it is, in fact, a presentation.

**Definition**
A **business presentation** is the presenting of ideas to an individual or to a group. The presenter usually stands, although sometimes he sits. Remember, if someone is listening to you, you are making a presentation.

**Definition**
A **flipchart** is an easel that holds a pad of newsprint. It's easy to write ideas on a flipchart and then "flip" the paper over the top of the easel and start on a new page. The flipchart pages are often gathered after a meeting and someone summarizes the information on them into a memo or meeting notes handout.

5

## HOW FORMAL IS YOUR PRESENTATION?

Check the boxes that apply to the presentation you plan to give. Based on the boxes you've checked, you can decide what level of formality you'll be dealing with.

### FORMAL

☐ Presenter will stand.

☐ Listeners will sit.

☐ Presenter will use visual aids, usually slides or overhead transparencies.

☐ Q&A will probably be deferred to the end of the presentation.

☐ Agenda will be sent in advance.

☐ Presenter will have time to develop and perhaps rehearse presentation and visual aids.

### SEMI-FORMAL

☐ Presenter can stand or sit, but will probably stand.

☐ Listeners will sit.

☐ Presenter might use visual aids, perhaps overhead transparencies or flipchart.

☐ Q&A will occur throughout the presentation.

☐ Agenda will probably not be sent in advance.

☐ Presenter might not have a lot of time to develop presentation.

### INFORMAL

☐ Presenter will sit or stand, but will probably sit.

☐ Listeners will sit or stand, but will probably sit. Usually whatever the presenter does, they do.

☐ Presenter might use a flipchart.

☐ Q&A will be ongoing and casual, resembling a discussion.

☐ Agenda will probably not available.

☐ Presenter will probably not spend a great deal of time preparing.

It's almost impossible not to make a presentation if you share your ideas at work in any setting. The challenge for most of us is to communicate an idea and sound intelligent and informed, even if we're nervous speaking to a group and if we're less prepared than we want to be. The risk is enormous, and the potential benefit is equally enormous. A business presentation can help win support for ideas, or it can make people think an idea is dumb.

A presentation that is clear and well-supported makes you appear prepared—ready for action. A presentation that rambles and leaves open questions makes you appear sloppy, as if you don't think very clearly and didn't do your homework.

# Why Do We Have to Make Them?

Business thrives on information and presentations share information critical to a business. Whether formal or informal, a presentation allows you to tell someone something they want to know, need to know, or even might not want to know. Although dealing with the challenges of speaking to a group and responding effectively to questions can be intimidating, a presentation gives you the opportunity to shape the information to meet the needs of the listeners so that they can truly understand what you're saying.

If you're presenting unpleasant or challenging information, a presentation can be the best format because people get to discuss your ideas rather than just reject them, as they might with a document. During a presentation, you can see what's happening, how people are reacting, and you can modify the information and your delivery.

> **Beware**
> Don't ever underestimate the surroundings of a presentation. You might think you're having a casual conversation, but someone might be listening who is judging whether you're intelligent, professional, and logical. When you're at work, you are constantly being assessed as to whether you contribute and can think clearly.

# Opportunity to Share and Jointly Examine Information

Ideally, you make a business presentation on a topic people find interesting and relevant, so the presentation is an opportunity to explore that information. It's an opportunity to review the ideas, the facts, the analysis, and everyone's opinions.

# It Helps to Get Input

When you expect an idea or information to be well-received, it's easy to prepare and deliver an effective business presentation. Well before the presentation, you can ask people for their comments and suggestions. You can also check in advance to see what questions people have, and you can put together the presentation knowing that you're answering questions and clarifying ideas that people find appealing.

When a presentation is designed to share and jointly examine information, the process can be comfortable, allowing for give and take, discussions among the listeners, and further development of the important ideas you're presenting.

## You Need to Build Belief in an Idea

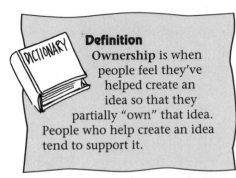

**Definition**
Ownership is when people feel they've helped create an idea so that they partially "own" that idea. People who help create an idea tend to support it.

Sometimes you'll be presenting an idea that is unfamiliar to people, but it's an appealing idea that listeners will support. The presentation gives you a chance to describe the idea and gather comments. It allows people to become involved in shaping the idea early in its existence, so that everyone feels a level of ownership.

Ownership goes a long way toward making something happen because everyone wants to see "their" idea succeed.

## You Can Showcase Your Contribution and Enthusiasm

One of the benefits of making a presentation is that you can show people your contributions. You can demonstrate your enthusiasm for an idea. Business presentations allow you to appear confident, enthusiastic, and well prepared.

## Opportunity to Share and Defend Information

Sometimes, you have to give a presentation because people need information, but they have their own opinions. In these presentations, you spend a lot of time defending your ideas, trying to integrate other people's viewpoints, and repeating key facts so that the listeners appreciate their importance. These presentations can be demanding and create terrible moments for you. But if you handle presentations well, you can appear to be in charge of ideas and of important information.

## It Helps to Get Input

When a presentation is on an unpleasant or new topic that people won't find appealing, you often have to get people's reactions first. You'll also find it useful to make sure the presentation has plenty of question and answer time, so that people can wrestle with ideas with your guidance. A presentation allows you to discuss difficult concepts and suggestions. It allows you to make recommendations and lets others discuss them enough so that often, people will begin to find the idea more appealing than it appeared at first.

## You Need to Clarify and Show Depth

During a difficult presentation, you hear what concerns people, so you can clarify the difficult points, give examples of how things will work, and demonstrate the thoroughness of your thinking on the subject. Presenting difficult ideas in writing doesn't always allow you to build your arguments exactly where they're needed. A presentation does.

Sometimes during a presentation, you realize that two people are talking intensely during a critical idea. If you have been sensitive to people's reactions throughout, and most presenters do pay close attention to people's reactions as they speak, you can check with them to see if you have been unclear about a point. Your willingness to recognize that someone is confused shows that you care about the audience. And your sensitivity to their reactions allows you to clarify a point that might otherwise have remained vague.

**Definition**
**Question and Answer, or Q&A** is the portion of the presentation, usually at the end, when listeners ask questions and the presenter responds. It's not unusual to have Q&A throughout a presentation, though. Q&A can be difficult to manage unless a presenter welcomes the questions as an opportunity to modify the presentation to suit the audience.

**Consider This**

Audiences respond very favorably to presenters who care about them. When a presenter chooses her words carefully, the listeners recognize that she values their reactions. When a presenter stops to ask if a point is clear, the listeners recognize that she cares more about clarity than about her performance.

You can only win if you spend more time worrying about the listeners' needs than about your own.

## Won't Writing Be Good Enough?

Many of us prefer to write. Almost anything is better than getting up in front of a group and talking! Writing is tough, but at least when you write, you don't have to worry about your facial expressions and your hand gestures and your timing. You don't have to look at angry or busy people and convince them you are worth listening to.

Unfortunately, with writing, if you are unclear, few people are going to call and ask for more information or to see if they've understood you. So writing can be efficient—if you're an effective writer. But writing also can be inefficient when the readers don't understand the writing or when they misinterpret your message.

# You Can't Shape a Written Argument to Fit Just So

Part of the difficulty writing creates is that you have to put the ideas in a sequence that makes sense to the reader. It's relatively easy to sequence information to meet your own needs, but you often don't know who will read a document, or how many people will read a document.

Even if the sequence of information makes sense to you, the sequence of information might be gobbledygook and ramble on for the reader. Or you might not include a key fact that would win the argument, which you consider to be a minor issue even though the reader considers it to be a major issue.

A presentation allows you to watch the listeners and immediately modify what you're saying and how you're saying it. A presentation allows you to skip a visual aid that is suddenly irrelevant or perhaps dangerous.

# Writing Takes A Lot of Time

Writing requires time, enough time to make sure that the words on the page convey the right message. First, you have to decide to write. Then you have to write the document, review it, make sure everything is correctly spelled and phrased, and then finally, send it. You can wait days and sometimes forever for a response.

Some people will read it. Some will carry it around for a long time, just in case they have time to read it. Others will avoid it by filing the document or putting it in the trash. Some ingenious people have layers of "in" boxes that allow them to pretend to themselves and others that they will read the documents in the third or fourth "in" box, as soon as they get around to it. Those are really "in" trash boxes.

## Consider This

Writing cleary depends on the connotation and denotation of every word and phrase you choose. *Denotation* is what the word actually means. Some words have many meanings, and often, people don't share the "correct" meanings other people have for the words.

*Connotation* is the "flavor" of the word, the emotional tone the word carries for a specific person. Connotation causes difficulties because no writer can control connotation. When connotation differs, the document is less easy to read and interpret accurately.

# Writing Is Formal

Writing has a lot of rules, and if you don't follow them, readers can easily misinterpret a document. And even if you do follow the rules, readers can easily misinterpret a document.

Recently, a presenter was explaining delivery requirements to a group and one of the listeners was uncertain what the presenter was demanding. Was the presenter saying there were two separate shipments with the same ship date? Or was the presenter saying there were two shipments with different ship dates? Because the listener could ask a question, the presenter could clarify that there were two separate shipments, each with the same ship date. Had the information been sent only in writing, the listener might have assumed she understood and failed to make sure the company met the shipping requirements.

> **Handy Hint**
> Always assume a reader will misinterpret a document you send him. Readers prefer to read about ideas they like, not about ideas that challenge them or their ideas.

Presenting and writing each have distinct advantages. You have to choose the appropriate one for the situation so that you meet your goal in communicating.

The advantages of presenting and writing are:

➤ Easy to modify content

➤ Easy to modify delivery if audience communicates confusion, dissatisfaction, or boredom

➤ Relatively easy to control who is going to listen to the presentation by tailoring the invitation list

➤ Can cover everything in the sequence you prefer, with the level of detail you think best

➤ Provides a permanent, unchanging record of an idea or discussion

➤ Can be delivered when you're somewhere else

Presenting and writing each present distinct disadvantages, too. When you consider which one to use to communicate, consider carefully.

The disadvantages of presenting are:

➤ You have to stand up and talk to people

➤ People can interrupt at any time, confusing you as you try to proceed sequentially through an explanation or argument.

➤ You might have to use equipment and visual aids

➤ Visual aids take time to design and prepare. Using visual aids effectively often requires practice. Visual aids machinery can malfunction.

The disadvantages of writing are:

➤ You don't know how people react and you might never receive any responses.

➤ You can't add or eliminate details and examples to meet a reader's needs.

➤ There are rules to follow, and readers often pay more attention to typographical errors and punctuation faults than to the content of a document.

➤ Lots of people are not effective readers or simply don't read, making written material useless.

Writing is valuable, and you need to be able to write well. If you're a good writer, you'll probably find that designing a presentation is relatively easy. It's just a lot easier to shape information in response to people's reactions than it is to write a perfect document and hope it gets read and interpreted correctly.

# The Least You Need to Know

➤ Business presentations are a constant throughout the business day. Expect to make business presentations frequently, and remember that if people are listening to you, you are being evaluated as a presenter. Reputations aren't necessarily lost over a coffee cup, but they can often be damaged or built.

➤ When you give a presentation, you can appear well-informed or you can appear be uninformed and unprepared.

➤ Presentations are ideal opportunities to share information and mutually shape ideas so that lots of people have ownership in the idea, giving it a better chance of success.

➤ Presentations give you the chance to make sure ideas and facts are clear and completely understood as you want them understood.

➤ Because presentations are "in person," you can modify the ideas, examples, visual aids, and delivery style as required to meet the needs of the listeners. The listeners will respond to you as you talk, and you can quickly alter the presentation if needed.

# Why Make the Presentation?

Most presentations have a persuasive element, but that doesn't mean you'll always be selling something. Usually, you're trying to persuade someone that you have relevant information or a perceptive insight that will help the business.

For example, you might be a new member of a team that has been working on a project for several months. Perhaps the team is developing a plan for reorganizing your office building. There are too many people for the space, and contractors need to decrease personal desk space. Also, the team needs to make sure that people who frequently work together are near each other. Plus, the team wants to minimize the disruption and frustration of a move.

So you join the team as an expert in organizing moves, not in organizing space. You have to make a presentation to the team about the logistics of the moving process. That's an informational presentation, but it will have persuasive elements. You'll be persuading the other team members that your information and perspective is relevant and accurate, but you'll be informing them about the logistics. You won't be selling anything.

**Beware**
Don't ever think that you're just delivering information. You are always persuading the listeners that you are well-informed and prepared. You are always sending a message about yourself, and you are always proving that your information is useful. Don't underestimate the opportunity to "win points" or "lose points" when you're making even an informal, impromptu presentation.

# Delivering Information

Among the most common presentations are ones where you have to give someone information he needs. You might have to let someone know what happened at a meeting. You might have to explain to someone how a specific event was planned and carried out. You might have to explain a change in company policy or a modification to a well-known procedure. Delivering information inevitably seems to be a minor task, and yet many people deliver information that doesn't make sense to the listeners and that makes them appear unclear.

## What's the Status?

One of the most common types of informational presentation is a status report. You need to tell a manager or other team members how a project or assignment is faring. Is everything going as planned? Is the team meeting each milestone on time? Is there a problem with the deliverables?

Status reports focus first on an overview of the status, such as, "We're on track" or "We're a month behind." Their second focus is on significant changes to the project, if any. And their third focus is on the solutions you'll be implementing to fix any problems that have occurred or could occur.

Status reports focus on:

➤ Overview of status of project

➤ Significant changes to project plan

➤ Solutions to existing or prospective problems

**Definition**
A **deliverable** is something tangible that you produce. It can be a report, a product sample, or a written procedure. A deliverable is always something that can physically be given to someone else.

Generally, status reports are brief, although projects that are difficult often generate considerable discussion. Your risk as a presenter is appearing nervous or uninformed.

# Show and Tell—Product Demonstrations

One of the more dynamic forms of informational presentations is product demonstrations. When you demonstrate a product, you usually have something to show and describe—a machine, a product of some sort, or at minimum, a pamphlet. Because you demonstrate a product by showing the listeners parts of the product or elements of the pamphlet, the listeners are often very interested in what they're seeing and less interested in you.

Product demonstrations are usually most effective if you explain how the listeners will use the item or why they need to know about the item. Avoid showing how the item works or reviewing the pamphlet until the listeners understand the item's relevance to them. It helps if you can give hand-outs of the item or the pamphlet.

Product demonstrations focus on:

➤ Use or relevance of product

➤ Sequence of how the products works

Product demonstrations can be brief or long. Your risks as a presenter are lack of clarity and appearing to lack knowledge about the thing you're demonstrating. Often, presenters who give product demonstrations fail because they don't explain the product using an action step sequence, for example: "First, open this compartment and check to ensure it is empty. Second, insert the filter and make sure the filter covers the grinder opening. Third, gently push the compartment into its holder."

# Business Plans and Strategies

The most challenging informational presentation is a business plan or a business strategy. These presentations are always persuasive but rarely permit actual selling. These presentations demand that you be thoroughly prepared with all the necessary data, an in-depth understanding of how the plan or strategy was developed, the context of the plan, and the implications of the plan. Many presenters fail when they present their business plans because they haven't considered the many ways their plan could fail.

**Handy Hint**
When you prepare a business plan, also prepare an argument against every element of that plan. Identify every reason it could fail. Then build into the plan elements that prevent those events from occurring or from causing damage. Include in your presentation brief references to ways to ensure success of the plan.

Business plan presentations are most effective when you open with a clear description of the strategic outcome of the plan. What will happen as a result of the plan, and why will the listeners care? Explain a business plan by reviewing its phases. After the listeners understand the outcome of the plan and the major phases involved, describe the resources needed to implement the plan. Then add any necessary explanations of how the plan works and why its elements make sense. The how and why should be the supporting detail, not the focus of the presentation.

Business plans focus on:

➤ Strategic outcome and advantage of the plan

➤ Major phases of implementing the plan

➤ Resources needed to implement the plan

➤ Detail about how and why the plan works

Business plans and business strategies are often lengthy presentations with extensive question-and-answer sessions. Sometimes, you can get the listeners to withhold questions until after the presentation, but more often, you find yourself responding to questions throughout the presentation. You usually have visual aids to support a business plan or strategy presentation. And always have handouts for the listeners to follow along with. Your major risks as a presenter are: appearing to have thought through the plan superficially, and not having identified the threats to the plan's success.

# Selling an Idea

Sometimes you'll need to sell an idea. You'll have thought of something that can help the organization. Or you might have been asked for your ideas on a project. When you sell an idea, you have to engage the listeners quickly in the advantages of the idea and then justify the value of the idea. Selling an idea is clearly persuasive and is most successful when you pay close attention to the listeners and respond very carefully to their questions and concerns.

**Handy Hint**
To the extent possible, schedule presentations so that the listeners don't have distractions.

When you sell an idea, prepare carefully and present the idea when people have time to pay attention. Avoid scheduling presentations that will have distractions—other meetings, imminent deadlines, start-up of vacation, or holiday.

**Consider This**

Listeners sometimes don't tell you what their concerns are. You often have to figure out that someone has a concern by reading her nonverbal behavior. Perhaps she is fidgety, or she appears to be thinking about something else. Perhaps she is looking at you and doesn't really see you.

When you're selling an idea, always pay close attention to each person's nonverbal behavior. However, don't assume that what appears to be lack of concern or attention actually is. Sometimes what you see is not what you think it is. You might need to ask the person if they need additional information.

If you think someone has a concern and that person isn't voicing it, stop the presentation and ask if anyone has any questions. If you know the listeners well, you can sometimes ask the person himself, "Joe, when I was explaining the capital we'll need for this project, you appeared concerned. Is there any information I can provide you to clarify the numbers?"

## Have I Got an Idea for You!

Let's say you work in a bank. You know a new way to produce a standard consumer report that requires fewer steps but will produce a report that is easier to read. If you make the presentation carelessly, you might offend your boss, who designed the current report and the procedure for producing it.

You're going to have to make your presentation diplomatically, showing the listeners why the new idea is of value and why the new idea is new for now and probably wasn't possible previously. You'll also have to be very clear about the appearance and contents of the new report and the procedure needed to create it.

Selling an idea focuses on:

➤ Benefits of the idea

➤ How the new idea relates to the old way

➤ Exactly what the new idea looks like

**Beware**
Always consider the people who will be affected by a new idea. If your new idea makes someone else look foolish, stupid, or old-fashioned, you will make an enemy.

Part 2 of this book talks about alternatives for structuring a persuasive presentation of this sort. But remember that what you say in the presentation of a new idea must never make previous ideas or methods seem bad.

Try to make a selling presentation brief. Engage the listeners in the idea. Be dynamic. Be persuasive. Be passionate if you can be and it's appropriate to the idea and the listeners. But don't spend a lot of time on the first presentation. Give enough detail to support the logic of the idea and give people more information in a second presentation or in a hand-out.

When you're selling an idea, you easily can sell too hard or too long, so be careful.

## You Might Want to Consider...

Sometimes you're going to want to suggest major changes in how your organization works. You're going to recognize that the company must change to grow, or must change to save money in a difficult market. Recommending major improvements and changes is risky.

What kinds of changes might you recommend? You might have figured out a way to reorganize the company to increase productivity. You might have discovered a new technology that could make your products number one in the market. You might have thought of a new methodology that can provide a competitive advantage. You might even have discovered that marketplace changes are placing your organization in jeopardy, and so your recommendations are to downsize and cut costs.

Recommending changes is usually a dramatic step, and how you explain the changes and gather champions for the recommendations can help you succeed or lead to failure.

**Definition**
A **benefit** is something that a buyer or an organization receives from a product or service. A benefit can be reduced costs, more profit, improved reputation, or better quality. Talk to the buyer about benefits that affect the buyer and also about the benefits to the organization. Whenever possible, quantify the benefits in dollars or percentages.

When you recommend major changes, you need to emphasize the opportunities and how they have grown out of past successes. You often can show how past successes depended on the ways you're trying to change. And you can then show how changing those older ways can lead to future successes. Always stress that improvements are a response to changes in the marketplace and avoid any statements that imply someone made a bad decision at some point in the past.

When recommending change focus on:

➤ Benefits of change

➤ How the change resembles past successes

➤ Environmental events that create the need to change

Keep presentations that recommend change long enough to make the need clear and to build support for the change. But don't expect the first presentation to convince the listeners that change is needed. Plan a series of presentations so that the first one provides a strategic overview and positions the changes as moving forward, not fixing the errors of the past. Use subsequent presentations to describe the logic of the changes and to build support for the changes.

Recommending changes is risky for the presenter even though potentially advantageous to the organization. Avoid over-selling, and get plenty of input from others as you structure your presentations. The more prework you do and the more you can integrate other people's insights and words, the more likely you'll be able to create support for the changes you're recommending.

**Definition**
A **feature** is a fact about the product or service. A feature might be the parts of the product, the appearance of the product, the warranty coverage, or the timing of the service. Features are not interesting unless a buyer thinks the benefits are interesting.

# Selling a Product or Service

Many people fear selling, and some people love selling. Selling a product or service is demanding, and the presenter needs to be able to handle a "no" response. When you sell, you will usually focus on the product's or service's benefits. After you have communicated the benefits, you can explain the features of the product or service.

Selling requires you to make a sales pitch focused on the needs of the buyer. Effective sales pitches often create a dialogue with the buyer so that the product or service becomes a solution to a problem, the pitch can be successful. Although we're not discussing sales techniques here, recognize that selling is a presentation with lots of questions and answers.

When selling, focus on:

➤ Benefits of the product or service

➤ Features of the product or service

**Consider This**

Selling by engaging the buyer is probably the most effective way to sell. If you use questions and answers to help the buyer describe the benefits she's looking for in the product or service and explain her needs, you then can more easily show how what you're selling provides those benefits and meets those needs.

Selling requires a great deal of resilience. You should never force a potential buyer to listen to you, but if you think the buyer is somewhat interested, be persistent. Encourage him to talk to you about his needs and priorities. Repeat the benefits of the product or service and ask him to comment on how he thinks the benefits meet his needs.

Selling is often more successful when it is less presentation and more discussion.

Chapter 9 looks at alternatives for shaping the selling presentation. But remember, the presentation itself is easier than the selling process overall.

## Selling to a Buyer Outside the Company

When you're selling to an outsider, you want to spend a lot of time on benefits first and features second. But you also should include details that show you understand how the buyer will see the benefits. Include facts about the buyer's organization and how the benefits relate to that organization.

For example, if you're selling an automated project management process, you might want to mention that one significant benefit of the process is its simplicity. Then you can describe how the buyer's organization has traditionally had to spend a lot of time and money on training when new processes have been purchased. Talk about how your process's simplicity means that the buyer won't have to also purchase training and enroll everyone in training programs. Show the buyer you understand his organization's needs.

**Handy Hint**

Do research about the buyer, the buyer's organization, and your competition. Don't go unprepared. Always include references to what the buyer's company is doing now and how your product or service can benefit them. Don't be afraid to ask the buyer whether the information you've gathered is accurate!

When selling to a buyer outside the company, focus on:

➤ Benefits of the product or service

➤ Specific elements of the buyer's organization and how the benefits relate to those elements

➤ Features of the product or service

The presentation segment of selling a product or service should be short so that you don't lose the buyer's attention. Your major risks come from focusing on features rather than on benefits and from not showing that you understand the buyer's organization. So focus on benefits and do your homework!

# Explaining Technical Information and Projects

In my experience, the most difficult presentations are the ones where you have to explain something technical to people who don't have a technical background. You want to review all the details you find relevant and interesting, and the listeners don't understand enough about the information to know why those details are relevant and interesting.

Consider the auditor who has to explain to management the problems in the new systems production and testing group. The auditor is going to know that the specific problems she saw are very relevant, without considering that management probably doesn't really understand what the production and testing group does. There's no way she can talk about production and testing and interest the management group.

She can, however, talk about the potential risks to the company of what's going on in the production and testing group. She can explain that because of certain events in production and testing, some of the software being used in the finance department might not work correctly, so the company might have errors in its financial statement.

The guideline for making a technical presentation to people who are not equally familiar with the technical area is to focus on the business implications of the technical facts. You can always add a few technical details, but try to describe the technical details using non-technical words.

When explaining technical information, focus on:

➤ Business outcomes of the technical facts

➤ Technical facts explained in non-technical terms

➤ Visual aids, hand-outs, examples, and analogies to explain the technical facts.

Keep technical presentations as short as possible unless the only listeners are the people who deal with that technical area. Technical people like lots of detail, although don't always assume they want to listen to a long presentation.

The risk you face in a technical presentation is being boring. You're boring when you present too many details, use too much technical language, and don't show how each fact you present affects a business situation.

Use the following worksheet to develop ideas for your presentations so that they are interesting and relevant to the listeners.

## Consider This

If you are presenting technical information, choose verbs that are clear and that describe the flow of events. Most nontechnical listeners can understand the action steps underlying the technical facts even if they don't understand what the "thingamajig" or "whatchamacallit" is.

For example, it's easy to understand that the body of the inductor coil disengaged from the aluminum mounting plate. It's even easier to understand that the body of the inductor coil stopped sticking to the aluminum mounting plate when the mechanical housing was stored in high humidity. But it would be difficult to understand what the presenter says if we hear, "The body of the inductor coil and the aluminum mounting plate didn't meet the rigorous testing for adhesion under humidity conditions."

Use lots of clear action verbs, and put the verbs early in the sentence if at all possible!

**EACH TYPE OF PRESENTATION CREATES CHALLENGES!**
How will you meet the challenge?  Use this worksheet to write some ideas.

**INFORMATIVE PRESENTATIONS**
*Challenge:  How can I make this presentation interesting and clear?*

Status reports
    Ideas:

Demonstrations
    Ideas:

Plans & Strategies
    Ideas:

**PERSUASIVE/SELLING PRESENTATIONS**
*Challenge:  How can I get agreement or close the sale?*

Ideas
    Ideas:

Changes
    Ideas:

Products/Services
    Ideas:

**TECHNICAL PRESENTATIONS**
*Challenge:  How can I be clear, accurate, and interesting?*

Technical Explanations
    Ideas:

Technical Demonstrations
    Ideas:

# The Least You Need To Know

➤ Presentations are usually either informative or persuasive.

➤ Every presentation has some element of persuasion because you have to convince the listeners that you are credible.

➤ Focus on the elements critical to the listeners, not on the elements you find most interesting.

➤ Make presentations shorter or longer depending on what you're trying to achieve with the presentation. Remember your purpose!

# Chapter 3

# Presentations Take Many Shapes

## In This Chapter

➤ What situations affect how you present your information?

➤ How do you determine the level of formality of a presentation?

➤ What is a multisite presentation?

Presentations take many shapes depending on how many people will be presenting, how many people will be listening, how formal or informal the presentation should be to achieve its purpose, and what your relationship is to the listeners. To increase the challenge, you may have to deal with multisite presentations in which some of the listeners—and maybe some of the presenters—participate by telephone.

And as video conferencing gets more sophisticated and becomes more common, you'll probably have to participate in video conference presentations in which some of the listeners and presenters are listening, watching, and presenting from remote locations.

**Handy Hint**
As you plan the presentation, consider the formality of your idea, the number of presenters, the size of your audience, and the location of the presentation. Then decide how formal or informal your presentation can be.

# How Many Presenters Are There?

Other presenters can simplify or complicate your job. It's always nice to have other people help; this decreases the pressure on you. But it can be very confusing for the listeners to identify the person who can answer their questions. And it can be very frustrating to present or listen when the presenters don't seem to be communicating the same message. It's also uncomfortable for everyone involved when the presenters seem to compete for control of the presentation.

## Give a Solo

Solo presentations are traditionally the most common format. One person prepares and delivers a presentation to one or more listeners. Solo presentations are easy to control because the presenter himself makes all the critical decisions before, during, and after the presentation. He can skip material, reframe information depending on the responses of the listeners, and decide how to manage the information and visual aids if something goes wrong or causes confusion.

But a solo presentation also can be very difficult for some people who don't like to stand up in front of other people and talk. Solo presentations cause some people tremendous amounts of stress. And solo presentations don't show the listeners that a group of people support the information being given.

### Consider This

If you're making a presentation by yourself and you find speaking in front of groups nerve-wracking, make the presentation interactive. Get the listeners to participate so that their focus is on the ideas and their contributions and not on you.

Interactive presentations require skill on your part. You have to remember to listen to questions and rephrase them as needed, and you have to let the audience control the flow and pace of the presentation. But it's a great way to get them involved, and involvement is a sure winner when you're trying to persuade someone to do or think something. Even better, it gets you out of the spotlight!

## Participate In a Duet

Duets also are common. Two people prepare and deliver the presentation to one or more listeners. Duet presentations require careful preparation so that both presenters know:

➤ what the other is trying to achieve

➤ what each will cover

➤ who will answer questions

➤ which person should answer which difficult or specific content questions

For example, if one of the presenters is from finance and one from marketing, what are the messages and facts each will deliver? Will the finance person answer all finance questions, and will the marketing person answer all the marketing questions? Or will the finance person answer all questions unless she refers a question to the marketing person?

When you have more than one presenter, the presentation loses flexibility. With two presenters, one of them can't suddenly decide to skip a point or resequence facts. One presenter can't interrupt the other unless they have agreed in advance that it is okay and they understand each other's signals.

But a duet presentation can also help control the stress of presenting. Armed with the appropriate decisions and preparation, the presenters know how to hand off questions to the other person. Neither has to feel stranded in front of the listeners. The presenters can speak to each other briefly—even while the audience listens—to provide each other more information for responding to a specific question.

**Handy Hint**
You don't have to have all the answers. You just have to be sure you understand all the questions and respond appropriately and quickly after the presentation has concluded. Audiences prefer an "I don't know" to an incorrect or ambiguous response.

Best of all, when there are two presenters, there is less pressure for one presenter to have all the answers.

## Play with a Trio, a Quartet, or Quintet

When a presentation team grows to three, four, or five or more people, the organization of the presentation can become very challenging. However, if a team has produced work that needs to be presented, it is better to have the team make the presentation than to suggest to the listeners that only one or two people did the work.

There is nothing wrong with having one person present the team's ideas and recommendations. But as organizations use teamwork to increase the quality of work performed, it makes good sense to have the teams present their results and make it clear that the team is the contributor.

**Consider This**

Sometimes, you'll have one or two people on the team who are outstanding presenters. It's tempting to let them face the audience each time because you know they'll succeed and that the listeners will respond favorably to the ideas the team has produced. But it's difficult for listeners to recognize a team effort when the same people always present the information.

People who present well are considered strong contributors and clear thinkers. It's advantageous to present. But teams should assess whether the team's contributions are inadvertently being considered the ideas of only one or two of the team's members.

Good presenters don't try to steal the attention and glory, but they are often given attention and glory. Set up your team presentations to give the ideas—and all of the team members—the best shot at being heard, understood, and valued.

Presentations by teams of three or more demand careful planning:

➤ Who will open the presentation?

➤ Who will present which type of information?

➤ How will the control be handed to the next presenter?

➤ Will all the presenters stand together up front all the time?

➤ Who will manage the question and answer session so that the right person responds to questions?

➤ Who will create the visual aids to ensure that they look consistent and that they are prepared well in advance?

The team must be sure to ask and answer all these questions.

For some people, the advantage of team presentations is that there is rarely time for one person to have to stand alone in front of the presenters and "perform." The disadvantage of managing the multiple performances, however, can equal or outweigh that advantage for some people in certain situations.

# How Many Listeners?

The number of listeners significantly affects how a presentation is delivered. It also can affect how many people deliver the presentation. For example, you won't want to have a team of three or more presenters give a presentation to one or two listeners unless the situation is very formal and there is no chance that the number of presenters will overwhelm the number of listeners.

## Presenting to Large Groups

You're speaking to a **large group** when the number of listeners begins to exceed 35. Some people consider 35 a large group; some consider 50 a large group; others consider a large group over 100. If you get a sense that it is difficult to see each person in the audience as a separate person, that group is probably "large" for you.

Presentations to large groups are usually more formal and require that the presenter stand, often using a microphone, a lectern, and/or a TelePrompTer. Many presenters like to use notes when speaking to a large group, and the larger the group, the more likely the visual aids will need to be slides.

## Presenting to Small Groups

For most people, a **small group** has anywhere from one to 35 listeners. Consider your audience "small" if you could sit down and hold a casual discussion without having to raise your voice.

Presenting to small groups decreases the level of formality of the situation. It's hard to be extremely formal when you could be having a casual discussion because there aren't that many people participating.

In small group presentations, presenters are sometimes standing, sometimes seated. Also, small group presentations often accommodate ongoing questions and answers.

### Consider This

When a presentation audience includes more than a conversation group but doesn't require you to use a microphone, you'll have to decide how to handle it. If the situation is relatively significant or the topic sensitive, treat the presentation as if it is to a large group. Be more formal. If the situation would benefit from casual conversation and the topic is not sensitive, treat the presentation as if it is to a small group. Be less formal.

# One-to-One Presentations

A one-to-one presentation can be formal or informal. It can be extremely easy to manage or it can be challenging. Much depends on the relationship between the two people and on the level of sensitivity of the topic.

In one presentation to a senior executive, the stakes were high. A lot of money was going to be committed, and the presentation was either going to push to get the commitment made immediately or convince the senior executive that she should wait before making any commitments of resources. So the situation was formal going in. But the presenter, equipped with slides and a tightly structured presentation, established an informal setting by sitting next to the senior executive and creating a dialogue, examining each message and fact thoroughly before moving forward.

In another presentation to an executive who had to make a decision, the presenter only had a few visual aids, planned to promote discussion, and hoped to keep the presentation informal. However, the executive was more comfortable with the formalities of a presentation and requested that the presenter stand, present the visual aids, and complete the presentation before they discussed any of the issues.

In one-to-one presentations, the presenter has to be prepared for any changes. But that's true of all presenters in all presentations, it's just that the ability to fail personally is much higher in a one-to-one presentation.

As you begin planning your presentation, consider how the number of listeners affects some of your choices, as you see in the following figure.

*Know the size of your audience and which type of visual support will be useful.*

| THE SIZE OF THE AUDIENCE AFFECTS THE LEVEL OF FORMALITY OF THE PRESENTATION AND THE CHOICE OF VISUAL AID | | | |
|---|---|---|---|
| **Preferred Visual Aid / Group Size↔** ↕ | **Large Groups** | **Medium Groups** | **Small Groups** |
| **Slides (Standard or PC-Based)** | X | X | ? |
| **Overhead Transparencies** | ? | X | X |
| **Flipchart** | - | ? | X |

| KEY | |
|---|---|
| X | Appropriate choice |
| ? | Might work |
| - | Very difficult to make work |

# How Formal Is the Presentation?

Presentations are formal or informal, although there are many levels of formality and informality. Also, presentations differ depending on whether they occur only once or regularly, such as at weekly or monthly meetings.

## It's Formal!

A **formal** presentation is often like a performance. A presenter or presenters stand in front of the listeners and the quality of delivery is very important. The presenter must be clear and dynamic, and the presentation should be carefully structured. Q&A is often held at the end of a formal presentation.

During formal presentations, the presenter(s) stands and almost always uses visual aids, generally slides or overhead transparencies. There is sometimes an agenda sent to listeners in advance. Q&A is structured and deferred to the end so that the presenter is not interrupted.

## It's Informal...

An **informal** presentation is more like a discussion than a performance. The emphasis is on sharing ideas. The presenter must be effective but the presenter does not usually have to establish and maintain the energy level by himself.

Informal presentations accommodate seated or standing presentations and usually have overhead transparencies, computer-based slides, or even flipcharts. For some informal presentations, there will be an agenda sent in advance. For others, the agenda is announced at the beginning of the meeting or is developed as the first step during the meeting.

> **Handy Hint**
> If you can benefit from lots of discussion, keep the presentation more informal so that people are comfortable participating.

# Is This a One-Time or Regularly Scheduled Presentation?

Some presentations are one-time only, and others are regularly scheduled, such as presentations at monthly status meetings.

One-time presentations are often more formal because so much depends on making a good impression. These presentations benefit from a lot of question-and-answer time, although some people are uncomfortable if the listeners interrupt the presentation flow with questions. If you are uncomfortable being interrupted, ask the listeners to hold their questions to the end of the presentation. They will usually cooperate, although there's no guarantee.

**31**

Regularly scheduled presentations are often informal rather than formal because the context of the presentation is known and because the listeners are coworkers on a project or team. These presentations can easily be formal. For example, financial presentations are often formal even if they are part of a regularly scheduled monthly meeting. Presumably, the importance of the monthly financial information dictates for many people the use of more formality.

# Relationship to Listeners

A major factor to help determine the formality or informality of a presentation is your relationship to the listeners. Generally, you're either an insider or an outsider.

## You're an Insider

Insiders are presenting to people they know and with whom they work. An insider is usually a peer—a fellow member of the executive team, a fellow employee, a fellow supervisor. Insiders know the listeners, and the listeners know them. Consequently, presentations by insiders are less formal. Although the set-up itself might be formal, the tone of the presentation will be less formal.

If you are significantly lower or higher in your organization's hierarchy than the listeners, you are generally not considered an insider. You are considered an outsider.

## You're an Outsider

Outsiders present to people they don't know and don't work with. An outsider might be selling something to a group, sharing information at a conference, or facilitating a meeting. Outsiders create an impression as soon as they are visible, and because it is easier to manage the impression you make if you are more formal about the choices, outsider presentations are usually formal presentations.

Be sensitive to the expectations of the audience, however. Sometimes, you are an outsider presenting to a group that is in an informal setting. You'll need to appear informal while being extremely formal about your style of speaking, the clarity of your presentation, and the structuring of your presentation.

Use the following worksheet to determine the degree of formality you'll be facing in a presentation.

## HOW FORMAL IS THE PRESENTATION GOING TO BE?

*Conditions determine level of formality*
←Formal ---------- Informal→

**Need for lectern** _____ **No need for lectern**
(Notes/TelePrompTer needed)                              (no notes/minimal notes)

**Outsider** _____ **Insider**

**One-time** _____ **Regularly scheduled**

*Formality establishes how you manage your delivery of ideas*
←Formal ---------- Informal→

**Stand** _____ **Sit**

**Need projected visuals** _____ **Can use flipchart /interactivity**

**Agenda** _____ **No agenda**

### Consider This

If you are significantly lower in the hierarchy of your organization than the listeners are, you are generally considered an outsider. However, recognize that if you are significantly higher in the hierarchy of your organization than are the listeners, you will probably prepare an informal presentation. You will want the listeners to feel comfortable asking questions.

But don't underestimate the situation—it is a formal situation, and the listeners expect you to behave as an organization leader. That expectation imposes expectations of formality on the presentation.

The overall set-up might be informal, with flipcharts perhaps, and maybe with you as presenter seated. But it is a formal situation and requires formal choices when you explain ideas, when you manage questions and answers, and when you respond.

# Managing Multisite Presentations

Increasingly, presentations are made to listeners at multiple sites simultaneously. The tremendous advances in telecommunications permit us to have people at many different geographic sites participate in a presentation, listen to one, or even deliver one by telephone. The increasing sophistication and easy use—plus the decreasing costs—means video conferences are becoming almost as common as telephone conferences.

Part 5 of this book, "How Will I Ever Be Able to Stand Up There?" gives you suggestions on how to manage multisite presentations.

# Telephone Conferences

Telephone conferences are informal and are easier to manage if the number of sites and the number of participants is limited. However, it is not unusual to have a telephone conference with as many as six or seven sites listening and with as many as 20 or more people in the main meeting rooms.

Telephones are more capable of transmitting sound clearly and quickly, so that you now can participate in a telephone conference without any significant halts in the progress of the conversation.

Chapter 20, "Effective Presenters Focus," gives you some tips for managing telephone conferences.

# Video Conferences

Video conferences are often held with multiple sites and with 15 or more people in the main meeting room. Video conferences permit the various sites to share visual aids while also seeing people's nonverbal responses to statements and suggestions. As the technology improves—and it is improving rapidly—there will undoubtedly be more video conferences.

Probably the most challenging aspect of today's video conferences is the inability to have simultaneous conversation from two sites. The lag that results when the speaker at another site begins to talk can slow down the progress of the conversation enough to prevent some participants from feeling comfortable contributing. This technology is rapidly improving, however, and the lag will probably be eliminated within the next year. So expect to participate in more video conferences.

Chapter 23 will give you some suggestions on managing your participation in a video conference.

# The Least You Need to Know

➤ You have to understand the formality of the situation to shape the presentation elements effectively. Sometimes, what appears to be informal is really formal. Sometimes, what appears to be formal is really informal.

➤ Presentations differ according to the number of presenters, the number of listeners, the technology involved in the presentation, and the relationship of the presenter(s) to the listener(s).

➤ Multisite presentations are increasingly common. Managing the sites usually increases the level of formality of the presentation.

# Chapter 4

# I Didn't Go to Acting School!

**In This Chapter**

➤ How do business presentations differ from public speeches?

➤ You can trust your skills

➤ Business presentations are conversations that are clear and audible

School really doesn't prepare us for the real world of day-to-day business very well. People who attend presentation skills training constantly complain about how little they were taught about the demands and expectations of what we do every day in business.

In school, we study math or science or marketing and prepare thoroughly to analyze problems and develop solutions. But most of us probably didn't expect to spend most of our time communicating our ideas in meetings or in memos or by e-mail! Most of us didn't understand that brilliant problem analysis is useless if we can't persuade people to listen.

You spend a great deal of time in business communicating, and for many people, communicating by making business presentations is at best intimidating, and at worst, terrifying.

Business presentations usually require that you stand up in front of a group and appear well-prepared, intelligent, enthusiastic about the topic, and interested in people's questions. There are variations, but generally, making a presentation means "standing up in front of a bunch of people." You probably don't like standing up in front of people or you wouldn't be reading this book. And if you don't like standing up in front of a bunch of people, you're in good company, and you're undoubtedly wondering why the presentation course was an elective and not a requirement.

Granted, many business schools today now require that teams make presentations at the conclusion of major case studies. As a result, some people arrive in the full-time business world with some ability to develop and deliver presentations. But many of us don't. And realistically, even the practice in business school doesn't prepare us for the demands of making presentations in front of people who might make critical decisions based on how well we present.

**Handy Hint**
Think of a business presentation as a conversation with one person at a time. Focus on how well you communicate, not on how well you "perform."

The reality is that in business you make a lot of presentations, and it can be challenging to manage your own expectations of how to present as you manage the listeners.

Remember, though, the best presenters maintain a conversation with their listeners. Effective business presenters are not actors, they're communicators. You don't have to become someone else when you deliver information during a business presentation.

*It's about them, not about you.*

# Business Presentations Versus Public Speaking

This book focuses on business presentations, which are not public speaking events. Public speaking usually has a strong performance element. The audience expects to be entertained by a public speaker. Audience members expect the speaker to entertain and perhaps to tell some jokes; they expect the speaker to do most of the work by using an interesting voice, lots of movement, and probably a lot of visual aids.

One public speaker I know throws crumbled papers at the audience to keep their attention. Another has a slide show and music. Many use lots of rhetorical questions to make it appear as if there is an intense, high energy give-and-take between him and the audience. Most of the time, a public speaker orchestrates what she says, how she says it, and what she expects the audience to be doing in response to any statement or action. Most public speakers design their performance to elicit specific responses.

Public speakers are often motivational speakers who are trying to get the listeners to consider an idea or an opportunity. They're the ones brought in to inspire employees when change is imminent or when the sales group wants to reward its best salespeople. They're the ones asked to inspire us to make strong commitments to new products and new corporate campaigns and initiatives.

Public speakers generally don't have to make sure the listeners take away specific information or respond with specific action steps.

Business presenters almost always have to make sure the listeners take away specific information or respond with specific action. In fact, most of the time, the reason you make a presentation is to make sure the listeners know, think, or do something very specific that has impact on the business itself.

So where public speakers usually have to be entertaining, business presenters have to be clear, audible, relevant, and willing to discuss issues. The skills are similar, but the demands are different.

Whereas Josephine Public Speaker might be able to tell the tale of how she learned to have pride in herself, Josephine Business Presenter must convince the controller that the budget increase that she is requesting is a worthwhile investment for the company to make. Where Josephine Public Speaker can pace around the stage that she's standing on and tell amusing stories about her life, Josephine Business Presenter must stand near the computer projecting her slides to explain the validity of her request for an increased budget.

It's nice, it's even preferable, to have a business presenter be interesting to listen to and demonstrate great vocal skill, appropriate gestures, and a lively sense of how to communicate specific ideas and examples. But it's essential that the business presenter be understood. It's crucial that the listeners hear and thoroughly consider the ideas he presents.

It's not crucial that a business presenter be amusing. A formal presentation requires some good performance techniques, but not a full performance.

# Hallmarks of Effective Business Presentations

To be effective as a presenter, you must make sure the listeners hear and understand you, so you must be clear and audible. You must be able to demonstrate that your ideas are relevant to the listeners and you must be able to discuss the ideas when someone asks a question.

When Tom mumbles and spends a lot of time staring at the screen while showing his audience his visual aids, people don't listen. The listeners can certainly figure out that Tom is far more worried about his slide than about his listeners.

What is clear? Listeners expect you to pronounce words completely and carefully, speak in complete sentences, and present information in a sequence they can easily follow. Listeners generally don't dislike accents, but they do expect you to manage the accent to make their listening job easier. Chapter 19 gives you some suggestions about managing an accent.

What is audible? Listeners shouldn't have to work to hear you. You should speak loudly enough for everyone to comfortably hear you, and you should not speak so loudly that people think you're shouting.

Your ability to make ideas seem relevant will depend on how well you have prepared the structure of the presentation (which is discussed in Part 2). Business presenters who don't talk about the correct information in a sequence that suits the purpose of the presentation are bound to fail. An entertaining explanation of irrelevant or wrong information will not be effective!

Your ability to discuss ideas is often critical to convincing your listeners that your idea is credible. That is why the business presentation is difficult. You have to be convincing. You must appear confident, even if you don't know the answer to a question. You must have considered the objections to your ideas so that you have responses ready if someone raises objections. And you must clarify the questions asked so that everyone understands what is being discussed.

*Put the spotlight on your ideas; show-case your thinking.*

In Chapter 23, you'll have an opportunity to better understand how to deal with questions. But don't ever underestimate the power of the question and answer process to win or lose the point you want to make. Questions and answers can create a successful presentation or destroy one. Success means you communicated effectively, even if you don't win your point.

Just think about how Dale gave a brilliant presentation, well-supported with just enough of her analytical models to show that the new approach to marketing would pay off. Dale won her point. But then, the executive committee began to ask questions. Dale panicked. She was so nervous that one of the committee members would ask her to explain the one model that a consulting group had provided that she didn't pay very close attention to the questions she was actually being asked. Worse, she stopped being clear and audible as her attention wandered away from the listeners' needs.

By the end of the question and answer session, Dale's point was lost. The prior year's marketing concept was retained, and Dale's hard work was wasted. Her presentation failed because she didn't manage the question and answer session effectively, and that made the rest of the presentation appear weak.

If Dale had failed to convince the committee because they liked a different marketing approach, that would have been fine. But she clouded the value of her actual presentation with the weak management of the questions.

**Consider This**

The success of a presentation is not measured by whether you win your point. It is measured by whether the listeners thoroughly understand your point and give it a fair hearing.

Don't forget that people who communicate effectively are good listeners. One of the hallmarks of an effective business presenter is that he listens to the audience.

**Beware**

The true challenge to a business presenter is being a good listener. It's pretty easy to tell people something. It's difficult to "hear" their responses.

When you listen to the audience, you are aware of their responses to everything you say or do. You see people frowning or laughing. You see people daydreaming or falling asleep. You see people looking confused or shocked. You also hear what they say when they ask a question and remain aware of how others respond to the question and to your answer.

The requirement to listen carefully and respond appropriately is probably the most difficult challenge a business presenter faces. The actual delivery of information in front of a group is relatively easy.

## The Hallmarks of Public Speaking

Effective public speakers must do a great deal more than be sure listeners can hear and understand them. They must certainly be clear and audible, but they must also be exciting and engaging. The listeners must want to listen to them as much for their styles as for their subjects. There is a great expectation that the public speaker will be dramatic. So the public speaker is more of an actor than is the business presenter.

Luckily, most of you will not have to be great actors, just clear and logical presenters of relevant business ideas and data.

A public speaker must make sure her comments are relevant to the listeners, but she will rarely be worried about the implementation of her ideas. In fact, most public speakers focus on communicating ideas and not on requesting action. But most business presenters want the listeners to do something. They are seeking funding or staffing for projects they want to work on, so they are looking for money and/or people.

Public speakers usually want the listeners to think about something, to take away a concept, such as "You can win if you want," "You are only as good as your last great idea," or "Leaders are people who have complete lives." Public speakers generally don't have the luxury of taking audiences through precise logic and detailed analyses of the financial position of a project.

Think about public speakers you have listened to. They have great examples. They often have great slides or videos that they use to demonstrate ideas. They use quotations to get you thinking. They also often talk rapidly with a lot of vocal variations. They're loud for a while, then soft. They speak quickly, then they slow down.

Also, where a business presenter has to be a good listener, a public speaker usually doesn't have to listen extensively. Yes, if you make a public speech you should be able to recognize that the audience is restless or unhappy and adapt to their needs, but it's not nearly as difficult to respond to a restless audience as it is to listen carefully to the audience of a business presentation.

If you get frustrated by having to give a public speech and you keep thinking, "But I didn't go to acting school, I went to business school!" you'll get a lot of sympathy. It can be very difficult to entertain an audience, and there are lots of skills needed to do it well. But the typical business presenter is usually quite well-equipped to meet the listeners' expectations.

## Every Day, You Use Presentation Skills

If you didn't go to acting school and you think making a business presentation is a major challenge, remember that you use the basic skills of a presenter every day. Every single day that you go to work, you have to communicate with people. You know how to walk and how to sit. You know how to look at people and listen to them. You know how to say what you want to say. And whether you believe it or not, you already use the gestures you need.

Basically, you are already walking and talking! You are already using eye contact. You are already gesturing. You don't have a lot of new skills to learn, you just need to understand how to have a conversation with an audience by using the skills you have and use daily.

**Handy Hint**
If you think you don't gesture, have someone videotape you during an informal meeting. Everyone gestures to some degree, and effective business presenters use their natural patterns of gesturing. They might have to slightly modify their natural patterns, but they don't design new patterns or rehearse their gestures.

## You Persuade People to Listen Every Day

Being an effective business presenter has two components, the physical one of being heard and the substantive one of being understood. But you persuade people to listen every day. You share ideas with coworkers. You discuss ideas during lunch. You raise concerns with your supervisor.

You already know how to persuade people to listen to you, and you're probably very effective at getting people to believe your ideas are relevant. You know this already because it's unlikely you're employed if you're unable to persuade. And you know this because you go to work every day and make the right things happen. You can't be effective at work if you don't know how to persuade people to listen to you.

## You Share Information at Meetings All the Time

Do you go to meetings? If not, you have the best job in the country, and a lot of people would like to have it, so don't tell!

Meetings are a reality of the day-to-day work environment. And the more business has teams, the more business will take place during meetings. Meetings are scheduled all the time and are about sharing information and getting people to do things. So, if you go to meetings, you already know how to share information.

Perhaps the best way to think about a business presentation is to consider it a conversation during which you share information. When you have shared the information, people know, think, or do what you want them to know, think, or do (or at least you get a clear "no" because they've understood you).

### Consider This

A business presentation is a conversation. If the business presentation is effective, the listeners know, think, or do what you wanted them to know, think, or do. At minimum, they have understood what you wanted and refused, having given you a fair hearing.

## The Least You Need to Know

➤ You already have all the physical skills you need to make business presentations effectively.

➤ If you are asked to make a public speech, you will need to practice how to be amusing, engaging, and inspiring.

➤ If you have been clear and audible and your ideas were relevant and understood, you have been successful as a business presenter.

# Part 2
# What Do I Say?

*Having a credible presentation is critical to your comfort and reputation, and credibility depends on organizing the ideas to deliver a strategic message that your listeners recognize and care about. You have two alternatives to work with, and both can help you get control over all the ideas and facts you are going to deliver. Having the right structure for the presentation will also help you eliminate information that can make the presentation too long and boring. Structure makes sure the message you want to deliver gets through to each listener.*

# Chapter 5

# Know Who's Listening, Who's Deciding, and What You Want

## In This Chapter

➤ Learn how to preassess the audience

➤ Understand the dynamics of the listeners

➤ Assess the organization's impact on the idea you're presenting

Audiences create all kinds of challenges for presenters. You have to understand who is going to be listening, who influences the decision makers, and who is concerned about the impact of your idea on them.

Sometimes, the person who seems to be the decision-maker isn't really going to make the decision. She is going to depend on her staff to assess your idea and recommend a decision, and she's not going to change their decision. This might seem a bit unfair to the poor business presenter who is trying to meet the specific needs of each listener, particularly the needs of the decision-maker. However, it's a very plausible situation. If you do the preassessment of the listeners as discussed in this chapter, you'll be able to meet the needs of the "real" decision-maker.

Other times, the decision-maker is going to be influenced by market conditions or other projects that are competing for current resources. For example, you might be recommending that the company purchase new software, but the critical decision-maker knows that another department must invest in new technology or put the company at a competitive disadvantage.

You have to do some prework to analyze the situation you're walking into. Pre-work helps you present information that answers the audience's questions so that the decision maker and the influencers can comfortably say, "Yes."

# Who Is Listening?

The first step is to identify the people who will listen to your presentation:

> ➤ Who plans to attend? Develop a list of listeners.

> ➤ Who are they? Identify each listener's job.

> ➤ What is their relationship to the idea? Identify how each person will be affected by your ideas.

> ➤ Why are they attending?

You can figure out how to answer these important questions by asking other people in the company. Find out who has presented a similar concept or topic in the past. Talk to people who will be affected by the concept you're going to present, and ask them to answer these questions from their perspective.

If it's a meeting you attend regularly, you'll have the information readily available, but if it's a one-time meeting held for the presentation you're making, make sure you find out who will be listening so that you can figure out what their concerns will most likely be.

# Who Is the Critical Listener?

The most important person in the audience is the critical listener.

The critical listener is probably busy with a number of projects and concerns. And it is likely that when you are presenting, several crises are demanding the critical listener's attention.

The typical critical listener manages numerous projects simultaneously. For example, the person you identify as the critical listener for your idea (which is to eliminate all audit reports and substitute "Action Hit Lists") is also participating on a committee to design the re-engineering project the company is planning to begin in the new year in the manufacturing division. This person is also heading a task force designed to identify opportunities for improving quality and eliminating at least one step in the develoment process used by the Research and Development group.

This critical listener also has to manage his department day-to-day, and just last month, he was told he could hire no new professional or support staff for at least six months.

This critical listener is not someone who is going to listen to your idea with full attention unless you can fit your idea into his list of concerns. You're going to have to make your idea worthy of his attention, so you need to understand all of the things he's dealing with.

So find out everything you can about the critical listener. The worksheet, "Identify and Assess the Critical Listener" will help you think about the critical listener's biases and sensitivities.

Use the following worksheet to figure out how the critical listener will respond to your presentation so that you can frame your ideas to be relevant and appealing to him.

You always can talk to people who have presented to the critical listener in the past. They'll know what kinds of questions the critical listener tends to ask.

**Definition**
The **critical listener** is the person who makes the decision about your ideas. This person determines whether what you want to have the listeners know, think, or do gets known, thought, or done.

**Handy Hint**
If you're having trouble figuring out how to acquire some of this information, list all the people to whom you might send a memo on this subject. Who would be the person most likely to authorize the idea or request?

☞ **IDENTIFY AND ASSESS THE CRITICAL LISTENER**

**Who is the person who will say "yes" or "no" to your idea?** _____

**If s/he says, "yes," how does s/he benefit?**



**If s/he says, "no," how does s/he benefit?**



**If s/he says, "yes," how does s/he get hurt?**



**If s/he says, "no," how does s/he get hurt?**



**Has s/he ever championed a similar or contradictory idea in the past? What was that idea? What happened to the idea? What impact did having the idea have on this person's career?**



**Who in the organization considers this person to be important?**



**How would these people react to the critical listener's support or rejection of your idea?**

# Who Are the Influencers?

Influencers are powerful. They will tell the critical listener what they think, and the critical listener will listen to them. Often, influencers can change the mind of the critical listener.

The influencers are people who must believe your idea is relevant, valuable, and well-thought out. Their concerns and sensitivities can affect whether they support your ideas. For example, Glenn was giving a presentation about converting existing procedures manuals to hypertext. Glenn's purpose was to make procedures easier to write, maintain, and use. But Glenn didn't understand how powerful the head of the graphics group was. The head of the graphics group was not in favor of new technology and felt threatened by the rapid takeover of the print world by computers.

Glenn's idea was relevant, valuable, and well-thought through. But Glenn's idea failed to get implemented because the head of graphics was able to get the critical listener to pay close attention to the many risks presented by hypertext. Glenn was unable to build into the presentation responses to concerns over cost, design-time, and the power of outside firms to turn medium-sized projects into huge projects.

You always need to know who the influencers are, what they care about, and how they will be influenced by your ideas. Use the worksheet, "Identify and Analyze the Influencers" to plan your presentation. Don't get confused by people's titles, though. Sometimes, the most significant influencer does not appear anywhere on the formal organization chart because it's someone in a support position, or someone with whom the critical listener plays golf or tennis. Pay attention to the critical listener's habits. Who does she go to for information?

**Definition**
Influencers are people the critical listener trusts. These are the people the critical listener believes have his best interests at heart. Influencers might not have job titles that carry authority, although they often do. Influencers tend to have a good relationship with the critical listener. They're the ones he goes to lunch with, "just to chat."

**Handy Hint**
You might be able to get videotaped or audiotaped copies of presentations made to the critical listener or the influencers. Often, a company keeps a record of major presentations, and from these tapes you can get a good sense of the kinds of concerns these people have when they listen to business presentations such as yours.

To get an idea of who can influence the outcome of your presentation, answer the questions in the following figure.

☞ **IDENTIFY AND ANALYZE THE INFLUENCERS**

Who is going to attend the presentation?

Who can influence the critical listener, even if they aren't at the presentation?

How can these people benefit from your idea?

Which of these people could get hurt by your idea?

Which of these people might be offended by the idea?

Which of these people might be offended that you had the idea and s/he didn't?

What power do the influencers have? *Consider resources, right to veto, private time with critical listener.*

Whom might the critical listener depend on to make the decision?

People in the company will usually know and be quite willing to share with you information about the primary influencers on the critical listener. You also might want to find out who is on the critical listener's standard distribution list for memos and e-mail messages. Those are probably the people she depends on.

## What Information Does the Audience Need?

After you know the sensitivities of the critical listener and the influencers, you can start to decide what information will help them understand your presentation and how your ideas will affect them and the organization. Use an initial analysis to figure out what's important to the listeners. The worksheets on the next pages will help you prepare some of this information.

# What Is Happening That Could Affect Your Ideas?

Finally, you need to gather information about the context of your presentation. Your ideas must fit into the business conditions of the time. You'll want to know how the funding you're requesting affects the financial status of the organization and what competing projects could put strain on the company's finances.

You'll also want to know how your idea fits into other projects and ideas under consideration:

➤ Is your idea new and potentially intimidating? Perhaps you can suggest a way to implement the idea in phases.

➤ Is your idea familiar and well-understood but undervalued? How can you make the idea more appealing and dramatize its benefits to the organization or to the critical listener?

➤ Is your idea going to make anyone look bad or make a department appear as if they haven't been doing their job? How can you present the idea to make sure that no one looks bad?

**Beware**
Make sure you know what the competition is doing. If the competition is doing something similar to what you are suggesting, you need to know how well they're succeeding. If the competition is not doing what you're suggesting, why not? And make sure you prepare to respond to the questions, "How quickly can the competition respond if we do this? How large is our window of opportunity?"

☞ **PRE-THINK WHAT'S IMPORTANT TO THE LISTENERS**

**What information must the audience know to make a decision?**

**What kinds of information does the critical listener prefer to hear?  Budgets?  People involved?  Time lines?  How the idea affects current products, services, plans?**

**What kinds of information do the influencers prefer to hear?  Budgets?  People involved?  Time lines?  How the idea affects current products, services, plans?**

**What kinds of questions does the critical listener tend to ask?**

**What kinds of questions do the influencers tend to ask?**

**How unusual or unexpected is the presentation?**

☞**WHAT IS THE CONTEXT OF THE PRESENTATION?**

**What is happening in the market that is relevant to your idea?**

**What is happening inside the organization that could compete for resources or affect the success of your idea?**

**How are decisions made about the type of idea you're presenting? Who is involved? What is the organization's process for analyzing the information and reaching a decision?**

**How much of what you're presenting is new information or a new way to assess the situation?**

You usually can acquire this information by talking to people who have presented to this group in the past. You also can review the organization chart and figure out who is closest to the decision-maker and who will be most affected by any changes you're suggesting. You also will want to ask if any presentations about comparable products or ideas have been made to the group so that you can find out why the products or ideas presented were authorized or rejected.

The preparation for a business presentation can take a great deal of time and effort, but the process also will help you include all the relevant information needed by the listeners to give you a fair hearing. Preparation also will give you extra information so that the question and answer session proceeds smoothly, without your having to promise information.

# The Least You Need to Know

➤ Always know who the critical listeners and influencers are so that you can address their concerns as part of the presentation itself.

➤ Make sure you know what is happening competitively so that you can answer questions the listeners will ask about how your idea or product positions the company in the marketplace.

➤ Don't ever assume that the apparent decision-maker will make the decision without assistance. Influencers tend to have a significant impact on the decision, and sometimes, one of the influencers will make the decision even though the formal decision-maker is supposed to "own" the decision.

# Chapter 6

# Structure Always Wins

## In This Chapter

➤ How to decide between informational and persuasive structures of presentations

➤ Ways to persuade the influencers who need persuading

➤ Techniques for building in responses to objections

Although how you deliver a presentation is critical, if you deliver information that is irrelevant, poorly thought through, or wrong, the presentation will fail. Never underestimate the power of a strong delivery, but always base the delivery on a well-structured presentation. The challenge is to explain the information in a sequence that will make sense to the listeners and engage them in the logic of your thoughts.

Chapter 7 guides you through structuring an informative presentation, and Chapter 9 guides you through structuring a persuasive presentation. Chapter 8 shows you how to create either of the structures if you are having trouble sorting through lots of details. This chapter helps you identify information you need to include in the presentation and information you need to know before you begin to create a structure.

Your challenge is to make sense to each of the listeners, and unfortunately, it is rare that all of the listeners manage information the same way. They don't all listen the way you do, and they don't interpret words the way you do. They certainly don't use the logic you do. So you have to use the presentation structure to meet many people's needs effectively. This is no small task, especially if you don't have a lot of time to prepare.

Consider the situation where you arrive at work Tuesday morning knowing that your major task of the day is to prepare a presentation for the senior vice president of the new marketing unit on the West Coast. She is scheduled to arrive Thursday, and your presentation is scheduled for Friday morning. You've done some preliminary thinking about the presentation, but you haven't had a chance to prepare any materials.

When you review your voice mail, you discover that the senior vice president is arriving today because of a scheduling conflict in her office. Your presentation is going to be the second presentation of the afternoon and you have a lot of work to do.

Managing this type of emergency should be easy if you understand the power of structure and the power of knowing who the decision maker and influencers are. This chapter and the next three will help you structure presentations, even in emergencies!

## Choose a Structure to Meet the Listeners' Needs

We've been talking about the significance and roles of the decision-maker, or critical listener, and the influencers. The decision-maker is almost always the most important person, the one whose preferences and concerns determine how you structure information and what kinds of information you need to include or avoid. That's why the decision-maker is called the "critical listener."

In Chapter 5, the critical listener was defined as the one whose needs govern the choices you make as you prepare the presentation.

The influencers, though, can occasionally be as important or more important than the decision-maker. Before you prepare a presentation, try to understand who will affect the outcome of your presentation so that you can factor in their interests.

The influencers are very important. If you don't make your points clear to the influencers, or if you provide information that in any way hurts an influencer, you might discover that your well-structured, professionally and enthusiastically delivered presentation has failed.

**Beware**

Sometimes, the critical listener is one of the influencers, someone who works behind the scenes to help the apparent decision-maker sift through information and make a final decision. Always consider the needs of the critical listener first, but don't forget to examine the interests and issues of the influencers. Try to identify any hidden decision-makers on whom the apparent decision maker will rely.

Let's consider the situation Carl faced when he gave a carefully planned presentation to a group of his fellow division controllers. His major point was that the divisions had to rethink how the budgeting process involved all of the executives of each of the divisions. Carl's concern was that the executives at the division level weren't involved early enough, causing the budgeting process to take a lot longer than necessary and ultimately, to be a more costly process than necessary. Carl believed that a different process could produce a more accurate budget faster, with less argument and for less cost.

But Carl didn't know that one of the division controllers had already submitted a proposal to the chief financial officer of the corporation. That division controller, Arthur, had designed a process very similar to Carl's. But Arthur's hidden agenda was a major one. Arthur wanted his proposal to be the idea that propelled him into second position behind the chief financial officer so that when the CFO retired, Arthur would be the replacement.

So Carl's presentation failed because Arthur couldn't afford to let Carl's version of the proposal be accepted. Instead, Arthur argued the presentation points detail by detail and made Carl's proposal appear poorly thought through. Later, Arthur's proposal was reviewed and accepted.

> **Definition**
> A **hidden agenda** is a purpose someone has that he doesn't let anyone know about. Hidden agendas are dangerous for presenters because people who have them tend to argue about points that don't seem significant. If the presenter knows about a hidden agenda, the arguments then make sense. If the presenter knows about someone's hidden agenda, he can respond directly to the concern and keep the presentation on target.

## Focus On the Message

A message is something you need the listeners to know, think, or do. It is not a fact. It is a statement asking a listener to act, or to believe something is true. It can be a statement asking the listener to believe something is significant.

The message is the most important aspect of a presentation. The listeners, regardless of whether they are decision makers or influencers, want to hear about information relevant to them. The listeners want to hear about how the facts affect them, not just about the facts themselves.

For example, a presentation about quarterly variances can be a powerful presentation focused on business issues, or it can be a boring presentation telling the listeners facts they could easily acquire by reading the variance report.

Variances have significance to the business. What is the significance of each variance? Is the first one important because it suggests a shift in market strength? Is the second one important because it implies an opportunity to double sales for the next quarter if the company re-creates the conditions that caused the variance this quarter? Does the third variance represent a management opportunity to rethink how it approaches managing internal costs? Do the variances overall suggest a business problem that management must respond to quickly or risk a major business loss?

The question to consider when beginning to structure a presentation is, "What is the message I must deliver?" Usually, you make that decision based primarily on the concerns of the decision maker and secondarily on the concern of the influencers. Based on the message, you will know whether the presentation is predominantly informative or predominantly persuasive. Knowing the message will tell you whether you are telling or selling.

## The Presentation Is About Telling

A telling presentation is an informative presentation. You need the listeners to know something. You might need the listeners to respond with action, but the major portion of the presentation will be giving information and explaining messages with facts.

If you are going to be telling the listeners about something, you'll need to understand exactly what the listeners need to know or do when you complete the presentation. Must they understand a process? Should they be able to explain a decision to another group?

The message of a telling presentation will be the information they will know and maybe an action step the listeners will take in response to the presentation. The action step might be telling someone else about the idea, or it might be implementing an activity or project. The action step might be something the listeners will be able to do as proof they've understood what you've said. The listeners will gain knowledge and maybe act—they won't have to change their beliefs.

## The Presentation Is About Selling

A selling presentation is a persuasive presentation. You need the listeners to do something. You need the listeners to respond with action or with a change in their attitude or beliefs.

If you are going to be selling the listeners something, such as a product or an idea, you'll need to define exactly what the listeners must believe or do when you complete your presentation. Must they commit funds? Will they need to devote time or staff to a project? Must they be willing to authorize a new process or support a proposal? Are you asking them to say, "yes" to an idea or change in the organization?

The message of a selling presentation will be the action step the listeners will take in response to the presentation, or an attitude or belief they will hold as a result of the presentation. The action step will get taken only if the listeners are persuaded to act or change the status quo. The action step might be something the listeners have to commit, such as resources, or a signature or verbal approval of an idea. The attitude or belief might be full support of a new idea, or a new appreciation of the significance of an event or opportunity.

**Handy Hint**
Always find out what the influencers care about before structuring your presentation so that you can incorporate responses to their concerns into the presentation.

## Presell the Influencers

Before you begin to structure your presentation past the message stage, identify all the influencers and figure out what their concerns and attitudes are currently. You have to understand the decision maker's concerns, too. Chapter 5 presents a number of worksheets that will help you identify the influencers and their concerns.

One way to presell the influencers is to review the idea with them before you structure the presentation. Create a rough draft of the presentation before you make any final decisions about the structure or about visual aids. Keep yourself very flexible at this stage!

Ask the influencers you identified as potentially argumentative or difficult to sell if you can review some key ideas with them before the presentation itself. Meet with these influencers one by one. Review the ideas, the details, and the facts. Ask them for their comments and concerns. Ask them to help you understand how the decision maker will respond to your idea.

**Beware**
Don't ask for support from an influencer who you know is negative about your idea. Ask how you can make the idea clearer, stronger, or more relevant. But don't risk having the influencer take an early negative position.

If you think it appropriate, ask the influencer what she thinks about your idea and whether she will be comfortable supporting it.

If your discussions go well, you will have the opportunity to discuss each influencer's concerns well in advance of the presentation so each can be thinking about your idea. Yes, some of them will come to the

**Handy Hint**
The influencers who give you their comments will have helped shape the idea. People who help shape an idea are supporters.

presentation with more negative arguments. But often, they will come to the presentation more prepared to hear what you have to say. Some might even have started to change their minds. Also, because you have asked for their comments, some of them might begin to feel as if the idea is partially theirs. Listeners find it much easier to change their minds about an idea when they think they have helped shape it.

# Incorporate Responses to the Influencers' Concerns

When you know what the influencers are concerned about, create a list of questions they might ask. Don't forget to identify any hidden agendas!

Based on their possible questions and concerns, identify any additional type of information or detail you need to include in your presentation. There will be information and details you want to include, and information and details you plan to include. Use this preassessment step to identify any additional information or details you must include to address the influencers' concerns during the actual presentation.

For example, you might want to include information about how another company used an idea similar to yours to increase profitability by 30 percent on a dying line of products. You might plan to include a complete financial analysis of how the idea will produce the gain in profitability. But if you assess the concerns and hidden agendas of the influencers, and if you have thoroughly examined the concerns of the decision maker, you might discover that you have to include information about two alternative approaches to managing the dying line of products.

One influencer wants the dying line of products to be eliminated. This influencer has a great idea, his, about a new line of products that will help the company make more efficient use of an existing manufacturing facility. You'll probably have to build into your presentation some kind of analysis of alternative product lines and demonstrate why your idea is a better use of corporate resources.

Another influencer helped create the dying line of products, and you need to make sure you do not suggest in any way that the line is flawed. You might have to find a sensitive way to describe the problems the line has run into. Perhaps the focus will need to be on a competitor's overwhelming attack on the line and not on the irrelevance of the line given today's market for that type of product.

# Include Responses to Potential Arguments

As you identify influencers and their concerns, also identify the potential arguments you might face. You will want to build into the presentation itself responses to potential arguments. You won't want to spend a lot of time on the responses, but you will want to seed the ideas. You can always build on what you seed if someone raises the argument during the question and answer process.

Many of the arguments might arise from the influencers' concerns. But other arguments might come from their concerns over your logic, your facts, or the impact of your idea on their departments. Some might arise because of the way they think—pure details preferred or the big picture only preferred.

Figure out whether one of the influencers is passionate about detail levels when the financial position of a product is discussed. Know in advance that one of the influencers has a reputation for avoiding new technology. Be prepared to deal with arguments, and put some of the response into the presentation itself during the planning phase.

# Brainstorm Questions And Challenges

Brainstorming means listing every thought that could possibly be related to the issue. No matter how silly or illogical, list the questions, challenges, risks, and costs. Think of all the possibilities. Identify every potential area of impact so that you know how your brilliant idea might be squashed.

Sometimes, you know you have a perfect argument. It's difficult to imagine that the perfect argument has flaws, but it might! So before you structure the presentation, brainstorm all the questions and challenges that anyone might ask. Brainstorm all the risks and hidden costs that are embedded in your idea. Do everything you can to identify aspects of your idea or your persuasive argument that might hurt someone in the organization.

The goal is to know what you must include, what you must avoid, and how to say certain things so that the presentation itself creates the action or belief you are seeking.

At minimum, you will want to have prepared all the responses needed and have your facts ready as additional visual aids and/or handouts just in case someone raises an issue. Ideally, you will include some of these facts in the presentation itself so that your listeners can hear them as you present your idea logically.

Whether you're telling or selling, people will usually want to argue with you. Be prepared.

The following two checklists will help you think about some of the potential risks and hidden costs that could affect the success of your idea, or the attitude of the listeners.

**Handy Hint**
Always assume the listeners will want to argue with you. Assume your logic is flawed, the idea is dangerous, and you're presenting ideas that will upset people. Include responses in the presentation, or, at minimum, prepare back-up information and visual aids so that you can respond if the issues are raised.

## IDENTIFY THE RISKS

**Who/What could prevent the listeners from knowing or doing what you want them to know or do?**

**What market conditions could affect the success of your idea? How likely is it they could occur?**

**What can the company do to prevent these things from occurring in the market?**

**What can the company do to make the idea successful even if these conditions occur?**

**What disastrous events or forces could ruin your idea? Consider events or forces such as technology, competitive products or services, pricing choices, regulatory requirements? How would you counter them?**

## WHAT ARE THE HIDDEN COSTS?

Which aspects of your idea could create liability for the company? Consider factors such as safety, copyright or trademark violations, effectiveness of changes, and others that could require legal protection or create legal exposure, damage to market reputation, or injury to customers.

What changes might or will the company need to make to its existing organization structure, manufacturing facilities, union contracts, training programs, marketing programs?

What regulatory groups or tax codes will or could the company have to deal with as a result of your idea?

65

Most of the time, if you are prepared for objections and arguments, and if you build in responses to those objections and arguments to the presentation, you will have prepared what appears to be a very logical, well thought-out presentation. Often, just preparing for the worst arguments and including facts that refute them before anyone raises them will prevent the arguments from becoming major.

And in the unpleasant situation where you have prepared well but someone wants to argue, you'll be able to comment and respond intelligently and professionally. You won't need to panic, and you'll have the extra information ready to share as it becomes needed.

Focus first on the issues and concerns of the decision maker, and then make sure you do everything you can to get the influencers to support your idea or, at minimum, to make the influencers' concerns and hidden agendas weak. Then you will be prepared to create an effective structure for explaining your ideas. You'll be able to tell or sell and concentrate on the structure first and delivery second.

# The Least You Need to Know

➤ Before you begin to structure your presentation, make sure you know all the information that must be included.

➤ Figure out your message before you begin to draft the presentation. Know what you plan to include in the presentation in case you need to presell an influencer.

➤ Assume your idea is flawed, and list all the ways your argument could be faulty so that you can build in the appropriate responses when you structure the presentation.

➤ Plan to bring extra information so that you can respond to arguments raised during the question and answer session.

# Chapter 7

# Message-based℠ Always Works

## In This Chapter

➤ Understand how journalists focus on facts and business presenters focus on messages

➤ Use the context, message, and roadmap to guide your presentation structure

➤ Use the Message-based℠ structure to check the logic of your presentation

Part of the challenge of developing an effective business presentation is that you usually know a lot of facts about the topic, and sorting through the facts to identify the important and relevant ones is often difficult. It's particularly difficult to eliminate facts when you know how important they have been in forming your opinions. Somehow, you just know that the listeners must know each fact or they won't believe what you're saying. Listeners have to go through the steps you went through to form an opinion, or they won't see the logic of the opinion.

So you have to use a structure that helps you choose relevant facts, eliminate unneeded facts, and focus on the message.

# Message-based℠ Is Not Fact-Based

Chapter 6 reviewed the concept of a message. A message is something you need the listeners to know, think, or do. It is not a fact. It is a move to action, or a move to believe something is true. It can be a statement to believe something has significance.

A fact is something you know; a message is the significance of the fact:

➤ "*Avoid driving on the day before Thanksgiving* because it is the heaviest travel day of the year."

➤ "The checks are not kept in a secure cabinet, *so someone could steal them.*"

➤ "The taste test shows us that the new product formula tastes more like banana than the original product formula, *so we should conduct a market test of the new product formula.*"

In each instance, the message (in italic type) shows the listener a way to think about the fact.

## Journalists Focus on the 5Ws

Journalists present information by focusing on key facts: the 5Ws, or the "Who, What, When, Where, Why" of the story. Many of us were taught to write by focusing on the 5Ws and now many of us continue to use the 5Ws in presentations.

**Definition**
The **5Ws** are Who, What, When, Where, and Why. Journalists usually provide this information in the first paragraph of a news story.

But the 5Ws are generally not useful by themselves in a business presentation. Most decision makers listening to a business presentation want to hear how to deal with a problem, how to react to a situation, and what the facts suggest for a business opportunity. Decision makers assume that you know what you're talking about; they want to know how it affects them. What should they know, think, or do?

## Message-based℠ Focuses On What to Know, Think, or Do

Using the Message-based℠ structure makes facts secondary. The Message-based℠ structure creates an argument. The logic of the argument requires facts as support. The facts prove the message is sound and show how to do what needs to be done. The facts also make the message complete and clear.

Think of the work you do every day as a triangle sitting on its base, as shown in the following figure. Someone asks a question, you gather all sorts of data, and then you identify what it means—its message.

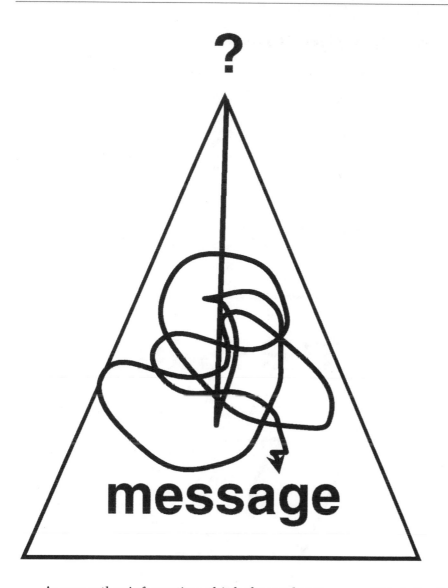

As you gather information, think about what it means. This is the thinking triangle, sitting on its base, right-side up. You are asked to do some research into a business opportunity, so you talk to a lot of people, read some material that is available on the Internet, and do some financial modeling of the opportunity. You speak to some people from other departments to verify some of your assumptions. Then, you must make a presentation to the senior vice president of marketing and explain the business opportunity.

You have just used the right-side up triangle, the one that sits on its base. You had a question, the top of the triangle. You know very little at this point, but you gathered information and enlarged your knowledge of the facts. Then, you landed on the answer—your message at the base of the triangle. In this case, let's say it's a "no." The business opportunity will not produce the return targeted by the company for all new ventures.

But the presentation needs to reverse the order of the information now available to you. The senior vice president of marketing really doesn't want to review with you all of the steps you have taken to produce your "no." She probably wouldn't have wanted you to do the research into the business opportunity if she didn't believe you capable of doing that research. The senior vice president of marketing wants the answer. She wants to know what she needs to know, think, or do about the business opportunity presented to the company.

So you'll use the upside-down triangle—the message, the base, is at the top. The following figure shows the upside-down triangle. It presents the message first and then the supporting logic and data in a logical sequence.

*Tell the listeners the message first.*

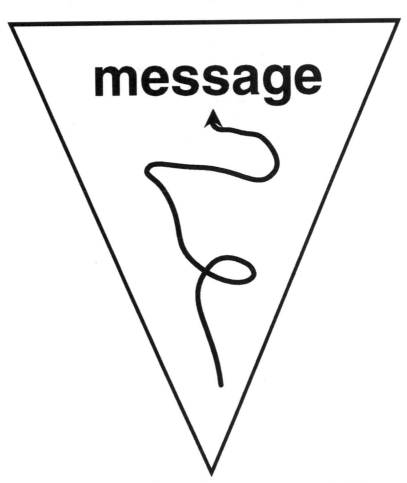

You're going to structure your presentation around the message, "We should not invest in this business opportunity because we cannot make the returns needed to justify the investment." This is the most important information, the top of the upside-down triangle, the message. The rest of the presentation will be a review of the facts that support that statement.

But when you develop the presentation, include only enough facts to make the message clear. You won't have to describe all the steps you took, all the facts you reviewed, and all the analysis you performed. You will select just enough of the facts to show that the business opportunity will not produce the targeted returns.

Which facts will you choose? Probably, you should include a discussion of how you calculated the returns based on varying assumptions. And you can include an explanation of the assumptions and their relevance to the company. This information will validate the work you've done and support the message you're delivering to the senior vice president of marketing.

You won't have to review all the information you found on the Internet, or the information you gathered by interviewing people with experience in comparable ventures. Why? Most of this information is not relevant to the message, which is "no." This information was important to you because it helped you determine whether the business opportunity was, in fact, an opportunity. You validated the opportunity.

> **Beware**
> Don't include facts just because they are powerful or important. Include facts only because they support the message. They help the listeners know why or how they should know, think, or do something.

But the message has nothing to do with how valid the opportunity is. The message is that the opportunity, however real, is not going to meet financial targets established by your company for new investments.

That's how the Message-based<sup>SM</sup> structure works. It helps you put together a presentation that focuses on what you want the decision maker to know, think, or do and then to select enough facts —the right facts—to support that knowledge, thought, or action.

## Message-based<sup>SM</sup> Structures Messages and Facts

As you can see, if you clearly define the message you want the decision maker to focus on, you can control the facts you need to include in the presentation.

This approach to structuring a presentation works whether you are telling people something or selling people something. Because you focus on what you want the listeners to know, think, or do, you help the listeners hear the facts as they relate to the message.

**Consider This**

People who are listening to presentations are usually busy and are generally thinking about many things when they arrive to hear you speak. Your listeners are intelligent and are used to gathering information rapidly, forming an opinion, and acting on that opinion.

If you explain a lot of facts to business listeners, they will probably hear the facts, decide what they mean, develop a "take-away"—an opinion about the significance of the facts—and stop listening. They will have designed, in effect, their own presentation based on the facts you have communicated to them.

But there's no way for you to control these listeners' thought processes. There's no way for you to make them stop thinking. So your best bet is to tell them what you want them to think (or know or do) so that as you present facts to them, they can line up those facts behind that message.

# Identify The Context, Message, and Roadmap

To develop a presentation, you must identify the context, message, and roadmap for the presentation.

In essence, the top of the upside-down triangle contains three types of information:

➤ **The context**  Why are you making this presentation? What situation exists or has occurred that brings everyone to this presentation today?

➤ **The message**  What must the listeners know, think, or do when you have completed your presentation?

➤ **The roadmap**  What topics or groups of facts must you review for the listeners so that they can know, think, or do what you want them to know, think, or do?

**Definition**
The **roadmap** is the sequence of topics you explain to support the message. The roadmap is the facts, grouped by topic. Each topic has its own message so that each time you begin to explain a new topic, or a new fact that is part of that topic, you explain to the listeners what they should know, think, or do about that topic or fact.

One of the values of using a roadmap is the guidance it gives the listeners. If you tell the listeners what type of information to listen for, they will usually pay attention so that they hear those topics. If you don't tell the listeners what type of information to listen for, they will often decide at some point that you've provided enough facts for them, and they will stop paying close attention to the information you're sharing.

Think of a roadmap as an explanation of the street signs to look for to follow the logic of your presentation. The roadmap defines the key topics that get the listeners to the right destination—the proof of the message, the substantiation of why or how they should know, think, or do something.

Let's look at an example.

>    **The context:** We recently completed the study you commissioned.
>
>    **The message:** You should build the new facility only if you can work with the architect and engineering firm responsible for the competitor's facility.
>
>    **The roadmap:** Facilities such as the one planned pose significant difficulties because there are environmental regulations, technological challenges, and few comparable facilities from which to learn.

The facts that you will review in this presentation are the environmental regulations, the technological challenges, and the competitor's facility—the only comparable facility successfully built to date. You also probably will want to include, as your fourth topic, a review of the architect and the engineering firm that built the competitor's facility.

Each of these four topics will become a subtriangle, opening with a message statement that tells the listeners what they should know, think, or do about the topic. The following figure shows the triangle structures for this presentation. The messages for each of the four roadmap topics appear below the figure.

**Handy Hint**
Don't include more than five topics in a presentation. Most listeners have the patience for two to three topics, and if you have a complex message, the listeners will probably remain attentive for as many as five topics. After five topics, the listeners will select the topics they'll remember. If you need 21 topics, by all means include them, but aim for five or fewer.

*Here's a graphical look at the presentation flow.*

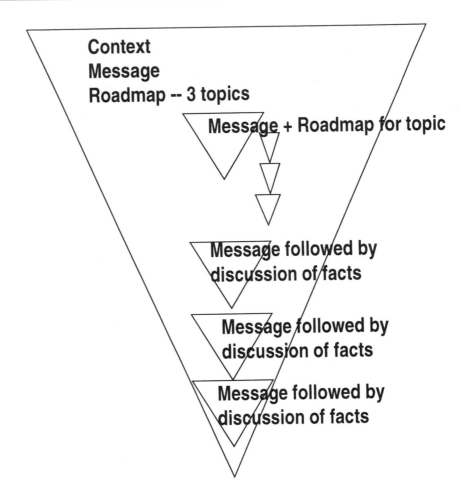

If there are subsets of facts, add a roadmap for each one:

### Roadmap Topic 1

The environmental regulations for this type of facility have increased dramatically in the last five years. Three regulations are particularly demanding.

This topic will have three sub-sub-triangles, each opening with a message statement explaining what the listeners will know, think, or do about those facts, followed by a presentation of the facts.

### Roadmap Topic 2

The technological challenges largely come from the chips used to run the computers that make such a facility feasible.

**Roadmap Topic 3**

Our competitor's facility has been successful because they worked closely with the architect and engineering firm to identify possible flaws, and therefore, they built into the plans most of the remedies for those flaws.

**Roadmap Topic 4**

The architect and engineering firm have a long record of success, and are the only ones who have conquered the many problems these types of facilities pose.

For the first sub-triangle, there will be sub-sub-triangles. For the other three sub-triangles, there will be only discussions of the message you plan to communicate about that topic.

You now have structured your presentation and can decide which facts to include.

> **Handy Hint**
> Limit the number of facts to five or fewer at each level whenever possible. For the presentation, use five or fewer topics. For each topic, use five or fewer sub-topics. It is almost always possible. Realistically, you can usually limit the facts to two or three.

## Fill In the Facts

After you have structured the presentation to focus on the message, you can select the facts you want to review with the listeners. Consider four guidelines:

> ➤ Stop adding facts once your point is clear.

> ➤ Sequence facts so that the most important ones are first and the less important ones follow.

> ➤ Sequence facts so that the bigger concepts are before the smaller ones.

> ➤ Present the facts chronologically only if chronology is important, such as in procedures, explanations of research, or descriptions of protocols.

If you open each segment of your presentation with a message, and if you choose facts according to these guidelines, you will quickly discover that you can easily tell when you have enough facts. Your Message-based℠ structure will help you select and sequence the facts you need to include.

## Consider This

The director of telecommunications in a large consumer products company was preparing a presentation to the executive committee. He was concerned about his preparation time because he had only a few hours. So much had been happening with his team that he just hadn't been able to do the planning he wanted to do. But the presentation was critical because he needed to get a 50 percent increase in his budget to implement some new technology. He knew that to prepare properly would take several days, and he had only a few hours.

So he decided to work with the Message-based℠ structure, hoping it might save some time. He knew he always had trouble sorting through facts and picking the right ones.

And it worked! He identified the message right away—"We need to increase our budget 50 percent." And he easily defined the context, "Given the new technology available, we can meet our goals two years earlier if we invest immediately in upgrading our telecommunications capabilities." And once he knew what the context and message were, he could select the types of facts that would win his point: the financial analysis of how the investment would produce the return—to show that a 50 percent budget increase would produce a return far greater than the investment, and a review of the technology with an overview of the steps needed to implement it.

He was able to create the presentation and deliver it successfully while working within the time constraints.

Everything you include in a presentation relates to the message. At the conclusion of the presentation, what will your listeners know, think, or do? Every topic opens with a message. After you have presented the topic, what will the listeners know, think, or do about the topic and its relationship to the presentation's message?

So how do you develop a presentation that is Message-based℠? Just follow these steps:

1. Identify the context.

    Why are you making a presentation?

2. Identify the message.

    What must the listeners know, think, or do when you have finished your presentation?

3. Create the roadmap.

    What topics and facts must you present to make sure the listeners can know, think, or do what you want them to know, think, or do?

Think of the process as filling in the upside-down triangle, which focuses on the message first, as shown here.

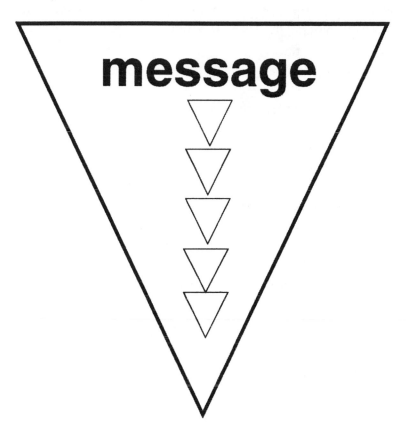

*The focus is on the message, supported by sub-messages and facts.*

About the only thing that could pose a challenge once you have create the upside-down triangle is the ending. If you don't know what you want to say at the end of your presentation, plan to tell the listeners who should do what next.

Let's look at some examples of presentation plans that use the Message-based<sup>SM</sup> structure.

In the example mapped below, the presenter is recommending that the division restructure its marketing and manufacturing. There are three topics to cover, as the roadmap statement makes clear. And the first topic has four sub-topics, while the second and third topics will be discussions of the messages with supporting facts. The second and third topics don't have any sub-messages.

Review the structure to see how it is Message-based[SM] and not fact-based.

**CONTEXT:** It has been difficult to meet profitability goals. So we conducted a study of the market and our competitors' best practices.

**MESSAGE:** We must re-structure our marketing function and manufacturing operations to decrease costs.

**ROADMAP:** If we re-structure marketing and manufacturing, we'll see significant savings and gain in quality and productivity.

**Sub-message 1:** Re-structure marketing and manufacturing carefully to produce measurable benefits.

**Sub-sub-message 1:** Re-structure marketing to gain . . .
**Sub-sub-message 2:** Re-structure marketing by . . .
**Sub-sub-message 3:** Re-structure manufacturing to gain . . .
**Sub-sub-message 4:** Re-structure manufacturing by . . .

**Sub-message 2:** Our quality will increase in several ways:

**Sub-message 3:** Our productivity will increase . . .

**WHO DOES WHAT NEXT WHEN?**
I'm suggesting we agree to hear a consulting report on our costs and the targeted benefits of this type of project. I've scheduled a meeting for Tuesday.

In the example mapped in the next figure, the presenter is assigning the departments responsibility for quality improvement. The presenter doesn't plan to review all the steps each group will need to take. She will discuss the three topics referred to in the roadmap statement, but she will not outline the steps and give lots of details. So there are not sub-sub-messages, just a discussion that is introduced by the sub-messages.

Review the structure to see how it focuses on the messages.

CONTEXT: We're not taking the steps necessary to remain competitive. Our services earn a premium because of their quality, so...

MESSAGE: You are each going to be responsible for quality improvement goals in your departments.

ROADMAP: Quality improvement is going to require assessment, problem definition, and the design and implementation of appropriate solutions.

Sub-message 1: By August 31st, 2 months from now, each department must design and complete an assessment of its quality, the competitors' quality, and the risks to our quality.

Sub-message 2: Once everyone has identified the quality issues at risk, each group must identify problems it must resolve so that we can eliminate the problems before they arise.

Sub-message 3: Ultimately, your creative challenge is to figure out how to prevent quality problems from occurring and how to improve our quality as we sell it today.

WHO DOES WHAT NEXT WHEN?
I'm asking that each of you send me your comments before our meeting next month.

79

In the following example, the message and roadmap are stated in one sentence. There are two topics to discuss, and the second has two sub-messages.

Review the structure to see how the presenter has built it on messages.

**CONTEXT:** We have nearly completed our review of your systems development process.

**MESSAGE/
ROADMAP:** No significant problems exist, although you might want to develop a more formal documentation standard.

**Sub-message 1:** Currently, your documentation standard requires . . .

**Sub-message 2:** Documentation is often more useful if prepared earlier in the process and if it is issued to reviewers earlier.
**Sub-sub-message:** Early preparation provides . . .
**Sub-sub-message:** Reviewers can suggest ways to clarify the documentation if they have more time to comment, so the earlier they receive it, the better.

**WHO DOES WHAT NEXT WHEN?**
If your department has any questions about how to develop a more formal standard, please let us know.

In the next example, the presenter is introducing new information and discussing the benefits of the new technology. Although the roadmap statement mentions only three topics, the first sub-triangle introduces a discussion of the new technology mentioned in the context statement. It is appropriate to provide a topic that reviews background or the problem or key definitions before presenting the sub-messages. But don't discuss the background or the problem until the message is clear—you might discover that the listeners are trying to solve the problem and aren't listening to you.

**CONTEXT:** Our new product line has dramatically new technology.

**MESSAGE/**

**ROADMAP:** The newer models will be less expensive and easier to maintain, and they'll require less space.

**Sub-message 1:** The new technology depends on sophisticated new chip designs . . .

**Sub-message 2:** The new equipment models are less expensive to purchase and to maintain.

**Sub-message 3:** The new technology makes the equipment easier to maintain.

**Sub-message 4:** The new models are smaller, requiring less space. . .

**WHO DOES WHAT NEXT WHEN?**
I'll leave the documentation for your review. If you have any questions about the equipment and its sophisticated new technology, please let us know.

Use the Message-based℠ structure anytime. Chapter 8 reviews a special approach for making selling presentations.

## The Least You Need to Know

➤ Identify the context, message, and roadmap of your presentation first so that you have the overall structure clear.

➤ Limit the roadmap and sub-topics to five or fewer items whenever possible.

➤ Use the Message-based℠ structure for any presentation, whether informative or persuasive.

# How Do I Put Together a Presentation?

| In This Chapter |
| --- |
| ➤ Sort through the information you have to present |
| ➤ Produce a Message based℠ presentation—the "grand sort" |
| ➤ Plan a presentation quickly and easily—the skeleton first |

You're probably wondering how you can ever take a lot of ideas and facts and create a presentation. How can you know what's really important when all you see are facts, facts, facts? This challenge faces everyone who has to put together a presentation, particularly if you are presenting an interim report, a status update, or the results of a complicated project or process.

You can't skip this step; you have to do the planning carefully, and you have to create a clear structure. Once you have the structure, you'll be able to make other decisions, such as what you need to create for visual aids.

## The "Grand Sort"—To a Message-based℠ Presentation

The "grand sort" is a straightforward, easy, reliable method you can use to identify, prioritize, and structure lots of facts. It's one of the easiest methods you can use to create a Message-based℠ presentation, one that will ensure that you and your listeners are focusing on relevant ideas—the messages—and not just on facts.

**Consider This**

Never give listeners "just facts" or "facts first," or they will start to figure out for themselves the significance of those facts. You might want to tell them the financial results for the quarter, the significant variances, and the major events that shaped the results and variances.

But your point might be that the quarter was unusual and that despite the unusual results, everything next quarter should even out and probably even exceed expectations. But by the time the listeners see the critical facts, they are likely to have concluded that the quarter was a disaster, the variances a major problem, and that perhaps you haven't done your job!

Always give listeners messages so that the facts support the messages and don't create new, unintended messages.

**Handy Hint**

Generally, it's easiest to use 3×5 cards or Post-it® notes because you can write one idea or fact on each one and then later, when you do the sorting, you can move the facts and ideas around quite easily.

The first step of the "grand sort" is to list all the ideas and facts you think you might want to include in the presentation.

Let's say the presentation you need to make to your executive committee is about a recently conducted customer satisfaction survey. You are unsure of how to handle the responses because there were so many strange ones. Some customers clearly think what you do is wonderful, others think it's terrible, and there were an awful lot of comments about how costly your products and services tend to be. In fact, some of the comments were pretty nasty, such as the one about the sales representatives wearing expensive suits!

When you sort through the information again, select 15 facts and comments you think are important, as shown in the figure on the next page.

Then, after you write each fact and idea on a separate 3×5 card, sort them into groups of similar or related comments. This sort, the "grand sort," can be a complicated process. Often, you will sort the information one way and then another way and then even another way, looking to find a meaningful pattern in the facts and ideas.

In our fictional situation, the sort is relatively straightforward, and you've found three different categories of information, the last one of which has two aspects.

# Customer Satisfaction Survey

*You select the facts you think you'll include in the presentation.*

| FACTS/IDEAS | | | |
|---|---|---|---|
| Your sales staff wears $1,000 suits | Cadillac services | How can you afford to send technicians so freely? | Hand-holding is superb |
| 20% think we are awful | Common write in: quallty hlgh but pricey | No longer In my prlce category | 50% think we're average |
| You anticipate my whims! | 25% gave ambiguous answers | You meet needs I didn't know I had | Standard comment: reliable but expensive |
| | 5% think we're great | Mercedes Benz quality | You're an 80s firm |

The first data set is a group of percentages. They fit together because they are all percentages and all are in the category of the actual responses to customer satisfaction. And they all seem to suggest that "Responses were varied, but the most interesting response is that customer reaction to our products and services is ambiguous." Group facts and identify a message: What should the listeners know, think, or do about these facts?

> 5% think we're great
>
> 20% think we are awful
>
> 50% think we're average
>
> 25% gave ambiguous answers

The second grouping includes one comment that doesn't make sense until it is grouped with another pair of comments. Together, they suggest an idea: "Customers seem to think we are providing luxurious excess."

> You're an 80s firm

> You meet needs
> I didn't know I had
>
> You anticipate
> my whims!

The third grouping has two sub-elements. First, there were comments about our quality. Second, there were comments about the costliness of our quality. Overall, these comments seem to suggest that "Our quality is high but it is pricey—perhaps the quality we provide is not worth the price we charge." The following shows how the facts lead to a message.

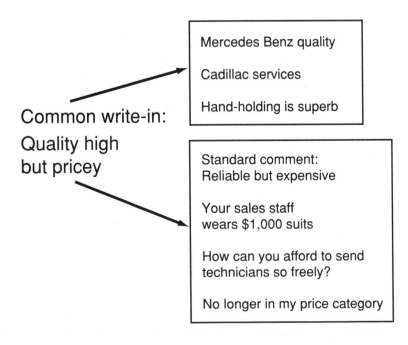

Common write-in:
Quality high
but pricey

Mercedes Benz quality

Cadillac services

Hand-holding is superb

Standard comment:
Reliable but expensive

Your sales staff
wears $1,000 suits

How can you afford to send
technicians so freely?

No longer in my price category

These facts were originally in two groups, but combined into one, they create an important message.

The messages seem to be:

➤ Responses varied, and most interesting was "ambiguous."

➤ Are we providers of luxurious excess?

➤ We seem to provide unexpected levels of quality and service and charge for the privilege.

The overall message seems to be that we are not meeting our customers' needs, as shown by three types of comments. So we end up with this plan for the presentation:

Context: We recently completed an extensive customer satisfaction survey.

Message: We are not meeting our customers' needs.

Roadmap: The responses send an ambiguous message, summarized by:

➤ We are providers of excess.

➤ We charge for that excess.

Now you can work on how you'll deliver the presentation and what kinds of visual aids you'll need.

# Skeleton First

In an ideal world, you would be able to sit down to prepare a presentation, think for a while, identify the main message and all the sub-messages, add the facts, and be finished with the structure of a Message-based℠ presentation! You probably don't think you can do this right now, and realistically, lots of times you won't be able to do this. But as you can see from this example, it's something you should be able to do for presentations that are not incredibly complicated.

Let's consider a different presentation. In this presentation, you know the message but not the facts. You have to announce to the employees at your corporate site a complete change in services and pricing in the corporate cafeteria.

The message is pretty straightforward: The company will re-vamp cafeteria services and change pricing effective May 1st. That's the easy part of this presentation.

But what must you include? The topics will probably be "why?" and "in what way?" You'll end up with a preliminary plan as seen in the following figure.

*Make preliminary notes.*

So, given the topics and the facts that explain them, you end up with the following plan.

*You begin to get a sense of the facts to include.*

## The company will re-vamp cafeteria services and change pricing effective May 1st.

### Services Today

Breakfast
Lunch
Dinner
Coffee
Catering

### Why?

IRS regulations
Tight market
No longer competitive re:
  compensation

### New Services

Breakfast
Lunch
Dinner
Coffee
Catering

### New Pricing

+ approximately 15%
Contractors will pay full price
No more discounts to senior
  management

But you'll need a context statement. The obvious context statement here is the information under "Why?" This information will need to be discussed, also, so you can plan to introduce the ideas of why the changes are occurring as the context statement and then discuss them as part of the presentation itself.

**The company will re-vamp cafeteria services and change pricing effective May 1st.**

*Your presentation is taking shape.*

**Services Today**

Breakfast
Lunch
Dinner
Coffee
Catering

**Why?**

Use this as the context.

IRS regulations
Tight market
No longer competitive re: compensation

**New Services**

Breakfast
Lunch
Dinner
Coffee
Catering

**New Pricing**

+ approximately 15%
Contractors will pay full price
No more discounts to senior management

Now you have to decide what sequence the information should appear in. Clearly, the big issue you identified up front is the pricing issue. The cost will be the issue most relevant to most of the employees; they'll then want to know what they'll be getting, so the new services will need to be second. And the new services will probably be most effectively understood in comparison to the old services, so you'll have to briefly review the old services.

**The company will re-vamp cafeteria services and change pricing effective May 1st.**

*R1 is the first topic you identify in the roadmap, R2 is the second, and so on.*

**Services Today**

R2    Breakfast
Lunch
Dinner
Coffee
Catering

**Why?**

R4    IRS regulations
Tight market
No longer competitive re: compensation

**New Services**

R3    Breakfast
Lunch
Dinner
Coffee
Catering

**New Pricing**

R1    + approximately 15%
Contractors will pay full price
No more discounts to senior management

89

You may want to include a comparison chart that will emphasize how much better the new services are. The information in the previous figure will be effective in chart form. The chart will help make the new, higher pricing look worthwhile.

Your final topic will need to be a quick review of why the changes are occurring.

This planning process produces a workable skeleton of the presentation. Now you can figure out how to deliver it and what kinds of visual aids you'll need.

## The Least You Need to Know

➤ If you don't know how to organize the presentation, use the "grand sort" to group similar facts and ideas and then develop the messages that explain them. Use these sub-messages to lead you to the overall message.

➤ If the presentation is relatively straightforward, identify the message, the topics that you will cover, and then the sequence of the topics that best presents and supports the message.

➤ Keep examining the facts and identifying, "What should the listeners know, think, or do about these facts?"

# Chapter 9

# Persuasive Structure Can Help Sell Ideas

**In This Chapter**

➤ When to use the persuasive structure

➤ How to use the persuasive structure

➤ How to develop the persuasive structure

Sometimes you know there is a problem or an opportunity and you want to make sure the organization or team does something in response to that problem or opportunity. But how do you present an idea without sounding like you're creating problems? How can you get people to listen to the idea, and not solve the problem itself? And how do you keep everyone's attention, particularly when they don't realize there's a problem?

The persuasive presentation works well when you don't have a lot of time to prepare. You have to write ten sentences, but that shouldn't take too much time.

## So You Have an Idea or a Solution?

You have figured out that a problem exists or that an opportunity exists. Perhaps you recognize that with current spending patterns, the team will have spent its budget by October, but its work won't be done before December or January. Or maybe you have figured out a new packaging concept that can increase consumer awareness of your company's oldest product.

What you need is to have key executives listen to your idea and understand that there is a need for action, preferably now.

You need a fast-paced presentation that presents the idea, shows the idea is needed, and demonstrates that you've thought through how to implement the idea. Normally, you'd rely on the Message-based[SM] structure to make the message clear and the logic well thought-out, but this time, you need something punchy.

# Wear a Listener's Hat

As you consider how to structure the presentation, ask yourself why anyone would care about this idea. They'll certainly care about costs and profitability. They'll care about the organization's image and reputation, or about customer service and quality products. They'll care about whether you know enough to be recommending this idea. How can you respond? How can you answer all their concerns, sound organized and well-informed, and keep the presentation simple and persuasive? That's where the persuasive structure comes in.

Most of us have a set of expectations when we begin to listen to a presenter. One of the major expectations, or hopes, you have is that you will find the presenter and the ideas interesting.

Most of us also want to know why we should bother to listen. We are all busy. We are all focused on getting too much done in too little time, so why should we spend time listening to someone?

**Handy Hint**
Listeners are people like you. You know what you find boring and irrelevant when listening to a presentation. You know when a presenter is presenting an idea that is poorly developed. Rely on yourself, but don't forget to do prework on your listeners, too.

First, put yourself in a listener's seat: You want to know what's going on that creates the need for a presentation. What's happening in the organization or market that says we need an idea right now?

Second, you want to know what needs to be done. What should you do? If you need an idea, then what are you supposed to do to respond to that idea?

Third, you always want to know how to accomplish the action step. What are the details of the idea?

Also, you have questions, such as what will this action step cost you? And what resources must you give to this idea? And everyone is wondering about the outcome and its impact. What benefits will you receive? If you are going to devote resources to an idea, there had better be a reward for your efforts and for expending those resources.

You'll want to know whether there's any guarantee you'll receive those benefits.

Also, don't forget that you will want to know about the risks. What can go wrong? How might the idea be flawed? And of course, you will want to know how you plan to eliminate, minimize, or respond to these risks.

Finally, you have questions about immediate action steps. What do you do right now, right after the presentation, or shortly afterward?

If you answer these questions concisely, you'll have presented a strong argument that a problem or opportunity exists and that you have a well-thought out action step that responds to the problem or opportunity.

The information you'll present is the sentences you will write in response to the key questions we just asked.

# The Key Questions to Answer to Persuade

1. Why should I listen to you?
2. What is going on?
3. What should we do?
4. How do we do that?
5. What will doing this cost us? What resources must we give to this?
6. What benefits will we receive?
7. How do I know we'll receive those benefits?
8. What could go wrong?
9. What do you want me to do? Why?
10. What do you want from me right now?

The persuasive structure is also great for responding to questions. Try memorizing the questions, and when someone asks a question during a presentation, respond to the question by responding to the 10 questions.

For example, someone might ask you, "How do you plan to introduce this new report so that the recipients think it's useful and will read it?"

You can respond:

1. The report hasn't been considered very useful by many readers.

2. The problem seems to be that it is very difficult to locate the conclusions of the data.

3. Let's move the conclusions section to the first page, at the top.

4. We can easily modify the template.

5. And because so few people work with this template, we won't have to spend much time making sure they know how to use the modified version.

6. We'll make the new report format appealing to the readers because the information they want first will appear first.

7. This approach to the problem is very similar to what the finance department did with their quarterly status reports a few months ago. The new format was received very favorably.

8. About the only risk is that the people who use the template might take a few attempts before they're comfortable with it. But I'm confident we can handle this small problem by speaking with these few people in person.

9. So let's modify the template to make the material more relevant and to make sure the readers can find what they're looking for.

10. Can we all agree to try the new format for the next report?

Let's review how to respond to each question in the list so that the structure contains all the information needed to present a clear argument.

# 1. Why Should I Listen to You?

Your listeners will want to know why they should listen to you. What is special about your idea?

Respond in one or two sentences to this opening question. Make a statement that draws attention to an opportunity or a benefit. Comment on an issue of current interest to the organization. Describe an event or a predicament.

Consider opening statements such as:

"We have a chance to make our product appealing to our most frequent customers, even as they age and retire."

"As many of you know, we have had a 200 percent increase in customer complaints since we reformulated our instant mixes."

"Our sales for our primary product have decreased an average of 7% quarterly for the past five quarters."

Your opening statement should directly answer the question, "Why should I listen to you?" The listener should hear the answer to that question clearly.

Your opening statement should last no more than 30 seconds. The listeners have a lot on their minds, and they will think about their own concerns, not yours, unless you make a strong case for listening.

## 2. What Is Going On?

The listeners need to know the context of your idea. You've opened with a statement that grabbed their attention and made your presentation issue seem relevant to them, but you have to prove it's relevant and make sure they know what you're talking about. Now you want to sketch a picture of the scenario behind the idea you're going to describe in step three.

Explain briefly, in less than a minute, what the situation is. There's a problem. There has been an event. Something has changed. Do not give lots of detail about the situation. If you describe the situation in detail, people will begin to try to solve the problem as they understand it. They will not be listening.

You could use these statements to explain briefly what's going on after you have opened any of the three presentations introduced in the preceding section.

**Beware**

Don't open a presentation with a comment about your topic! "Today we're going to talk about fire and safety regulations." Topic statements can be deadly! It's not interesting to hear what someone will talk about. It is interesting to get information about a benefit or opportunity —something that affects us as listeners. "New fire and safety regulations come into force the first of next month."

**Beware**

Limit your description of the context to three or four sentences. You are explaining the reason your idea is needed, and you don't want to create concern over a problem. People are very problem-oriented. People like to solve problems. Describe a problem, and you'll have a group of problem solvers listening to a solution that isn't theirs.

"Ten years ago, the average age of our most frequent customers was 30. In the coming years, the average age of our most frequent customers will be 59."

"We reformulated our mixes a year ago to extend their shelf life. That reformulation modified the product taste, although our test market seemed not to care."

"As you are fully aware, our technology is quickly becoming obsolete. When we committed to video, we assumed the market would never respond to the more expensive digital alternatives. We underestimated the speed of research that has made digital so inexpensive."

## 3. What Should We Do?

Listeners want to know what they will have to do, how they should act, to what they should consider committing, so you'll have to tell them what you're asking for. In one sentence, tell the listeners exactly what you want them to do. What is your idea?

These sentences build the presentations further.

"I'm here today to ask you to commit $1.5 million to modify the handles and buttons on all our products."

"We need to modify our mix again, and that will take an executive directive to reexamine the alternatives and then executive authorization to increase product cost by $.03 per SKU, representing a 2% price increase or a decrease in profit margins."

"I'm asking you to underwrite a major market research study and to create a new products research group so that we can have products ready to replace our current line-up."

Don't discuss the idea yet, just present it. Be prepared for some strong reaction to the idea because no one yet understands it. Ideally, state the idea in words that make an action step clear. Spend no more than 15 to 30 seconds on the idea, and move quickly to answer the next key question.

## 4. How Do We Do That?

Because you've asked for an action response, the listeners are going to want to know what that action response requires of them. So review the major action steps and then discuss the details of the idea. Give an overview of how the idea will be implemented, and follow the overview with a review of the key steps.

"The process will be relatively simple, requiring industrial design studies and recommendations. Based on the recommendations, we can assess the retooling costs and marketing requirements to shift our focus to this new segment. So we'll also have to do some market research."

"The product research will be an additional burden on our existing staff, but it's a classic process that presents no new requirements other than staffing."

"Setting up the research work is relatively easy, and our market research group is ready to begin as soon as you say, 'yes.' But we'll want to do a benchmark study on new product research groups before we commit to a structure and know what kind of talent we'll look for."

## 5. What Will Doing This Cost Us, and What Resources Must We Give to This?

Your description of the action steps needed will raise many questions about costs. So explain, briefly, the costs of the idea. Even if the idea does not have financial costs, explain how and why there are no financial costs. Also explain what resources the idea requires.

"The cost for the industrial design studies is $X, which we can fund from our existing research budget. But the market research funding will have to be an increase from our current budget. Also, some of the work might have to be done by consultants, so we'll probably be looking at an addition to our annual budget of $10 million once we factor in the consulting fees, their space requirements, and the increase in our computing capacity."

"The research work will require about $400,000, including taste testing and financial analysis of the implications of the results."

"The market research will cost $250,000. The benchmarking study will cost an additional $150,000. Our understanding is that the information is available, although we will need to purchase access to it. After we have this information, we can prepare a financial analysis of the costs and returns for a new product research group."

**Handy Hint**
When you figure out the costs of a proposal, identify all the resources required. What kinds of money must be committed? How many hours or work days will be required? What is the length of time needed to produce results? Are there requirements for space? Equipment? Consultants?

## 6. What Benefits Will We Receive?

You've now built a clear explanation of why you're speaking to the group, what you want, and what they have to give you if they say "yes." So they'll want to know what they get in return. What benefits will the listeners receive from the idea? Describe traditional business benefits: cost reduction, resource reduction, increased sales and profits, productivity increases, and efficiencies. If you can describe benefits that you know are personally relevant to the listeners, you'll have a stronger argument.

For example, some ideas might increase sales and profits, and those benefits are very important. But the ideas also might polish an organization's reputation, show how a department is unusually innovative, or showcase a new executive's talents and contributions.

"The primary benefit of modifying the handles and buttons on our products is an increased market in our new, primary targeted segment. But these changes also will position us to add an additional segment, the physically challenged group of consumers who will find easier to use tools and implements appealing. We'll also be positioning ourselves for product extensions. And the benefits will show up on our bottom line quickly, helping us recoup our costs within the first 18 months."

"The primary benefit of our efforts will be an improved product that can rebuild our market base without sacrificing the shelf life increase we consider essential to remaining in this market."

"The benefit is simple. Either we move forward with the times and invest in the future, or we won't be here next decade."

## 7. How Do I Know We'll Receive Those Benefits?

Benefits are appealing. We get something. But benefits are easy to promise and not always so easy to deliver. Your listeners will want to know how reliable your promises are.

After you've explained which benefits the idea will produce, describe how you know those benefits will result from the idea. Has the idea worked elsewhere? Does market research show a strong likelihood of success for the idea? Are the financial analyses so well thought out that the logic of the idea is easy to see?

"We've done some preliminary market research and have identified an enormous need for modified handles and buttons. And once we factor in all the costs versus the increase in sales, the benefits are easy to quantify and become quite appealing."

"The only way I can convince you to commit the funding to this additional research work is to get you to consider the alternative—a decreasing market share. The benefit is a given—with knowledge will come a better decision, a better product, a better product position with our customer."

"This is a life and death situation for our organization. We move forward or die."

## 8. What Can Go Wrong?

The eighth question is a dangerous one. If you respond to it, you can raise issues that ruin your presentation. If you ignore it, you might appear slick, or you might seem to have avoided key issues. Briefly raise one or more issues that are risky in the idea. Don't raise major risks that will take lengthy discussion to resolve.

After raising the issues, answer them. Be very brief. Show the listeners how you have prethought solutions to potential problems.

To raise the issues, use phrases such as:

"Some of you might be wondering how we'll handle…"

"It occurred to me as I prepared this presentation that some of you might wonder whether…"

"One question that might need to be examined here is…."

How can you weave this issue into your presentation?

> **Beware**
> Before making any presentation, brainstorm all the possible objections and risks. Put answers to the objections and risks into the presentation structure. If there are any critical issues, prepare responses and have that information ready. The eighth question is not the place to get the listeners thinking about the high risk aspects of your idea.

"Some of you might be concerned that modifying our product will threaten our current customers. But we've verified with our current market research efforts that our existing customers would respond quite favorably to tools and implements that are easier to grasp and work."

"It has occurred to me as I've been wrestling with this problem that we might not find an answer. Our shelf life requirement might make the taste factor less important. But we won't know if there are flavor modifications that can help us retrieve our market share unless we do the research."

"It is possible that we won't be able to develop attractive new products for our future, but we won't know until we try. The alternative is certainly less expensive, but also unappealing."

## 9. So What Do You Want Me to Do? Why?

You'll have covered a lot of information at this point, and your listeners will need to be brought back to the basic concerns. What are you asking them to do, and why? Review the idea, step three, and briefly review the benefits of the idea, step six.

"I'm asking you today to take a big step, commit $1.5 million to a major change in our products to capture a larger market that represents significantly increased profitability for us."

"So I'm asking you to authorize the research work and then use the results to assess alternatives. It seems better to limit our profit margins somewhat and regain market share than to continue to lose market share."

"I'm asking you to underwrite these costs, effective immediately."

## 10. What Do You Want from Me Right Now?

The listeners are now ready to respond, and you have to decide how big a step they're ready to take. Are they ready to make the big commitment you've asked for in step three? Or will they need time to discuss the idea and review information? Ask for a response, but don't ask for a big response unless they're prepared.

> "I'm asking that you spend time this week reviewing the handouts I've provided so that you fully understand what we need to do and the accompanying costs. I'll be calling you next Monday to see if we can begin the project."

> "Can I have your authorization?"

> "Shall we move forward today?"

# How Can You Prepare the Presentation and Notes?

**Handy Hint**
Be sure that when you read aloud, the ten basic sentences that answer the questions about the situation, idea, and logic are clear.

To prepare a persuasive presentation, write a one sentence response to each question. Add details as needed to support and clarify the sentences for questions 2, 4, 5, 6, 7, 8, and 9.

As you'll see in the two examples here and from the three outlined previously, the "one sentence" rule is not strict. But it is helpful when you begin to structure your presentation to write a single sentence that summarizes what you'll actually say so that you can be sure you're making sense.

Let's look at two high-level presentations.

## Presentation Example One

1. Why should I listen to you?

   "Many of you probably don't realize that the smallest store in our chain sees twice as much foot traffic daily as our newest store."

2. What is going on?

   "There is a major shift today away from large suburban malls to smaller, boutique-oriented mini-malls."

3. What should we do?

   "I'm recommending that we consider closing our newest store and turning it into a mini-mall. I'm here today to ask you to fund a study to assess the feasibility of this idea."

4. How do we do that?

   "The process of turning a store into a mini-mall is relatively straightforward. It will involve modifying our structures, altering how we present our brands, and repositioning our market. But the important step is to assess the feasability of this dramatic change."

5. What will doing this cost us? What resources must we give to this?

   "The study will cost $350,000. The study will tell us what the costs will be for the transformation of our newest store into a mini-mall."

6. What benefits will we receive?

   "We'll find out whether we can increase our "sales per store" by changing our idea of what a store is."

7. How do I know we'll receive those benefits?

   "At worst, we'll discover that the mini-mall idea is not a good one, and we'll know it's worth our while to be creative about ways to make our newest store more profitable."

8. What could go wrong?

   "You might be concerned about the costs of this study, but with a multimillion dollar facility involved, that cost seems minimal."

9. What do you want me to do? Why?

   "So I'm asking you to fund the study and see if we should modify our newest store to become a mini-mall to capture the market and profits of the future."

10. What do you want from me right now?

    "What do you think? Should I move ahead with the study?"

## Presentation Example Two

1. Why should I listen to you?

   "No one here today has ever ridden a camel."

2. What is going on?

   "We have a tradition in this firm of being unadventurous, even staid."

3. What should we do?

   "I'm suggesting we sponsor a culture-busting event and introduce some humor into our company."

4. How do we do that?

   "We should schedule the 'Corporate Follies' for our holiday party."

5. What will doing this cost us? What resources must we give to this?

   "For a Saturday in the prime holiday period, we'll have to pay $500,000 plus provide an administrative assistant for all the logistics work."

6. What benefits will we receive?

   "We stand to gain employees who think we care and a new outlook on ourselves."

7. How do I know we'll receive those benefits?

   "The research I've done into this group says they're exactly the group we need to get us to begin being less staid for the new year."

8. What could go wrong?

   "Some of you might be concerned that this is an expensive, unusual step, and you'd be right."

9. What do you want me to do? Why?

   "I'm asking you to spend a great deal of money, $500,000, to begin to change the atmosphere around here."

10. What do you want from me right now?

    "Here are some brochures for you to review so that you can discuss the idea and give me your response this afternoon."

## The Least You Need to Know

➤ If you have a great idea or a solution to a problem, you'll need a fluid, concise, strategic presentation that catches the attention of the listeners. Prepare the presentation by responding to the ten questions.

➤ Each question needs a complete sentence that fully answers the question. Add the details later.

➤ Always check to make sure the ten sentences are clear and logical.

# Part 3
# Support—Space and Visual Aids

*Presenters need to be comfortable using the space they're given for the presentation and the equipment they need to use visual aids effectively. Many presenters underestimate the amount of preparation it takes to look effective in front of an audience. Always know how the room will be set up so that you can do as much as possible to make the space meet your needs. Choose your visual aids medium carefully so that it provides support and doesn't become a circus. And figure out well in advance how to handle handouts.*

# Chapter 10

# Be Sure the Room is Presentation-Friendly

## In This Chapter

➤ Check the room and do everything you can to make sure it suits your needs and makes it easy to present.

➤ Choose a seating configuration to permit the listeners to listen comfortably to your message and respond as you want them to.

➤ Set up a team presentation so that it runs smoothly.

All too often, you'll be thrown into a situation when you have to make a presentation, but you won't have much time to prepare for it or to check the room where you'll be presenting. The audio visual equipment might be awful, the room too small or too large, unattractive, and perhaps decorated with mirrors. And sometimes, even worse, the room could be so wonderful, with a great view of a gorgeous landscape, that you won't be able to hold anyone's attention for long.

Always remember that you should be fully prepared for your presentation. Knowing the room you'll be working in is a part of preparing. Most of the time you'll know the room, or you'll have an opportunity to visit the room in advance and make sure the set-up will meet your needs. Take advantage of every opportunity to be prepared so that if something does go wrong, you know how to handle the problem.

Make sure you know how a room is set up so that you can use the space comfortably and keep the focus on the ideas in the presentation, not on the room, its lighting, its comfort, or the machinery you're using.

*You're* the presentation. It's up to you to get everything set up so that *you* are the point of interest. It's not helpful to have the room and its peculiarities be the point of interest.

## Consider This

One presenter, let's call her Tracy, had to make a presentation to a group of six people. Tracy was flying in from another city and couldn't get to the room until early on the morning of the presentation, and the presentation began at 8:00 a.m. Tracy discovered at 7:00 a.m. that the room was a small, narrow bar room often used during conferences. The room was approximately 12' by 20', with a bar permanently installed on one side. Tracy's presentation required video and flipcharts. The table was a conference table, and the participants needed tables for note taking. There was almost no space for walking or standing.

Tracy asked for an alternative room and was told there was none. Due to construction at the hotel, the floor normally used was unavailable. In fact, Tracy discovered that the construction project was just getting underway—with jack hammers going full force on that floor, just above the one she was on.

Tracy had to move from the front of the room, which accommodated the video equipment, to the back of the room, which had just enough space for the flipchart. She had to move from front to back via the bar area, which required climbing over the bar and walking out its opening to get to the front, and walking back through the opening and climbing over the end to get to the back.

So Tracy gave her presentation, did a lot of climbing, and spoke very loudly to make sure she could be heard over the jackhammers.

An unusual situation? Yes. But it did happen. It helped that Tracy had a good sense of humor. And besides, from Tracy's perspective, the presentation had to go on. Luckily, Tracy was the presentation and didn't let the environmental challenges become her message. She kept the listeners focused on her and on her message.

# Know Your Room

The room is the first major challenge for most speakers. If the room is too small, the listeners will be uncomfortable, and if you stand, they might find you intimidating. If the room is too big, the listeners could sit too far apart or too closely together. When too far apart, the presentation environment quickly becomes cold and socially distant. When too close together in a large space, the listeners quickly become a group of buddies huddled together—potentially against the speaker.

Of course, if the room is too big, it's awfully difficult to appear enthusiastic and credible because you'll need to shout to be heard adequately.

If you have a choice, select a room that provides just enough space for everyone to sit comfortably and see the visual aids you'll be using.

Set up the room so that the seating creates the interaction you want. If there will be lots of note-taking, use tables and chairs as shown in the following figure.

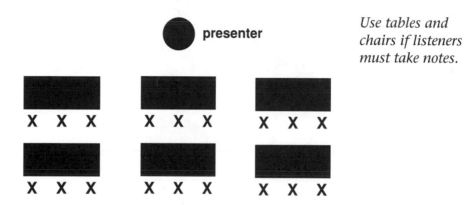

*Use tables and chairs if listeners must take notes.*

If there will be limited note-taking and most of the presentation will feature you as the speaker, use chairs and place them auditorium style.

But consider that many people want to take notes, and that most people prefer to sit with access to a table so that they can take notes comfortably. Of course, with a formal presentation in a large room, tables won't work, so use chairs set up auditorium style as illustrated in the following figure.

*Use auditorium seating for presenter-focused presentations.*

107

If you want interaction among groups, use chairs with or without tables, in groups of five to eight or, with a large group, use a U-shaped configuration.

Why groups of five to eight? Discussion seems to be easiest when there are enough people to create some energy among the group and not so many people that participants are intimidated by the number of listeners. So a group of five to eight works best for discussion (see the following figures).

*The "U" configuration helps people see the visual aids and encourages discussion.*

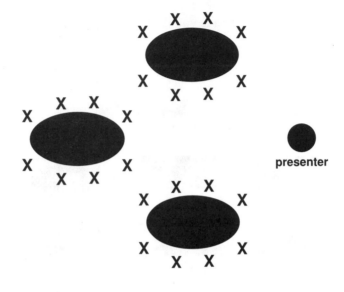

*Group the listeners to encourage discussion.*

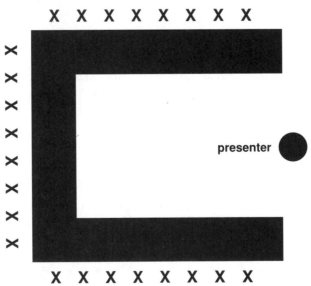

Also, if you'll be using visual aids, set up the room to make it easy for everyone to see the visuals. If you're using tables, slant them so that people can see the screen. Position the chairs so that each listener can see the visuals.

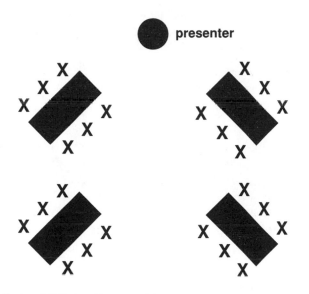

*Slant the tables to help listeners see visual aids.*

Frequently, you'll find that the room you've been assigned has an enormous conference room table in the middle, with chairs around it. You have no choice about any set-up beyond what you've been given. In this instance, make sure your style of delivery is so engaging that the listeners forget about the room and concentrate on what you're saying. And consider delivering the presentation from the middle of the table rather than from the end.

## Check Machines, Bring Backup, or Know Where Backup Is

Before the presentation begins, review all the equipment you plan to use for the presentation.

If you'll be using an overhead projector and screen, examine the projector in advance and find out where the on/off switch is located. Check the screen to ensure it is large enough and in good enough condition to project clean images. Focus the image of the visual.

If you'll be using computer-based slides projected on a screen, set up all the connections and try the entire presentation to make sure the images are clear and big enough to see.

> ## Consider This
>
> One presenter found out the hard way that although most computer-based presentations are easy to deliver, the "auto slide advance" option must be disabled unless you plan to use it. As he talked about the information presented on his first slide, the computer continued through the slide show. Because he hadn't checked the presentation in advance using the equipment in the room, he didn't discover that someone else had reviewed the presentation and set it up as a slide show.
>
> Slide-show capability can be very appealing if you want the presentation timed a certain way. But if you want the presentation to be something that you control, you have to make certain that the equipment works with you, not against you.

If you plan to work with a flipchart, test it to ensure that it is sturdy and positioned for everyone to see. Ensure that the markers provided are usable and not dried out. Also be sure to have more than one color pen so you can emphasize or point something out using a different color.

Make sure you have colors that will be easy to see, such as black, blue, dark purple, bright green, and red. These colors are easy to read from a distance, although red is not useful for anything except highlighting small bits of important data because it hurts the eyes after a while. So take notes with the deeper colors and use red as an accent.

Be aware that many corporations are trying to cut costs by buying only the kind of markers that are designed for use on white boards. White board markers usually have a noxious odor and dry out fast if used on paper. Also, some corporations don't provide markers, so you should plan to bring your own. Other corporations provide lots of markers, all black. So bring some other colors with you if you're going to be highlighting information on a flipchart during your presentation.

If you plan to use a slide projector, work with it in advance to make sure the auto-focus works. If it's not working quite right, disable auto-focus and focus each slide yourself. Check the remote control to see if it is wired (attached with a cord) or wireless. Make sure that "forward" means "forward" and that "backward" means "backward." Sometimes the wiring no longer works correctly, and you can push forward but the projector goes to the previous slide.

### Consider This

One of the funniest presentations ever given at a controller's conference was not meant to be funny. The presenter, the divisional controller in the confectionary division, was reviewing the process of coating candy. The slides were photographs of the plant and showed the entire process of coating candy.

But as the controller talked about each slide, the projector was trying to locate "focus." The result was that each slide would go all the way past focus to out of focus, return to focus and pass by it to out of focus the other way. The colorful photographs of the candy going through the coating stages became a color and light show.

The problem was that the slides were warped. Because the slides were not flat, the projector's auto-focus couldn't figure out how to focus them. Parts of the slide were closer to the mechanism than others, creating the constant search for a focal point.

Unfortunately, the controller didn't know how to stop the floating focus or how to get a backup machine. The presentation was funny, but no one learned much about the coating process.

Always bring backup equipment or know where to get it:

➤ Get the phone number of the service staff at the hotel or conference center.

➤ Know the extension of the visual aids group at the site where you're presenting.

➤ Ask the visual aids support staff where the extra equipment is.

➤ Check to see that extra bulbs are in the machine and that those extra bulbs still work!

And while you're getting the physical lay-out just right for your presentation, mark the position of the machinery and the tables with masking tape. Often, you'll discover that someone has come into the room and moved the equipment, repositioning it on its cart, making all your pre-work useless. What should you mark?

➤ Put a masking-tape "X" next to three corners of the machine on its cart, whether the machine is an overhead projector or slide projector.

➤ Put a masking-tape "X" next to three of the cart legs on the floor or carpet.

➤ And if needed, put masking tape at the point on the projector arm where the focus arm/mechanism sits.

This way, if someone moves the cart, the equipment, or the focus arm, you can put them back the way you wanted without having to do so in front of all your listeners.

## Set Up Sound and Lights

When you prepare the room, set the sound and light controls that will make your presentation easy to listen to and see. Sit where the listeners will sit and make sure you can see around the equipment and past you, the speaker, to the visual aids.

If you'll be using equipment with sound, set up the sound controls so that everyone can hear and no one has to sit near a speaker that is overly loud. People shouldn't cringe when you turn on the sound, but they also shouldn't turn their ears toward the equipment straining to hear.

Remember that sound gets absorbed by bodies, clothing, tables, curtains, walls, and so on. Set the volume to be a little bit louder than appears necessary when the room is empty.

**Handy Hint**
Mark the volume-control position with tape or washable marker so that just before the presentation you can check to make sure no one has changed the controls.

If you're using a room with lighting controls, find out which controls darken the room only where the projection screen sits so that the projected images can be bright but the audience can sit in lighted areas.

If the lighting controls give you options only to make the room all bright or all dark, try to have bulbs removed, if possible. If you ask the support group to remove a few bulbs for you, they will often help willingly. But don't remove bulbs yourself unless you know how, can do so safely, and aren't violating any site-specific and/or union regulations.

# Carefully Plan How a Team Presentation Will Flow

Team presentations are potentially interesting for the listeners because different people speak and bring different styles, voices, language choices, and perspectives. But team presentations are hard to orchestrate.

Individual presentations are easier to set up and deliver than team presentations because you are the only person who has to deal with the content, the visual aids, and the audience. But team presentations are central to today's team-based organizations.

# Assign Roles Strategically

When you prepare the team presentation:

➤ Make sure all the presenters practice and help set up together.

➤ Pick the person with the strongest presentation style and credibility level for the opening.

➤ Put the weaker presenters in the middle of the presentation.

➤ Place a stronger presenter as the last speaker.

Make sure everyone has a clear role for the presentation:

➤ Who will handle the visual aids, change them, and make sure they're clear?

➤ Who will take notes on questions asked during the presentation that will be responded to at the end of the presentation?

➤ Decide how each presenter will hand over the presentation to the next speaker. Decide how introductions will be made—all at once at the beginning, or will each speaker introduce the next speaker?

Write introductions for each presenter so that the information provided is short, consistent, and relevant.

## Consider This

Remember the last presentation you sat through when the introductions took the first 15 minutes? The "host" read the complete biography of the each of the five speakers, where they went to school and which awards they received 25 years ago. Not only did you not care, you probably couldn't remember each person's biography when they got up to speak.

Limit biographical information to a few key facts that show why a speaker is credible on the topic to be discussed. Hand out biographical information in advance if it's something the listeners might want. Keep the introductions short, sweet, and to the point.

Assign someone to manage the question and answer session. Who will determine who responds to each type of question? Who will make sure that all the questions are responded to so that one audience member doesn't dominate the question-and-answer session?

Determine how differences of opinion among the presenters will be handled: Will the manager of the question-and-answer session be responsible for telling the presenters to stop? Will the presenters be allowed to respond only if the question-and-answer manager calls on them?

Assign each presenter responsibility for bringing extra information on his/her topics in case extra information is needed. Assign the responsibilities appropriately so that the person who is best able to deal with each issue is the one in charge of it. Use the team's strengths!

## Establish Ground Rules for Contributions and Transitions

Also, with a team presentation, the team members should decide what hand signals they will use to communicate with one another:

➤ What hand signal will tell the current speaker to be louder or softer?

➤ What hand signal will tell the current speaker to slow down or speed up?

➤ What hand signal will tell the current speaker to stop for a moment to handle questions and concerns.

## Preparing Scripts and Notes

Part of preparing a presentation is creating the necessary script or notes. Scripts are generally not a good idea because the presenter will have a tendency to read the script word-for-word. But sometimes, such as when you use a Teleprompter, you'll have to have a script.

More often, you'll have notes you'll want to use during the presentation.

**Handy Hint**
Try using 5×8 note cards or regular paper rather than 3×5 cards. If you use the larger cards, the writing on them can be bigger, and the reading is a lot easier. Paper permits even larger writing and easier reading.

First, create an outline of the presentation. What are you going to say? What are your messages and the supporting facts? Second, draft the script as if you are saying exactly what you want to say. Pick the words you'll want to use. Include the examples. Write in a style that represents your speaking, not your writing.

Third, read the script out loud several times. If you have several days between the preparation and the delivery of the presentation, read the script out loud several times each day. Get familiar with the sequence, the flow of words, and the word choices you prefer.

Then, just before the presentation, create notes for that presentation.

You'll often modify the sequence at this point, but that's normal. Just make sure you resequence any visual aids affected.

Notes should be key words only, preferably a lot of nouns and verbs. Use print rather than script writing. If you're using a printer to produce the notes, make the words bold and large, and use an easy-to-read font.

You'll want to include key facts such as dollars, numbers, percentages, and quotes. Ideally, of course, the facts appear on the visual aids and you won't have to keep track of them on note cards, but if you do, make sure you have them.

Many speakers who are working with overhead transparencies will put cardboard frames around the transparencies, write the notes on 5×8 cards, and tape the cards to the frames. In doing so, they eliminate the need to work with a lectern and still keep their notes where they can easily see them. Plus, the notes are attached to the relevant images.

**Definition**

A **lectern** is the stand you put your notes on. Lecterns are often large, wooden furniture with lights and buttons for controlling the audio visual machinery. Sometimes they are lightweight and portable—and can easily collapse if you lean on them. Others are half-height and sit on tables.

A **podium** is a wooden structure you stand on top of. Podiums can be solid or flimsy. They can permit you to stand still or they can make your every minor movement look big to the listeners. Podiums help you stand above the listeners so that it is easier for a large group to see you.

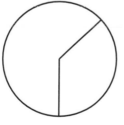

**We have a significant share of the market.**

market up 15%

our share up 25% to 40%

Expect repeat this year

*Tape a 5×8 notecard with your notes on it to the transparency frame.*

Speakers who are working with slide projectors or computer-based images will usually have a lectern so that the notes can sit on a surface and be read without having the speaker hold the notes throughout the presentation.

Can you hold notes during a presentation? Of course, but it's easier not to because you'll want to use hand gestures and concentrate visually on the audience, as you'll see in Part 4 of this book.

## Sometimes You'll Have to Use a Script

Many speakers use scripts because they worry they might not say the right words. In fact, listeners prefer to hear a message clearly, and the specific words are not the only carriers of a message.

If you are going to use a script, especially with a Teleprompter, mark the script with notes to guide you. Make sure you group the basic elements of the sentences so that you speak the subject and verb and object together. Mark the prepositional phrases so that you speak the preposition and its noun together.

**Consider This**

Speakers using scripts often speak unnaturally. They pronounce words they are reading, not words they are speaking. They don't "hear" the words they're using, so they divide the sentence units unnaturally.

Sometimes you'll hear a politician, for example, say things such as, "We are [pause] going to [pause] make a [pause] difference in this community." This speaking pattern makes the point sound odd and often will prevent the listeners from hearing, "We are going to make a difference [pause] in this community."

If you do use a script, be animated and listen to what you're saying so that the meaning of each word is clear and each grammatical unit is hooked together so that listeners hear your point, not just your words.

## The Least You Need to Know

➤ Prepare for every presentation as much as you can.

➤ Set up the room, the equipment, the seating, and the speakers, if you have more than one, so that the listeners can hear the message you came to deliver.

➤ Prepare your notes or script to enable you to be clear and to minimize the audience's awareness of your notes or script.

# Chapter 11

# Visual Support Helps Deliver the Message

---

**In This Chapter**

➤ Why use visual aids?

➤ When do you choose word visuals versus graphic visuals?

➤ How do you design visual aids so that they serve their purpose?

---

You use visual aids to help the listeners understand and remember important messages and facts. Visual aids are supportive. They don't send the message or convey the facts. They *do* make the message clearer and more memorable.

You need to help your listeners understand and remember messages and facts. When you make a presentation, you do a lot of talking, and people might try to remember everything you say, but they won't be able to. Some people won't even want to hear what you're saying or remember it later. So use visual aids to make messages visible and to clarify the messages you're sending, the facts you're sharing, and the ideas you want remembered.

Unfortunately, one of the biggest errors people make is to create visually stunning slides or transparencies—the audience leaves the presentation thinking of how visually stunning the presentation was, and not about the message. Or the presenter creates an exciting multimedia presentation, and the audience is impressed by the gadgetry and not the content.

This chapter helps you design visual aids that support the message you're sending, and Chapter 12 will help you select and use the media for creating those visual aids.

# When and How Many Visual Aids to Use

Use visual aids any time you want the listeners to remember and understand a message or fact, or review details of an explanation or concept that must be seen to be understood. Also use visual aids to signal to the audience that you're talking about a new topic or message.

*Visual aids support your presentation.*

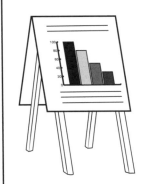

**USE VISUAL AIDS TO HELP LISTENERS**

- **Remember facts,**

- **Understand ideas, numerical relationships, physical layouts, and**

- **Recognize that you're discussing a new topic.**

**Handy Hint**

There are no rules for how many visual aids you should have in a presentation, but consider the reaction of the audience. If you walk in with 50 overhead transparencies for a 30-minute presentation, the audience will feel overwhelmed before you even begin.

One visual aid for every 3 to 5 minutes of presentation is a reasonable guideline.

If you're not aiming to get the listeners to remember or understand a piece of information, you don't need a visual aid.

Be considerate, too, when using visual aids. If you try to include too many visual aids, the information blurs and the audience will become confused.

You might want to use a visual aid to make sure a message is heard and remembered. The following figure conveys a key message you want listeners to remember.

**WE MUST FOCUS ON
HOLIDAY SALES**

*Notice the message
title of the visual
aid.*

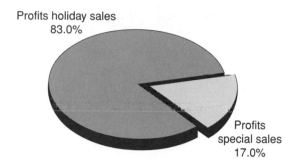

Or you might want to use a visual aid to help the listeners understand how a piece of equipment works or how a building's floorplan will look. The following figure is typical of this type of visual aid.

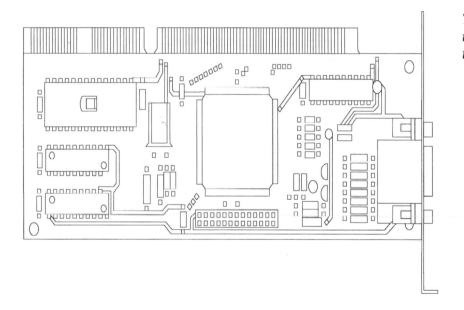

*This visual aid
uses a message
title, too.*

You can use visual aids to signal a switch in topics, too, as you can see in the next figure.

One of the first questions you'll need to answer for each visual aid is whether you're trying to get the listeners to remember action steps or key words, or whether you want them to remember a concept. And you'll want to make sure that regardless of the content of a visual aid, you use a message title that tells the listeners how to interpret the information on the visual aid.

*You would show
the agenda and say,
"Let's switch to our
third topic."*

---

## AGENDA

- Outcomes accomplished 1st quarter

- Expectations for 2nd quarter

- Possible constraints for 3rd quarter

- Immediate action steps required

*"Let's switch to our third topic..."*

---

# Use Message Titles with Clear Verbs

Use a message title for every visual aid you create. A *message title* is a brief sentence that summarizes the message the visual aid is sending. For example:

"Sales have been decreasing since 2nd quarter."

"Fewer children are attending preschools in the northeast."

"Use 5 steps to submit claims."

**Handy Hint**

Some people use flow charts to explain a process. Flow charts can be very helpful, but you might want to join a flow chart to the word-based description of the flow of events so that the listeners remember the words and visually understand the steps of the process.

The message title answers the question, "What must the listeners know, think, or do about the information presented in the visual aid?"

If you provide a message title for each visual aid, the listeners will understand how to interpret the information provided.

The listeners should be able to read only the message title and skip the content and understand what kind of content you covered, even if they don't know the details.

Using message titles helps you provide usable hand-outs, too. Whenever the listeners review the handouts, the message titles help them to remember how you explained the information.

# Use Words for Action Steps and Key Terminology

Use words when you want the listeners to remember action steps and key words. If the visual aid will help them remember the five-step process they need to follow to submit an insurance claim, as shown in the figure below, use words.

---

**FILE INSURANCE CLAIMS PROMPTLY:**

- Write name, home address, claim number in boxes on top of form.

- Describe accident in box 7.

- Sign form on signature line, bottom of page.

- Staple accident report to form.

- Mail form to Home Office address listed on form.

---

*The message title tells the listeners what to do.*

If you want the listeners to remember the words themselves, such as an ad campaign's, "Think bright!" or terminology such as the name of chemicals, a company, of people, or of competitors' products, use words as in the next figure.

---

**TWO PRODUCTS THREATEN OUR FRANCHISE WITH THE ELDERLY**

- **SEE-AROWND-IT**
- **SPEAK-LOWDER**

---

*You want the listeners to remember the product names.*

# Keep Bullets Parallel

If you do use words—and they make visual aids easy to create, especially with the formats provided by today's graphics software—make sure you keep the information "parallel." Parallel means that if you are using more than one line of words, each of those lines has to match the others' grammar.

For example, if you're listing product attributes, you would list all adjectives:

➤ Easy-to-prepare

➤ Flavorful

➤ Colorful

➤ Bubbly

You wouldn't want to list product attributes with a mix of a noun and adjectives as shown here because the first one, the noun, is what the product is, not an attribute of the product:

➤ Beverage

➤ Flavorful

➤ Colorful

➤ Bubbly

As another example, you might want to explain a process for submitting ideas to management for cost reductions. You could describe the process using a series of statements beginning with active verbs:

➤ Describe the idea you're recommending, using form 32XZ.

➤ Send the form to the Chief Technologist at maildrop 1LN17.

➤ Check the bulletin board outside the lunch room three days later to see if the Chief Technologist would like additional information about the idea.

If you presented this process with a mix of grammatical structures, you would not be clear to the listeners:

➤ Form 32XZ

➤ Send the form to the Chief Technologist at maildrop 1LN17

➤ Additional information posted on board outside lunch room within one week

## Pick Great Verbs

If you use words for your visual aids, use the most interesting verbs you can find. Try to use verbs that create pictures of actions so that what you're describing creates those pictures in the minds of the listeners.

---

## SALES DROPPED 38%

- **Frequency of sales calls decreased from 3/month to 1/month**

- **Competitive products entered the market**

- **Sales training decreased**

*Many visual aids would say "Sales down 38%," which is not as powerful as, "Sales dropped 38%."*

## UNEXPECTEDLY BAD WEATHER THREATENS OUR PROFITABILITY

- **Tornadoes assaulted the region in mid-year.**

- **Flooding drowned the region in early fall.**

- **Early blizzards blanketed the region before the holiday season.**

*Threatens is a verb that calls many images to mind.*

## WIGAMIGAME CAPTURED 12% OF THE MARKET

- **Game attracts junior high students.**

- **Packaging appeals to younger teens.**

- **Teens dominate the game-buying audience.**

*Captured is a verb that conveys a clear picture.*

# Use Pictures and Graphs for Concepts

If you want the listeners to remember a concept, use pictures and graphs. If you want the listeners to remember a comparison, use a graph showing the comparison. If you want the listeners to remember that the sales trend is increasing or decreasing, show the sales trend increasing or decreasing with a trend line chart.

**Handy Hint**

People think in pictures, so if you provide pictures that convey your concept, you stand a good chance of getting the listeners to remember the concept.

If you discuss cereal, listeners see boxes or bowls of cereal, not the word, "cereal." And if you want them to see boxes of it, not bowls of it, show them the boxes.

## Make Sure the Message Title Tells the Story

Because people think in pictures but we don't all think the same thoughts based on the same pictures, visual aids with pictures and graphs are not always easy to understand. Pictures and graphs are often very easy to misinterpret. Using a message title for each visual aid helps the listeners know exactly how you want them to interpret the information provided.

You don't have to create a message title for "Objectives" or "Agenda," but try to have a message title for the visual aids that clarify information or that you want the listener to remember.

# Choose the Picture and Graph Based on Clear Verbs

It can be difficult to figure out how to communicate a concept using a picture or graph. If you write the message title for each visual aid first, you'll have a sense of whether you need a word slide or a picture/graph slide. Then, if you need a picture or graph, use the verb of the message to guide you.

➤ Does the verb talk about a trend? Use a trend line.

➤ Does the verb talk about growth or shrinking? Use an up or down arrow.

➤ Does the verb focus on comparison? Use a bar chart.

➤ Does the verb focus on segmenting? Use a pie chart.

➤ Does the verb refer to a human relationship or people activity? Use a cartoon.

With graphics software making it easier for all of us to use pictures and tables, it is important to remember that the message is why you're using a visual aid. Your purpose is to get the listeners to know, think, or do something. Make the visual aids serve your purpose and avoid getting so involved in making things visually powerful that the visual aid becomes a message all by itself. Keep visual aids simple—use the graphics and pictures to make things clear, not just to use them.

# Simplify

Keep visual aids simple. Simplicity doesn't mean primitive, sloppy, or incomplete. Simple means that you should provide the information needed to communicate the message and no more than that.

The message title should clarify what the listeners need to know, think, or do about the information presented by the visual aid. It tells them what to take away from the visual aid. If the listeners have to spend a great deal of time examining the visual aid to understand it, then the visual aid is overly complex and not useful.

## Consider This

If you are presenting information on one slide and you want to talk about each element, consider a "build slide." Build slides have one item on the opening slide and additional slides add more items. Build slides allow you to keep the listeners focused on the information you're discussing.

First, create the slide—preferably with no more than five bullets of information on it. Make sure all the wording is parallel.

Second, create the first build slide so that it has only the message title and first bullet on it.

Third, create the second build slide so that the first bullet is a lighter color and the new bullet is in the primary text color.

Fourth, create the third build slide so that the first two bullets are in the lighter color and the third bullet is in the primary text color.

Follow this process until you have the complete slide that you originally created as the "summary" slide, with all the bulleted items in the primary text color.

For computer-generated slides, do the build automatically with a simple command in the tools menu.

# Eliminate Any Non-Essentials

Whether you're using words or pictures and graphs, create the message title and then the visual aid itself. Then, eliminate all the words or graphics elements that you can without damaging the message itself. The following figures are examples of simplification.

*This chart is accurate, but it contains a lot of information.*

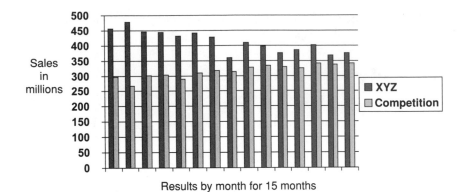

*This version of the chart eliminates some information and is easy to understand.*

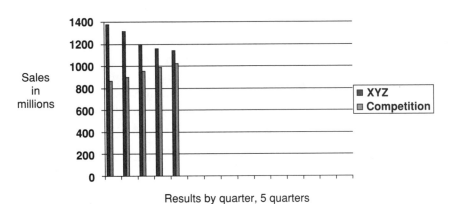

*This chart is very simple and makes a clear, easy-to-understand point.*

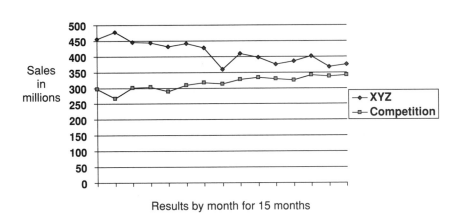

## Limit Items to Five or Fewer

Avoid describing more than five details at a time on one visual aid. Fewer is better!

Most people have trouble remembering lots of details, so they just forget some of them or decide which ones are actually important, and remember only those. Sometimes the listeners remember only the first few details, assuming the presenter is talking about the most important details first.

This behavior can cause lots of trouble for the presenter if she wants the listeners to remember all the details or if she hasn't presented the ideas from "most important" to "least important."

If you use bullets, use five or fewer on each visual aid. If you use a graph, try to use five or fewer bars or pie segments. You can, of course, use as many as you need to communicate accurately the correct information, but listeners probably won't pay much attention to details if there are more than five.

**Beware**
Do not use red for numbers because being "in the red" financially is negative. It means you're losing money.

## Use Color

Color makes visual aids appealing and easier to remember. If a listener must mentally process more than black-and-white, he has done more work with the visual aid and is more likely to remember it.

Don't use a lot of color, but do use three or four colors. Choose bright, easy-to-read colors such as green, blue, or purple. Avoid challenging colors such as yellow. And try not to use red for words because red is hard on the eyes.

If the presentation is relatively long (maybe 30 minutes or so) use different colors for the backgrounds of the visual aids for each different topic. Maybe the first topic can have a blue background, the second topic a green background, the third topic a purple background. The audience will find it easier to know that you're on a different topic if the background colors change as the topics change.

**Consider This**

You can color-code a complicated visual aid. This technique permits you to make the figures or words larger and easier to read, and it eliminates the other figures the listeners might try to read while you're speaking.

For example, if you are presenting a balance sheet, you can show a visual aid with the entire balance sheet on it, but make the segment backgrounds different colors so that you can direct the listeners to focus on the segment you want to discuss. Then create visual aids showing the subsets of the balance sheet, with the corresponding colored backgrounds.

If you wanted the listeners to focus on the first line, you could highlight the first line of the overall balance sheet blue. Then create a visual aid with a blue background that contains only the first line of information.

# The Least You Need to Know

➤ Use visual aids to help listeners remember content, understand content, or recognize that a new topic is being presented.

➤ Keep visual aids simple so that the listeners can easily understand them.

➤ Use message titles so that the listeners know how to interpret each visual aid.

# Chapter 12

# Choose the Visual-Aids Medium Carefully

## In This Chapter

➤ How to choose the medium that suits the size of the audience

➤ Using the simplest medium

➤ Which medium will meet your needs?

Whenever you design a visual aid, the guidelines presented in the preceding chapter will work. You should always use a visual aid to make something memorable or understandable, and you should always keep the visual aid simple, but "visual" enough that it is interesting, readable, and clear.

Given today's technology, though, you'll have to choose a medium that is suitable and that your organization supports. If your company or your manager believes in using only PC-based visual aids, you don't have much choice. If your company or manager doesn't believe in using cardboard frames around overhead transparencies, then you probably won't use them either. If your company doesn't use flipcharts or doesn't like slides, you won't use them.

Ideally, you choose the medium that best suits the size of the audience and the formality level of the presentation. Realistically, however, you use what your corporate culture says to use.

What are some of the advantages and risks of the media choices available to you?

# Overhead Transparencies Are Common

Overhead transparencies are traditionally the workhorses of the corporate presentation. They are:

➤ Low-tech

➤ Easy to create and can usually be prepared quickly and at the last minute

➤ Good for small to medium-sized audiences

➤ Good for both informal and formal presentations

With overhead transparencies it used to be difficult to create anything but black images on clear acetate. These were black-and-white when projected. Even today, many presentations using overhead transparencies are boring, visually unappealing, and essentially ineffective because the information is presented as a lot of words in relatively small-sized print.

**Beware**
Don't confuse visually powerful visual aids with a clear, well-structured presentation. If you have to choose between the two, choose the clear and well-structured content.

**Beware**
Less is more! Remember, *you* are the presentation. Visual aids support what you are saying and help the listeners follow along. Put only enough on the visual aid to support, not to deliver the information. If the listeners are staring at the visual aids, reading or trying to interpret them, the visual aids are visual blockages.

Think, for example, of the traditional financial presentation with its columns of numbers presented as tiny numbers printed in black on clear. These are not message-sending visual aids!

Black-and-clear might be appropriate for a brief presentation at a meeting that has as its focus discussion and information sharing, not message-sending. But at least make sure that the standard black-and-clear overhead transparencies are easy to read.

Today, we use color printers that can make the images vivid and readable, as long as the words, numbers, and images are few and kept simple and large. Gone are the days when you had to purchase sticky, colored acetate sheets, cut out images, and stick those images to clear acetate sheets to create color. And gone are the days when color was provided by special marking pens to work on the acetate sheets.

If you use overhead transparencies, try to keep the letters and numbers at least 1/4" tall. Choose a font that is simple, and use bold if it helps make the letters and numbers easier to read from the audience's perspective. Choose a serif font over a non-serif font because serif fonts are easier to read, particularly if you put a lot of words on a visual aid. Non-serif fonts are easy to read if the letters are large and the number of words few.

**Choose fonts for readability:**

■ **This is a serif style.**

■ **It has marks at the end of each letter.**

*Serif fonts tend to be easy to read.*

**Choose fonts for readability:**

■ **This is a sans serif style.**

■ **It has no marks at the end of each letter.**

*Sans-serif fonts are often hard to read.*

Limit the number of lines of words to five or fewer. Provide lots of space around images and words.

Transparencies work best when used with frames. You can use the cardboard frames we've all used for years or the "flip" frames that provide a border at the top and bottom. The borders help eliminate the light from all the area except the image itself, providing visual focus.

The borders of the frames also provide a space for you to write notes to yourself.

**Handy Hint**
The graphics software programs today provide templates for visual aids. The templates predetermine the fonts, the sizes of the images, and the spacing of information if you're using words. Let those templates be your guide! If you find yourself having to shrink the letters to fit more onto the visual aid, you're probably overloading the visual aid. Simplify it. Make it into two or three visuals.

# Overhead Transparencies Provide Flexibility

One advantage of using overhead transparencies is that if you decide to resequence the visual aids or skip one or two of them, you can do so without the listeners being aware of what you're doing. Of course, if they have a hand-out showing all the visual aids, they'll know. But often you won't provide a hand-out, and you will want to skip a visual that turns out to be redundant, dangerous, or irrelevant.

You can't skip a slide in a slide projector carousel or in a PC-based presentation. At minimum, the listeners know you skipped something or are skipping around instead of proceeding sequentially.

# Use Overhead Transparencies for Informal Presentations

Overhead transparencies work well for informal presentations because usually you can leave the lights all the way on and still see the image clearly. And if for some reason you do have to dim the lights to see the images, you can turn off the machine and turn on the lights to accommodate an impromptu discussion.

Overhead transparencies are not inappropriate for formal presentations, but they tend not to be "slick." There is just something informal about placing a piece of acetate on top of a machine.

Also, there is an informality about the process of switching transparencies. You can always ask someone to switch them for you, but then you can't control which transparencies you use, when you use them, and when you might want to skip one or two of them. And having someone else switch the transparencies doesn't make the presentation more formal.

Somehow, switching transparencies almost always forces the person doing the switching to move the new one around until the image is straight and centered. This process alone tends to keep overhead transparencies in the "less formal" category.

If a presentation is formal, though, and you will be using overhead transparencies, make sure the projection equipment works well, the image is clean, clear, and easy to read, and that you use cardboard or flip frames around the image to "package" the image.

**Handy Hint**
Use the frames so that you can preset the positioning of the transparency images. Place an index card at the top of the glass near the projection arm in the space between the glass and the metal of the machine. Position the machine so that when you slide the transparency onto the glass, it is stopped by the card. This minimizes the amount of repositioning you have to do when switching transparencies.

You also can use masking tape to mark where one of the corners of the transparency fits to get the right image. You'll have to pay close attention when you place the transparency onto the glass, but you can trust that the position of the image will be correct.

Remember, too, that today's technology enables you to make overhead transparencies of photographic images. These are more affordable today than they were five years ago. So if you need to use a photograph of a new piece of equipment or of a new manufacturing facility, you can do so using scanners and color printers.

## Use for Small to Medium-Sized Groups

Because an overhead transparency can be projected easily onto a large screen, it is useful for most groups unless there are so many people that you need an auditorium with a stage—and therefore need to use slides.

One of the challenges of using overhead transparencies can be the screen used. If the screen is not set up correctly, the image "keystones."

Keystoning gets worse the larger the image. So if you are going to use overhead transparencies with large groups, you will need a large screen. Make sure you get the screen set up to prevent or minimize keystoning.

Many portable screens have a hook at the top of the screen arm. That hook, if provided, is usually there to hold the top of the screen out further than the bottom of the screen. This mechanism enables you to control keystoning to some degree, as long as the distance between the projector and screen is controlled. Work with the set up in advance so that you get the best image possible.

## Use Transparencies for Small to Medium-Sized Rooms

Overhead transparencies work well for small and medium-sized rooms because the audience can see the screen and the overhead is easy to read from the screens used.

**Definition**
Keystoning is the distortion of the image so that the top section of the image is wider than the bottom section of the image.

**Beware**
Some hotels have invested in small screens that can be permanently installed in small areas of rooms rented for corporate presentations. If the screen you'll be using is too small, ask for a free-standing screen that is suitable to the audience size and the image size you need to make the visual aids useful.

But be ready to work with whatever you're given. Remember that if a hotel has invested in small screens, they probably don't value the needs of the presenter as much as they do their own needs. They are probably trying to eliminate the costs of purchasing, storing, maintaining, setting up, and removing the larger screens.

# Slides Are Easy to Transport, Hard to Control

Slides are traditionally the most formal of the visual aids media and the standard for public presentations and formal presentations. Slides are:

➤ Low-tech

➤ Easy to create, but require preparation time

➤ Good for medium-sized to large audiences

➤ Better for formal, but okay for informal presentations

Slides are slick, easy to read, and colorful. However, they do require lead time. You have to figure out what you want each slide to say and then have someone create the slide. It no longer takes weeks to get slides prepared, but it does take some time. It can also be expensive.

**Beware**
Don't plan to use slides if you're preparing a presentation at the last minute. There are ways to create slides at the last minute, but these slides are not as clear. Always check with the graphics service or department you use to see how much lead time they need to give you high-quality slides.

Keep slides simple, and remember that it is difficult to skip over a slide if you decide it's not a good one to spend time on. Audiences will want to know what you skipped—and why.

The guidelines provided for creating readable overhead transparencies apply equally to preparing readable slides. Trust a graphics software program to guide you in drafting slides. Or work with your visual aids support group to create easy to read slides with just enough words and images on them to be appealing, readable, and supportive of what you're going to say.

## Use Slides for Formal Meetings

Slides are useful for formal meetings because they project well and they can be projected so that no machinery sits between the audience and the image on screen. With slides, you as the presenter can position yourself to see the image and make sure you are on track.

One of the detractions of overhead transparencies is that the projection arm of the machine often blocks the image from the audience. Also, the need to change the transparencies can place the presenter between the audience and the image. Slides can usually be set up to eliminate these difficulties.

# Use for Large Groups and Large Rooms

Slides are appropriate for large groups because they can be projected to be enormous images without creating visual distortion. With overhead transparencies, as the image gets larger, you often have to deal with fuzzy images and keystoning.

If you'll be presenting at a large conference and there will be a visual aids or production support group, these professionals can help you set up the equipment to get the best image available.

Trust them. They manage visual-aid equipment for a living and they know what they're doing!

**Handy Hint**
Many presenters don't realize their slides are ahead of or behind their notes. Position yourself so that you can see the projected image by turning your head just a little. When the image changes, say nothing. Turn your head and check the image. Then turn your head back to the audience and deliver the next segment of information.

# PC-Based Presentations Pose Risks

PC-based slides are the new standard of the corporate presentation. PC-based slides are:

➤ Easy to create if you have the software

➤ Easy to transport if you're already carrying a laptop computer anyway

➤ Good for small to medium-sized audiences

➤ Good for informal and formal presentations

PC-based slides are quickly becoming the standard that overhead transparencies used to be. They have color, can be modified just before you begin speaking, and can be projected.

But you need to make sure that the images project well. Many images are not clean and clear. Many presenters put too much on each slide. And there are many types of projectors, some of which don't project images as clearly and easily as needed.

With PC-based slides:

➤ Make sure the images are bright, clear, and easy to read.

➤ Check to make sure the image is readable.

➤ Try bolding the letters.

➤ Don't shrink the size of the letters to fit more on each slide—use more slides.

➤ Use enough contrast between the background and the image to make it easy to read.

➤ Don't clutter the slides with lots of graphics unless the graphics make the point clearer.

**135**

**Handy Hint**
Always consider if graphics images used as backgrounds will enhance the presentation. Use consistent images in all slides so that if you establish one image as the theme—an hourglass for time, for example—it remains the one image for that theme.

Remember, too, that visual aids are designed to support the presentation. If you're presenting at a meeting and the purpose of the meeting is to discuss ideas and reach consensus, consider whether fancy slides are useful. Are bullet slides just as good—and will the simple bullet slides keep the focus on the discussion and not on the presentation's show aspects?

Today's PC-based presentations can quickly and easily become shows all by themselves. Focus on your message and purpose. If the presentation becomes the message, you're not delivering a message effectively. Use the tools wisely and for the right purpose. And use your time well, too.

# Flipcharts Are Flexible and Interactive

Flipcharts are traditionally used during meetings and workshops to help capture comments made during the meeting or workshop by participants. They also are useful for informal and impromptu presentations. Flipcharts are:

➤ Low-tech

➤ Easy to create, although your handwriting or spelling can ruin your professional image!

➤ Good for small to medium-sized audiences

➤ Good for informal presentations

## Use Flipcharts for Last-Minute, Informal Meetings

Flipcharts are informal tools and work fine for last-minute meetings. You can write the items on the flipchart just before the meeting, or you can write them on the flipchart with the audience watching—or even have them help.

If you're going to have the group create an agenda with you for the meeting, for example, the flipchart is the best tool available.

If you use the flipchart, write big and fast. Make the letters 1" to 2" tall. Ask the audience in the back if they can read what's being written.

Use easy-to-read colors such as black, blue, green, purple, brown, and red. Avoid orange, yellow, pale green, and any other "highlighter" color available. Those boxes of 12 and 16 markers with lots of colors are appealing, but many of those colors are hard to read from a distance.

If you value the interaction of the meeting, have masking tape ready so that you can hang the flipchart pages on the wall.

Watch out for flimsy flipcharts. Your presentation might be excellent, but the audience will remember (more than anything you say) the flipchart that falls or the flipchart whose telescoping legs collapsed!

## Use a Flipchart for an Interactive Meeting

Flipcharts foster interaction. They enable audiences to work with you and to contribute ideas.

Flipcharts are particularly useful for presentations in which you want interaction and intend to provide feedback after the meeting. After the presentation, you can carry the flipchart pages away and have their contents typed into manageable sets for distribution to the listeners.

## Multimedia Can Make or Break a Presentation

Multimedia is the future, and the future is today for most of us. Multimedia presentations have been around for years and the challenges of multimedia remain the same today as they were when multimedia was brand new.

Multimedia means you're using more than one visual-aids technique. Usually, you'll be using video plus slides. And you might be using more than one slide machine so that you can cross-feed images and fade one into the other. Increasingly, of course, many multimedia effects are being put onto a computer and projected from there—the cross-fading, the mixing of video with slide images, the sound. But a lot of what multimedia means in your organization depends on your production support group or on the visual aids support group.

If you're using multimedia, you'll probably be presenting at a formal event with a large audience. You'll have excellent production support from people who know how to set up the machinery and make sure the images and sounds are available when you need them.

**Beware**
Use multimedia if you gain something from it. If your presentation needs slides, video, and special effects, multimedia is for you. But remember, multimedia multiplies the dangers: errors, bad timing, broken or stuck machinery. Choose multimedia if you need it to deliver the message. Avoid multimedia if you can deliver the message effectively without it.

But *you* remain the presentation. Make sure multimedia presentation doesn't take over the process of delivering the message. Your job is to deliver a clear, relevant message so that the listeners will know, think, or do something when you're finished.

### Consider This

A presentation coach who worked with the CEO of a Fortune 10 company frequently tells a story of the day the CEO stood up to deliver a multimedia presentation at the annual stockholders' meeting. These meetings are formal, important, and potentially uncomfortable if there are lots of stockholder issues to be dealt with. Few CEOs approach them confident that all will go well. CEOs are very well-prepared and expect the multimedia presentation to support them—to work without hitches.

Unfortunately, this CEO encountered the worst-case scenario. Nothing worked. The machinery did not cooperate. The production group couldn't fix what was wrong. The presentation stopped.

The CEO had discussed contingencies with the coach, and the coach had always reinforced the concept: You are the presentation. The multimedia supports you. Deliver your message and the rest is all background. It's fun and exciting and appealing, but it's all background.

So the CEO asked the audience to wait a moment, had someone bring a flipchart, and delivered his presentation, supported with home-grown visual aids he prepared on the flipchart as he spoke. He illustrated certain points he wanted to clarify and emphasize, but he focused on the presentation and delivered his message.

That CEO has not returned to using multimedia because he discovered that the connection he made with that audience created a positive result: credibility for his message and trust in him. The presentation based on *him* made delivering his message easier.

If you plan to use multimedia, or if you're told to use multimedia for a presentation, make sure you create the structure of the presentation first so that the message is clear and well-supported, and then work with the production people to take advantage of the power of multimedia without letting the power take over.

## Multimedia Can Become Its Own Show

Multimedia presentations are great when the audience expects to see a show. Multimedia presentations are:

➤ High-tech and powerful

➤ Dangerous because they often don't work as planned

➤ Challenging to create and run without glitches

➤ Good for large audiences

➤ Good for formal, slick presentations

# Use Video Selectively and Purposefully

Video is a great medium for demonstrating and teaching things; it also is expensive and requires a lot of preparation. Video is:

➤ Low- to medium-tech

➤ Challenging to create and requires a lot of time and money

➤ Good for small to medium-sized audiences unless the projection equipment is outstanding or supplied in multiple sets so that each audience group can easily see the monitor screen

➤ Good for informal and formal presentations

You will not design your own video, but you might need to introduce a video segment into a presentation. Always explain to the listeners the message you want them to take away from the video before the video begins. After the video, talk through the major points the video presented. Don't let the video's content hang over the audience without reference. Refer to it. Weave what it said into your presentation points.

Also, if you are going to use video, make sure the video set up is easy to use. If you have to turn it on, where is the machine? Where are the relevant buttons? Preset the sound so that the listeners can hear it and you don't have to fix the sound levels while they watch and listen to you. Make sure everyone can see a monitor easily. Make the operating of the video segment easy for yourself, or don't use it.

# The Least You Need to Know

➤ You are the presentation and the visual aids support you. They should not take over the presentation. And they can't be the deliverer of the message.

➤ Assume you will have to deliver the presentation with no visual aids. Be fully prepared to give an energetic, well-structured presentation that focuses on a message that you want your audience to know, think, or do.

➤ Use all the technology you want and that you trust, but make sure the technology supports you. Don't let the technology dominate you.

# Chapter 13

# Offer Handouts

## In This Chapter

➤ Why listeners take notes

➤ Why presenters don't like to provide handouts

➤ Why presenters need to give the listeners handouts and live with the consequences

During a recent presentation, the speaker, Pat, was disturbed that none of the listeners were paying attention to her. Pat was trying hard to share eye contact, but she couldn't get any of the listeners to look up from their notes. She tried for several minutes and then decided to stop the presentation and ask if there was a problem. The listeners responded that no, there was no problem, but they wanted to make sure they had all the information she was presenting, so they were busy taking notes and copying the information contained on her visual aids.

Pat had spent a lot of time before the presentation agonizing over whether she should provide copies of her presentation to the listeners. Because the presentation was about a new strategic direction she was recommending the company take, she decided to control the information in the presentation and did not provide hand-outs of her visual aids. Pat believed that she had to walk the audience through the ideas carefully, and she didn't want them skipping ahead.

She certainly made the right decision if her goal was to feed the information to the listeners bit by bit so that she could build her case. But Pat forgot a crucial fact of corporate life: The listeners will hear what they want to hear, and they will follow information they find of interest, but they also will meet their needs first. If they want to "own" the information, they will take notes if they are not provided first. Often they will copy all of the information on each visual.

Listeners cannot "own" information unless they can write it down, take notes on it, and take it back to their offices for the files. They need to know they can use it for reference later, even if they never use it.

So did Pat make an error? No. Pat did, however, make a decision that affected the atmosphere of the presentation. She inadvertently set up a situation in which the listeners took notes and looked at their paper rather than at her. She had to be a powerful, highly energetic speaker to hold the group's attention, and few speakers are that energetic. In this presentation, Pat encountered one of the difficult issues presenters face: Handouts? No handouts? Handouts when?

# Why Provide Handouts?

**Definition**
Handouts are copies of the visual aids.
Sometimes handouts include an outline of the presentation and information such as additional or more detailed charts and tables. Some speakers also provide copies of the script they work from, if there is one.

You might be asking, "Why would you provide handouts to the listeners? Why can't they just listen to me, ask questions at the end, and be satisfied?" You also might be thinking, "If I give out handouts at the beginning of my presentation, they'll read ahead and I'll lose their attention. Worse, I won't be able to build my case the way I've planned. And what if they ask me questions about the data toward the end of the presentation when I'm not ready to deal with any of it yet?"

These questions are ones you must always consider. The answers are not appealing to most of us, but the answers are probably essential to understand and accept.

## Listeners Like to Follow

**"Why would you provide handouts to the listeners?"**   Listeners like to be able to take notes on copies of the visual aids you use. They find it easier to remember information presented when notes about it are attached to the visual aids that you used to help explain your ideas.

**"Why can't they just listen to me, ask questions at the end, and be satisfied?"**   It's hard to listen, and people learn, just as you have, that if you work with the information you're hearing, you're more likely to hear it and remember it. A lot of people who take notes during a presentation are using the process of taking notes to be more effective listeners. They can certainly take notes without handouts, but they prefer to take notes on the handouts and follow along with you. This process helps them hear and remember what you're saying.

> ### Consider This
>
> Business presenters almost always find it difficult to determine when to give people handouts and whether giving handouts is worthwhile. We don't like to waste time making copies of visual aids and find out later that everyone left them in the meeting room. We don't like to waste the paper. And above all, we don't like to think that if we give handouts, people won't listen to us.

**"If I give out handouts at the beginning of my presentation, they'll read ahead and I'll lose their attention."** A lot of listeners will read ahead and will not cooperate with you. Most business people are busy and work hard at acquiring information rapidly so that they can "keep moving" to get work done. So if you provide handouts, you'll have to accept that some people will read ahead.

But the people who read ahead are often very interested in what you're saying, so if reading ahead keeps them interested, it's okay. Of course, some people are not at all interested in what you're saying, and they read ahead so that they can stop listening. These people aren't helpful listeners anyway, so don't worry about it.

**"I won't be able to build my case the way I've planned."** You are right that if someone reads ahead, they won't be responding to the information you're providing in the sequence you're providing it. Consider, though, maybe the sequence you're using isn't effective. If everyone keeps reading ahead when you present, maybe you aren't putting the message first.

Consider, too, maybe the overall structure of the presentation is effective for most of your listeners, just not for all your listeners. The larger the group, the more likely people will be interested in different facts. These people will find a way to meet their needs. It's not something to worry about.

**"What if they ask me questions about the data toward the end of the presentation when I'm not ready to deal with any of it yet?"** People, especially corporate executives, do have a tendency to find something in a presentation and ask questions about it immediately. Sometimes, you can ask that they hold the question until later. And sometimes, you can give them a quick, high-level response and then return to the presentation as planned. Then you can discuss the fact in detail later, as planned.

Always, though, consider why they are asking you about that data. If that data is what the group is interested in, it is possible you have placed it too late in the presentation. You might want to stop and deal with the listeners' concerns so that they can begin listening to the rest of the presentation again.

## Consider This

If the listeners you encounter are frequently asking questions about information you plan to provide later, you might want to check whether you're sequencing information in the most useful way. Perhaps you are holding off giving the bad news or the price because you believe you must build an argument before the bad news or price will be acceptable.

Consider, though, that most people know bad news is coming, and most of us know there's a price attached to a recommendation or sales pitch. Why not quickly answer the questions everyone has and then support the answer with relevant facts? Why ignore the primary information needs of the listeners and try to force them to cooperate with the way you prefer to present information? Do you gain anything? Can you achieve your real purpose by trying to enforce behavior and force people to pay attention to your logic the way you want to present it?

# Handouts Prevent Listeners from Having to Take Notes

## Handy Hint

When you start to worry about whether the listeners will read ahead or listen at all if you give them handouts, focus instead on your role. Your job is to deliver a clear message. Focus on what you're saying and how you're saying it. Let the listeners do what they choose to do. Be compelling, and they won't be distracted by handouts!

One advantage of giving people copies of the visual aids is that they can pay attention to you. They won't have to copy all the information on each visual aid. And let's face it, some people just have to take away all the information on each visual aid so that they "own" the information. It's just the way some listeners are.

But think about your role. You're speaking in front of a lot of people. Do you want them staring at a piece of paper and taking notes, or do you want them making eye contact with you so that you can engage them in your ideas and convince them to know, think, or do what you came to convince them to know, think, or do?

Should you be a powerful and highly energetic show person or do you want to be focused and enthusiastic and pay close attention to getting your message across?

## Handouts Makes Listeners Happy

Handouts are useful, even if the presentation you're giving doesn't have a lot of details and doesn't consist of tables and graphs. People today prefer to have a copy of the visual aids. Think about all the corporate conferences and the multitude of copies of each presenter's visual aids. People drag home enormously thick binders holding presentation handouts. Some of those binders are so thick that people have to mail them back to the office because they can't be carried onto the airplane. You've probably done this yourself.

Do people read those handouts later? Does anyone share the handouts with anyone else? Occasionally, yes. There are some visual aids that people review and share with others. But most of the handouts stay in those binders until someone cleans the office and throws them away.

Why do we give people handouts if the handouts aren't full of content and aren't meant to be used again in the future? People like to believe they "own" the information they heard, and they "own" it when they have the handout.

# What Kinds of Handouts Should You Provide?

So you need to figure out what kind of handout you'll provide. The choice is between giving everyone full-page copies of each visual aid or giving them a version that will enable them to take notes next to each visual aid.

### Consider This

Thomas, an engineer who had been making a number of presentations at professional conferences, was recently stopped by one of the listeners at the presentation he had just made. The listener told him that he found Thomas's handouts unusually effective. He explained that he had heard Thomas present several times previously.

The listener complained that so often, when he is at a conference and listening to a presentation that he finds very pertinent to his career, he finds the lack of a handout very frustrating.

He commented in particular about Thomas's handouts. He said, "Every time I've heard you present, you've provided handouts that I can use to follow your talk and take notes on. You always give handouts with three visuals per page on the left side of the paper and open paper on the right for my notes."

Graphics software packages make it quite easy to create the style of handout that Thomas's listener found so useful.

# Use Copies of Visuals, Three Per Page

The method that seems to work well for most presenters in most situations is to provide copies of the visual aids printed three visuals per page on the left or right side of paper so that the other half of the page is available for notes, as shown here.

*Three visuals per page leave room for notes.*

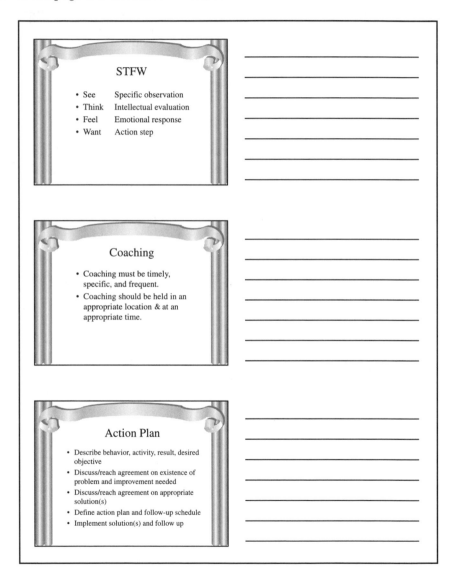

146

Most graphics software today offers options to print handouts with two, three, or six visuals per page. The two-per-page option shown here usually allows no room for notes. Although, if you're presenting a lot of charts that contain a lot of data, you might find the two per page option useful. People can take notes on the copy of the visual aid itself, and the words and numbers printed on an image this large are usually large enough to read easily.

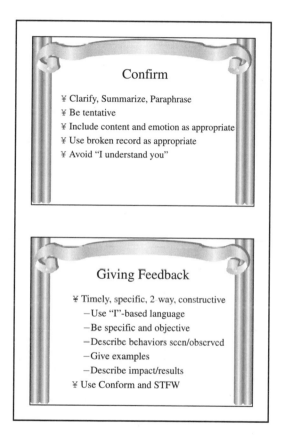

*Two per page creates a larger, easier to read copy of the visual aids.*

The six visuals per page option, as shown in the following figure, is appropriate if the visuals are not carrying a lot of information and there are few charts. If not, they are too small to be useful.

*With six per page, details are difficult to read.*

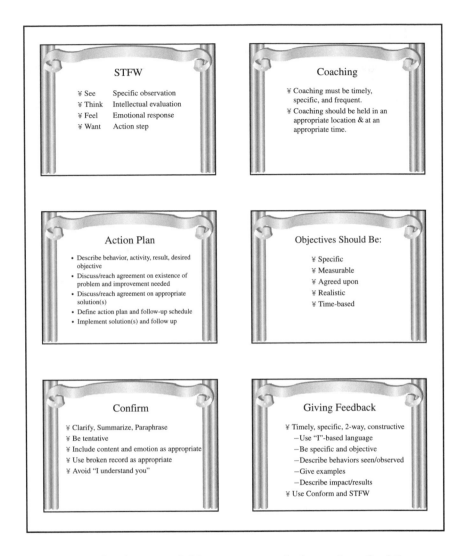

The full-page copies of the visual aids are useful for many people, but others find they create an awful lot of paper and little room for notes.

## Provide Extra Information on the Handouts

Handouts can include extra information that you don't plan to provide during the presentation. For example, if you're keeping your visual aids simple, you'll probably eliminate a lot of the labeling and data that doesn't directly help carry the message you're delivering. You might want to provide a copy of the visual you use during the presentation, followed by a more detailed chart or graph that contains all the labels and data.

Also, it can be useful to provide charts and graphs that you won't cover during the presentation but which further explain the ideas you're describing or support the message you want the listeners to take away.

## Follow Up with a Script or Outline

One technique some presenters use well is to provide an outline of their presentation. If there is a script, you can give people the script, too. Generally, though, you can withhold the script until after the presentation. Some people will want it, and others will not.

## When Should You Distribute Handouts?

To distribute the handouts before or after the presentation is a challenge for each presenter to decide. Consider the listeners and their needs. Consider your needs as a listener. And consider whether you want people sharing eye contact with you or feverishly taking notes.

Almost always, give the handouts at the beginning of the presentation. Just give them the handouts and live with whatever happens.

You can, of course, ask that the listeners try to stay with you rather than read ahead, and some will cooperate. Others will not. It is better, though, to give people what they "need" than it is to try to control them. Your job is to communicate and support a message, not to control your listeners' behavior.

## What If They Read While I Talk?

> **Handy Hint**
> If you're going to offer the listeners a copy of the outline or script, place the handouts on a table in the back of the room just before you begin speaking. Or ask someone to place them there after you begin speaking. During the presentation, mention they are available, and the people who want the handouts will take them afterward.

> **Handy Hint**
> Give handouts at the beginning of the presentation. It is more rewarding to make the majority of the listeners happy and to ignore the listeners who become readers than it is to annoy the true listeners and risk losing their attention. The people who want to listen to you will do so, and the others weren't going to listen anyway.

If your listeners are reading the handouts while you are talking, be more energetic in your delivery. Think about whether you've withheld the "good" information until the end, so that the listeners are reading ahead to find what they came to hear. Consider asking them what they're most interested in and giving them that information immediately.

Talk about the interesting information as soon as possible in your presentation. Meet the audience's needs, not yours.

If your listeners are distracted by handouts, by side conversations among other listeners, or by noise in the hallway, it is possible you are not being interesting enough for them.

**Beware**
Don't try to make listeners behave. Adults do what they want to do. Your job is to effectively and professionally prepare and deliver a clear, message-based presentation.

Perhaps you are not engaging them in the message and supporting information. You might be allowing the listeners to become distracted. Give them the information they want to hear quickly. Be appropriately energetic. Use eye contact!

Ask yourself whether you're speaking loudly enough and enthusiastically enough to engage the listeners. Are they bored and therefore find it more interesting to read than to listen?

## What If They Want to Talk about Ideas Before I'm Ready to?

What if someone does ask a question you hadn't planned on answering until the end of the presentation? And what if someone wants to discuss ideas before you've presented everything you want to present?

Ask yourself, "What is the message I'm delivering? What is the best way to get people to engage with that message and to know, think, or do what I want them to know, think, or do?"

Your job as a presenter is to deliver a message and make it clear so that people can respond appropriately. Presentations are not about behavior, they're about communication.

So provide the handouts in a format that makes them easy to use during and after the presentation. Assume some people will read ahead. Others will interrupt you and ask questions about material you hadn't planned to cover or were reserving for later. People are going to behave the way they prefer to behave. Concentrate on being clear, enthusiastic, and professional, and let the listeners do what they need to do to listen effectively.

## The Least You Need to Know

➤ Provide handouts to the listeners before you begin the presentation.

➤ If listeners aren't paying attention to you, make sure you're delivering the presentation with enough energy and clarity.

➤ Don't worry about listeners who "do their own thing" and read ahead or take notes or refuse to share eye contact with you. They are meeting their own needs.

➤ Remember that your job is to make an effective business presentation, not to control the listeners' behavior.

# Part 4
# Getting Ready

*Preparing a presentation takes many steps, such as deciding what message you want to send with your clothing and how to manage the virtually inevitable nervousness. And what about eating before a presentation? Should you? Shouldn't you? And should you rehearse? Should you do any pre-work with the listeners who will sit in on the presentation?*

# Chapter 14

# Getting Ready

## In This Chapter

➤ Choose clothing that makes you look professional

➤ Make sure you are dressed at the appropriate level of formality or informality

➤ Choose clothing that allows you to feel confident

We would all prefer to live in a world where appearances don't count, but they do. When you make a presentation, you are being judged by what you say and by how you say it. You also are being judged by how you look.

One presenter who used to be asked to make presentations at major national conferences of his engineering association was notorious for showing up in dirty blue jeans and his undershirt. Yes, his undershirt—and according to the stories, sometimes that undershirt was less than clean. He didn't think it was important, apparently, to dress professionally.

People did ask him why he was always so casually dressed, and he explained that because he was an expert, people knew not to focus on his clothing. He found his casual clothing more comfortable. He firmly believed that as long as he was the expert in his field, he could expect the listeners to listen and not find his clothing or speaking style relevant. As you can imagine, he was not asked back to association meetings, and his career as a presenter was short-lived.

If you're thinking, "I'd never do that," be careful. You probably wouldn't make as severely an inappropriate choice, but you might make a choice about your appearance that would send a wrong message.

As unimportant as appearance ought to be, it has a lot to do with how you're perceived. Very few people would match the expert's arrogance—most of us know to dress appropriately, but consider all the little decisions you can make to ensure your appearance is not an issue. Or if it is an issue, make sure it's the right issue!

# Shaping a Look

As you prepare to make a presentation, consider how you want to look. There are many options, and you can select clothing that sends the message you want your listeners to take away.

### Consider This

The business suit is designed to make the person wearing it look like everyone else so that the focus of attention is on the person's contributions and not on the clothing. Of course, business suits also have symbolic attributes, and there's no mistaking a very expensive, beautifully cut custom suit for a standard, more affordable or inexpensive suit.

But the fact is, when you put everyone in basically the same clothing, the clothing becomes a minor issue and the individual's contributions become a major differentiator.

You might not like business suits, but it's nice to have people focus on what you create and contribute and not on what you wear.

The best guideline for making choices affecting your appearance is to choose so that the listeners focus on what you're saying and your ideas. Avoid shaping your appearance to call attention to it. You don't want to be nondescript, and you don't want to look dramatic, unless you're discussing a topic that calls for you to be nondescript or to look dramatic!

# What Message Do You Want to Send?

The key question is, "What message do you want to send?" Do you want to say, "I'm a professional"? Do you want to say, "I'm one of you"? Do you want to say, "Relax and have fun"?

# Dress Low-Key

For most corporate presentations, you will want to be low key. You will want to send the message, "I am a professional, and my ideas are important." For men, most corporate environments expect a low key look: a suit in a basic color such as navy, light or dark gray, or black. Some suits have stripes or quiet plaids.

Shirts provide color and personal accents, and they have symbolic value. You already know if you work in a "white shirt" company, where blue shirts are overly daring. You also know if you work in a company where a white shirt is considered boring. You also know if wearing a short-sleeved shirt is permissible in your organization, or if short-sleeved shirts are highly inappropriate.

Comply with the corporate norm if you are making a presentation on a typical business topic. Business suits are pretty easy to define as appropriate or inappropriate. You're already used to choosing business suits to meet the corporate environment you're in, so comply with the norm. And when you are making a standard business presentation in a typical organization, you'll probably choose from among the normal shirt colors and styles.

For women, these choices can be more complicated. But for most presentations, you'll want to make choices that match the corporate norms. You'll want to choose clothing that doesn't call attention to itself and colors that make it easy to focus on your face.

## Consider This

You might be thinking that as a woman, having to comply with corporate norms for dress is restrictive. But women have a broad range of choices available that might meet the corporate norms. You know, just as men know, whether the norm is a conservative business suit or highly fashionable clothing. And you know your own style.

Some women can wear highly fashionable clothing and very feminine accessories and make powerful business presentations. Others might wear highly fashionable clothing and be unable to make a powerful business presentation.

You need to make choices that suit you, and you need to make those choices with full consideration of the impact of each choice.

Don't ever try to be someone you're not and use clothing as a costume. Your value as a business professional is you! Make sure it is you that *you* are showcasing.

But also consider whether you can be more effective as a business presenter by making conservative clothing and style choices or by making choices of clothing and accessories that are unique. You have to decide; there is no right answer.

## What If I'm in a "Business Casual" Environment?

Unfortunately for many professionals, "business casual" is increasingly common. It's far more difficult to choose an appropriate business-casual outfit to wear when you present than it is to choose a standard corporate suit to wear at a presentation.

Always make your choices to match the norm. But consider, also, whether you want to be at the same level of formality as the listeners, or whether it might be useful to be a bit more formal.

## Make a Statement?

Sometimes when you're making a presentation, you want to be dramatic. The material or the environment is dramatic. Perhaps you're presenting at an annual sales meeting set up to celebrate an outstanding year of sales. Or perhaps you're presenting at a medical conference celebrating a major breakthrough you helped achieve.

If the topic and setting are dramatic, you might want to have a dramatic appearance. But always ask yourself, should the listeners leave the presentation with a concept or with a clear memory of my appearance?

For example, at an important annual conference for over 1,000 business women, a former beauty queen was discussing how to be successful. She wore a bright red dress—one that was cut dramatically to emphasize her height. She also wore high heels, not the typical one- or two-inch heels, and she focused most of her presentation on how she had become successful. The red dress and high heels were appropriate, dramatic, and almost a central element of her presentation. No listener in that audience would have separated the woman from her topic. But had she been discussing the financial requirements for cleaning up toxic-waste sites, the dramatic appearance might have seemed distracting to the audience.

## Reassure and Establish Credibility

Your appearance provides a level of reassurance to the listeners. It can help them believe in you because you look the way they expect you to look. When the audience's expectations are met, they can focus quickly and easily on the content you're delivering.

For example, people think that traditional medical professionals should look traditional, and that nontraditional medical professionals should look nontraditional. So if you're a heart surgeon discussing new surgical methods, you will probably want to select a traditional suit with traditional accessories. If you're a new age practitioner, you can probably choose a more relaxed outfit.

For any discretionary decisions you will make about your appearance as a presenter, decide what message you want to send and what you want the listeners to focus on. Make the choices that send those messages and help the listeners focus.

However, always appear as yourself. You should never have to violate your sense of self. Don't, however, mistake the very essential and important "sense of self" with a wish to make a personal statement that will distract the audience from the message you want them to take away from the presentation.

> **Beware!**
> We live in a diverse world in which differences are more obvious all the time. Differences can be of great value and shouldn't be disguised. You shouldn't have to modify your clothing and accessories to match expectations that don't suit you. If you have a national costume or religious norms to meet, you should make those appropriate choices. Audiences are not inflexible.

# What Level of Formality?

A challenge to all presenters is to appear appropriately formal. You don't want to be in a formal business suit and present to a group that is in shorts and blue jeans. And you certainly don't want to be in blue jeans and present to a group that is in traditional business clothing—not unless you are presenting a topic that is nontraditional and you are considered an expert in your field.

Audiences do judge speakers on their appearance, and generally, you'll want to be dressed at about the same level of formality as the audience.

## Match the Formality of Your Audience

A convenient guideline is to find out in advance what level of formality is expected of the audience and match it. If they wear suits, you wear a suit. If they are wearing khakis and blazers, you wear khakis and a blazer. If they are wearing uniforms, wear a traditional business suit.

## Step Up One Level

You might, though, want to be one level above the listeners' level of formality. Sometimes, you'll be asked to speak at a conference where business casual is the rule. But you'll want to be the expert, so dress one level up.

If they're wearing standard business suits, you might want to wear the most formal of business suits. For men, the most traditional suit is usually dark navy blue or slate gray with a white or blue shirt and a traditional tie. For women, the most traditional suit is usually a dark color with a jacket that matches the skirt, with a blouse buttoned to the collar or with a high neck or crew neck.

If the listeners will be wearing casual clothing, choose an outfit that is one step more formal. If the listeners wear khakis and a blazer, choose either a navy blazer with grey slacks or a business suit. If the listeners wear blue jeans and shorts, wear khakis and a blazer.

These clothing choices are classified according to men's choices. Women have more options and more challenges. As a woman, to make these choices, aim for comparable choices.

A woman's formal business suit usually has a jacket and skirt of identical fabric. However, a formal suit might have a jacket that does not match the skirt—but the jacket would obviously be a jacket designed to be worn with the skirt. A woman's informal suit is usually a mix-and-match choice such as a grey skirt with a navy blazer, a black skirt with a red blazer, or a solid skirt with a printed blazer that you can match to several different skirts in your wardrobe.

If you come from a culture that does not consider the western business suit a standard, choose your clothing to match the level of formality of the audience.

# Colors

Choosing colors is straightforward: pick the colors you wear to work, or pick a color that is similar to the colors the listeners will wear. Generally, select bright colors for clothing accents and sober colors such as navy, grey, and black for the dominant colors.

Men and women should always choose colors that make them appear attractive and professional and that do not distract the audience. For example, very few people in business can wear chartreuse without having the audience be very aware of the chartreuse. Very few people in business can wear all magenta and have an audience remain unaware of the brightness of the color. It can be hard to hear when your eyes are concentrating on the person's clothing choice. These two colors might be excellent accessory colors, but might not be appropriate for the suit or dress color.

# Be Yourself, But...

You don't need to dress in a way that is unnatural or uncomfortable for you. If you're presenting at a business conference, but you are a marketing consultant known for developing highly creative, high-tech marketing campaigns, you can certainly dress more creatively than your audience will be dressed. Be a bit dramatic, but match the level of formality of the listeners.

### Consider This

A young female professional with a creative background was preparing to make a presentation to a large audience of "pinstripes," as she thought of them, bankers who considered blue shirts wildly creative. She asked for advice on what to wear because she wanted to wear a fuschia silk dress. She knew that the people she worked with usually wore suits when they presented.

The presentation was a major opportunity for her. She was going to review with the audience their current marketing campaign and alternatives for a new marketing campaign aimed at a new audience for the bank, a young audience. People suggested she consider wearing a traditional business suit and a brightly colored blouse—a boring choice, perhaps, and one she resisted.

And then someone caught her attention. "Do you want the audience to remember your dress or the recommendations for the new marketing campaign?" She compromised and wore the dress with a long, very fashionably cut slate-gray jacket.

## Be Wary of Lighting

As you select your clothing, be wary of lighting. Many rooms have lighting that can turn beige suits into a sickly gray, or give a red suit an orange look.

If you don't know the room in which you will be speaking, avoid wearing colors that can become different colors. Choose grey or navy, for example, because they rarely look anything but grey or navy.

## Be Wary of Prints, Plaids, and Optical Illusions

As you choose your clothing for a presentation, consider how it will look from a distance. Try on the clothes and all the accessories, and look at yourself in a mirror from across a room.

Does your expensive glen plaid suit appear to be checked? Does the print create optical illusions or look like blotches of color? Does your pinstripe suit that is attractive up close make you look like a '50s gangster? Does the styling of your clothing look more or less attractive?

### Handy Hint

You also can ask someone to videotape you in the room where you'll speak—perhaps during a practice session. Look at that videotape critically. How do the clothes and accessories look? Is that how you want to look? If an accessory looks odd on tape, don't wear it. If the accessory interferes with your presentation, don't wear it.

Unfortunately, fabric can "read" differently from a distance than from up close. Some ties become graphic statements or optical illusions from a distance. Some prints become unattractive from a distance. Some plaids and checks gain high contrast from a distance and make the clothing look cheap rather than professional. The following figure gives an example of how a print can potentially create a visual distraction. The pattern on the left could easily create an optical illusion, as if the pattern is in motion. The one on the right is less likely to create an optical illusion.

*Clothing with the pattern on the right won't distract the reader.*

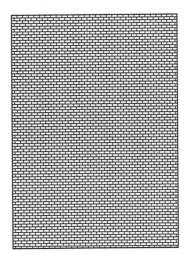 

Don't assume that expensive clothing will always look good or that discount clothing can't. Try it on, stand far away from a mirror in a well-lit room, and look in the mirror. If the colors, textures, patterns, fabric, or style look different in the mirror, decide whether what you see in the mirror is desirable for the audience to see.

## Do Real Women Use Cosmetics?

Cosmetics are a challenge for many women, and can be for men, too, usually in broadcast situations. Generally, you will want to use enough makeup to look good, but not so much that people are consciously aware you're "made up."

Remember that if you're making a presentation that will be videotaped or broadcast, work with the production people and follow their advice. They know how to use cosmetics to make you look good on tape. Follow their advice—they're professionals and know how to work with the medium. Your job is to present well. Their job is to make you look and sound good.

## Consider This

Men usually wear makeup for broadcasts, so don't be surprised if you're asked to go to the makeup experts before a television interview.

Think about the infamous story of Richard Nixon's loss in a political debate—he refused to wear makeup during a television debate with John F. Kennedy, and ended up having a dark shadow from his beard. He looked terrible and lost some credibility, and many historians have suggested that his loss in that debate contributed to his losing that election.

# Minimum Is Usually Useful

Many women avoid wearing cosmetics because they don't want to place a lot of emphasis on their femaleness. In day-to-day business, you should make the choice that suits you. But when making a presentation, consider using some makeup: eyeliner, mascara, lipstick, blush. If you'll be presenting in a room with bright lights, consider using a light layer of foundation.

Used carefully, cosmetics can help you make sure that the lights don't make you look unnatural. Lights go through the top layers of skin. But using a foundation establishes a layer of color that reflects the light—ensuring that the normal skin surface retains a normal color. Using some eyeliner, mascara, lipstick, and some blush makes you look healthy.

Choose colors that accent and highlight, and experiment with your makeup. Always look carefully in a mirror from a distance:

➤ Make sure the eyeliner helps emphasize the eye but doesn't become a dark circle around your eye.

➤ Make sure the mascara doesn't become a statement of its own.

➤ Make sure the lipstick color doesn't make you appear to be all mouth or make your lips look like a wound.

➤ Use blush carefully so that you don't appear to have stripes on your cheeks.

## Beware!

If you're going to be taped or appear on television, always ask the production staff for advice on makeup and clothing. They can guide you in choosing clothing and makeup that look right and work with the medium.

## Dramatic Is Usually Not Useful

If you usually wear cosmetics and enjoy having a relatively dramatic "look," consider whether it will look right when you are presenting. In a presentation in a small room, whatever you normally wear will probably be appropriate. But in larger rooms, what looks good from 12 to 18 feet often doesn't look quite the same.

➤ Watch out for heavy eyeliner that fully circles the eyes.

➤ Avoid colored eye shadow that the audience can see is blue or green.

➤ Avoid sparkling eye shadow colors because they don't work well from the audience's viewpoint—they reflect light.

# Accessories: Minimize Those Distractions!

Accessories can be the statement that makes or breaks your presentation. The guideline is simple, "Avoid adding accessories that create distraction." But the challenge is to figure out what things distract. Always remember that what looks great when you're speaking with someone one-to-one might be distracting when viewed by an audience from a distance. Check the following:

➤ Review your accessories by looking in a mirror.

➤ Consider videotaping your presentation and wearing the accessories during the practice session.

➤ Choose simpler accessories rather than more complicated ones.

## Shiny Things That Move or Reflect

As you select accessories such as belts, ties, pins, earrings, bracelets, watches, and scarves, consider how the accessory will look from the audience.

Will the belt you want to wear become a huge, shiny belt buckle that creates a mini light show as it reflects the lighting? Will the audience remember the huge belt buckle and wonder if it was really silver?

Think carefully:

➤ Will the tie you want to wear become an optical illusion?

➤ Will the tie tack or tie bar with the tiny diamond accent become the focal point for the audience, who will wonder why you can afford a diamond?

➤ Or will the audience spend the presentation time trying to figure out what is on your tie or tie bar or tie tack?

Think about distractions:

➤ Will the pin or earrings move and reflect light?

➤ Will your presentation be remembered because the earrings jangled or because your bracelet kept making noise?

## Consider This

One presenter chose to be himself, so he remained true to his Southwestern background. He wore a black suit with a western shirt, a string tie, and a western belt with a unique belt buckle. That belt buckle was enormous—all silver and turquoise and probably three to four inches high and four to five inches wide. The western look was fine. The presenter was probably interesting. But the audience was fascinated with the stunning belt buckle.

Consider in advance questions such as, "Will the earrings you've chosen disappear from a distance—and would you benefit from wearing larger earrings?"

If you decide to wear diamond stud earrings, will the audience be fascinated with how you can afford them and question your credibility as a speaker? Will they shine and sparkle so much, as diamonds can, and become a presentation of their own or do they make just the right statement?

Will your scarf be flowing and wavy, creating a fascinating show of its own? Will it wave in the breeze in the auditorium where you're speaking?

Will your watch catch the light, or is it so enormous that people will want to know its brand?

There are no rules for what you can or cannot wear in a presentation. Choose to wear something that makes you comfortable while you're speaking, sends the message you want to send, and keeps the listeners focusing on what you want them focusing on.

**Handy Hint**
As you choose your accessories, choose them to look good, and choose them so that you send the message you want to send. Make sure your audience has the opportunity to focus on you as the presentation, not you as the person who has flamboyant jewelry or fascinating accessories.

# The Least You Need to Know

➤ Don't assume that what you normally wear and how you normally accessorize will look the same from a distance as from close up.

➤ Consider the message that you are sending with your clothing and accessory choices—choose conservatively in most situations.

➤ Try to match the clothing and accessory choices of your audience, or dress slightly more formally unless the presentation you are making demands a specific style.

➤ Be sensitive to the cultural norms of the audience that will be listening to you.

➤ Make choices that will keep the focus of the listeners on your ideas.

# I Shouldn't Be Nervous!

There's a story about a young business professional who made his first presentation to a large group of executives. He was very nervous, and he had practiced and practiced. Unfortunately, he didn't take charge of his nervousness in front of the audience, so he didn't pay attention to how he was standing when he began his presentation. He rushed into the beginning of his presentation.

But he was not centered on his feet, and as he began to talk, physically off center, he tipped over. Yes, right over.

Before you panic and say, "What if that happened to me? I won't ever make a presentation," think about how this presenter could have used his nervous energy to be effective. Think instead about how he let his nervousness win so that he made a bad decision. If you use your nervous energy to appear energetic, you can be very effective. But if you get caught up in your nervous energy, it can control you.

## It's Worse to Be Calm

It's actually much worse to be calm than it is to be nervous. If you are calm before a presentation, you are either underjudging the challenges of the audience, or you are so nervous that you have buried your emotions. Neither will work.

If you are calm entering a presentation, you will have to work hard to communicate your message enthusiastically and clearly. So don't get more nervous just because you're feeling nervous. Instead, use your nervous energy to appear interested in the topic and focused on the audience.

## Appreciate the Risk of Being Calm

When speakers are completely calm entering a presentation room, they risk speaking with low energy. They risk not paying close attention to the audience members. It takes a lot of energy to stay calm, and it takes a lot of energy to speak in a lively manner and listen to the audience. You only have so much energy, and you have to decide whether to spend that energy controlling nervousness or being an interesting speaker.

Calmness, then, is not desirable. Confidence in your ability to be clear and make sense to the audience is the goal. Building your ability to manage your nervousness is part of building that confidence.

If you're very calm, ask why. Figure out whether you're burying your emotions. Ask yourself whether you've thought through the possible challenges the listeners might have in response to your presentation. Think about whether you're entering a situation in which you should be very high-energy to enliven a potentially boring topic.

And always think about whether you're fully prepared to appear professional, prepared, and enthusiastic. Are you ready to listen to the audience as they respond verbally and nonverbally? Presenters need to bring a lot of energy to the presentation, so calmness before a presentation can be a sign of trouble.

Maybe you're calm because you think the audience is an easy one or the topic a "no-brainer," one that's so easy to talk about that you don't even have to pay attention until you arrive at the presentation. Be careful! Don't underestimate the power of an audience. The topic might be simple, and the setting normal, but you are always being judged for your credibility and professionalism. You don't have to be perfect, but you have to respect that a group of people is looking at you, and they expect you to make sense and be appropriately enthusiastic.

But maybe you're really nervous. Maybe you are really anxious about having to present to a group. This happens to all presenters. Even speakers who get paid to make presentations can get nervous.

Just don't bury your emotions. If you're so nervous that you must bury your emotions to continue working on the presentation, get assistance. Find a way to rehearse with a practice audience. Use all the tips in this chapter. Realistically, if you're burying your emotions, you're not going to have the energy you'll need to pay close attention to your audience's needs.

## Having an Edge Can Be a Benefit

If you're nervous, be thankful. You appreciate the importance of the presentation, and you have energy readily available to devote to the audience. Stop worrying about you, and start thinking about them. Shift the focus of your energies to the audience and what they need from you:

➤ What will they want to know?

➤ What will concern them?

➤ What will bore them?

➤ What stories do you know that can illustrate key points?

➤ How will you engage them in the subject?

Good presenters focus all their energy on the listeners. They constantly ask themselves:

➤ "Can they hear me?"

➤ "Did they understand that?"

➤ "Do they need an example?"

➤ "Are they believing me?"

➤ "How can I illustrate this point just for him?"

➤ "How can I bring home this point just for her?"

## Nervousness Can Be a Tool to Communicate Enthusiasm

Think about what nervousness does. How do you know that someone is nervous? Generally, they speak rapidly, blink their eyes a lot, have a shallow and irregular breathing pattern, and speak with a tight or constrained voice. Nervous speakers "squeak." They run out of air in the middle of a sentence or word. Their speaking pattern is not normal.

You can use your nervous energy to communicate enthusiasm. But to do so, you have to convert the irregular patterns of speaking and breathing into regular patterns.

As you'll learn in Part 5, when you use your eyes and voice well, you send the audience the messages clearly and effectively. So use the nervous energy to create a lively pace of speaking, and remember to pronounce each word carefully and completely. Don't speak slowly, just make sure you pronounce each of the sounds of every word.

Use your eyes to talk to each person individually so that you establish and maintain a conversation with every person you look at.

If the pattern of how you breathe, share eye contact, and shape words communicates nervousness, modify your breathing, eye contact, and words to communicate enthusiasm and a clear message.

Breathing, sharing eye contact, and pronouncing words and phrases fully help you harness the energy you have from being nervous and make you appear fully engaged with the topic and listeners.

# Talk to Your Attitude

If you are nervous, have a conversation with yourself. Seriously. Emotions are powerful, and if you try to suppress them, they build and erupt when you least need them. So you have to acknowledge your emotions and direct them.

Talk to yourself: Say out loud, "I am nervous, and I intend to use this energy to be clear and interesting."

Consider your nervousness a healthy sign of respect for the audience. Review your notes, think through the major points, and then speak with conviction to each person in the audience, one by one.

# Few People Are Lousy Presenters

One of the major sources of nerves is the notion that you must be a perfect presenter. What is a perfect presenter? Is there one set of traits that makes someone "great" or "perfect" as a presenter? No.

Consider all the people you've seen present during your career. Some were interesting. Some were boring. Some were great. They were probably each different, and what made them interesting or boring or great was probably different, too.

Chances are you are just fine as a presenter. You could probably be better, and you can probably be great. But right now, you are probably just fine. So start worrying about the listeners. It's more productive to worry about listeners. And they like to be worried about!

## Consider This

Typically, people who attend training workshops on presentation skills are videotaped during a number of different presentations. Usually, the first presentation is a benchmark presentation that documents how the person presents right then. After the workshop is over, each person is taped again so that they can compare the "before" and "after" skills.

Maybe 85 to 90 percent of the time, people who are taped do not like the way they present at the beginning, but they are amazed at how good they really are in the initial presentation. They can see that improvement would help them, but they rarely consider their skills to be embarrassing. They can see that they make sense, sound credible, and look fine. They usually need to work on energy, clarity, and focus.

# Remember That Everyone Listening Is a Real Person

If you suffer from nervousness when you are getting ready to present, keep in mind that everyone in the audience is a real person. Each one has made a presentation, and each one has probably had successes and failures as a presenter. Those listeners want you to succeed.

You can choose to have the listeners concentrate on your discomfort. You do this by thinking about how nervous you are. Or you can choose to concentrate on the message you came to deliver and on the listeners and their needs and responses. If you focus on the message and on the listeners, they'll focus on the message. If you focus on how uncomfortable you are and how nervous you are, they'll focus on you and your discomfort.

**Handy Hint**
Audiences that are worried about you are difficult audiences to get a message across to. Audiences that listen to your message are usually very easy to work with.

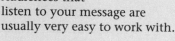

You get to choose what you want from your audience. Do you want empathy? Sympathy? Or do you want them to help you successfully deliver a message?

# Use Breathing to Focus

Realistically, some people find that nervousness overwhelms them. They cannot to reframe the situation and make nervousness a great source of positive energy, and they are focused on all the negativity of nervousness. So what do you do to get control? You breathe.

If you are nervous before you begin your presentation, concentrate on deep breathing. Even if you are sitting in an auditorium with a lot of people, sit straight. Pay attention to your breathing. Breathe deeply and slowly, in through your nose and out through your mouth. Do this quietly, not energetically. Concentrate on your breathing! But don't breathe in an obvious way so that your neighbors know what you're doing.

As you concentrate and get into a slow rhythm of inhaling and exhaling, you will begin to calm down.

## Breathe and Swallow—Swallow and Breathe

If you are dry in the mouth, swallow. Certainly, try and get some water to sip. But if you don't have access to water, concentrate on the breathing and occasionally swallow.

It is helpful to remember to "breathe and swallow," then "swallow and breathe." It's a pattern that helps you get control of your breathing. It prepares you for using your voice effectively, too.

Remember how people tell you to count to 10 so that you can calm down when you're angry? Counting to 10 is great for helping you refocus a feeling that is counter productive. You can practice slowly counting to 10 when you're nervous. It works. Because you concentrate on the counting, you stop paying attention to your nervous energy, and you begin to get control of it.

But counting to 10 is hard when you're extremely aware of how angry you are, or of how nervous you are. Breathe and swallow. Swallow and breathe. These steps are pretty easy no matter how emotional you're feeling.

Concentrate on your physical feelings and take control of the breathing. You will then take control of the nervousness.

> **Handy Hint**
>
> If you blush when you're nervous, concentrate on your breathing. If you keep your concentration on the breathing, the blushing will end sooner and at some point in your career, you might discover that you don't blush at all anymore.

## Use Eye Contact

After you have your breathing under control, use your eyes. Look at each listener, one at a time. Throughout your presentation, have an extended conversation with one person at a time.

# Prepare Before the Audience Arrives

If you have an opportunity before you speak to tour the room, do so. For example, if the audience is going to have lunch or take a break just before you speak, return to the room earlier than the listeners do and walk around the speaker's area. Get familiar with it. Get a sense of how the listeners will look as they watch you.

## Become Familiar with the Machinery

Place your notes where they will be most convenient, and practice using them. Check out the equipment so that it is very familiar to you. Review your visual aids, reading out loud the messages in order so that you review their sequence and practice being loud enough and clear for the room.

### Consider This

Do you remember in school, that moment in the fall when teachers would enter the classroom for the first time? Some teachers began talking immediately. Some of these teachers were able to quickly grab our attention and convince us that they were in charge. But some of these teachers didn't appear very confident, and we knew it. Those teachers suffered.

Other teachers took their time. They walked to the desk, arranged papers, carefully picked up the enrollment list, and after a time, would begin to speak with us. The teachers who took their time tended to look organized and confident.

Your challenge as a presenter is similar. If you begin by showing you are in charge of the pace and the environment, the listeners assume you are in charge, and they relax and let you present your message. But if you show you are not in charge, they either try to take over, worry about your discomfort, or wonder about your credibility.

## Stand in the Presenter's Spot While People Arrive

If appropriate, as people begin to arrive, greet them from the front of the room. Get comfortable with how loud you need to be for the listeners in the back of the room. Unfortunately, if someone is going to announce you and you'll be expected to come to the front of the room only after you've been announced, you won't be able to greet people.

If you're really nervous, though, you might be able to negotiate a less formal introduction.

Whenever possible, have a conversation with the listeners while everyone waits for the rest of the audience. After you've gotten used to conversing with them in the exact setting of the presentation, it's far easier to focus on the presentation and forget about nervousness.

# Don't Begin Until You're Ready

**Beware**

Do not let your nervous energy win. Prepare for the presentation, even as the listeners watch you. Make a decision to start only when you are ready—with all the handouts, visual aids, notes, lights, and so on. Take the time to get ready, and then take charge.

One of the biggest errors speakers make is that they begin right away. It's their turn, so they start.

But you don't have to start until you're ready. You need to take the time to get set up, to know who's in the audience, to identify the friendly listeners—the ones who give you eye contact in return. You need to demonstrate to the listeners that you are comfortable and in charge of the pace of the presentation. If you're in charge, get ready first. When you are ready, then you should share eye contact with one person and speak directly to that person.

What other ways can you get ready, as the listeners watch you, and take control of your nervous energy?

## Look at Your Listeners Before You Begin

One great way to begin a presentation is to spend some time establishing eye contact—maybe for a full five seconds per person. Establish eye contact with two or three separate people before you say anything. Get the pattern established and keep concentrating on your breathing.

Look at one person and count slowly to five while you breathe deeply and rhythmically.

Look at a second person and count slowly to five while you breathe deeply and rhythmically.

Look at a third person and count slowly to five while you breathe deeply and rhythmically.

Somewhere between person two and three, you'll be aware that you are in charge of the nervous energy and then you can decide when you begin.

## Check All the Corners

When you decide to begin, look first at the person in a back corner of the room. Have a conversation with her. Look next at the person in the opposite back corner of the room. Have a conversation with him. Then have a conversation with a person in the front corner. Then have a conversation with the person in the opposite front corner. And finally look into the center of the audience, and speak to a person in the center.

The following figure shows you how to check all the corners.

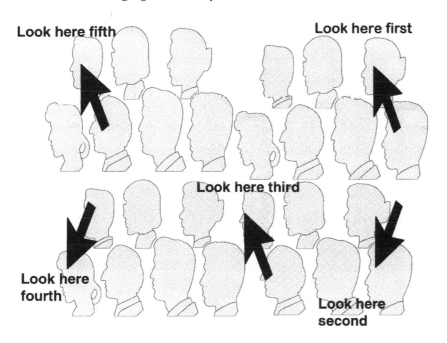

*Look at people from all the areas of the room.*

You will find that by concentrating on your breathing and eye contact, and by using a predetermined pattern for your eye contact, you will get your focus on the audience and the message, and your nervousness will disappear or become part of your energy as a presenter.

173

## Look at One Person Until You Calm Down

Another technique for controlling nervousness while you speak is to concentrate on the breathing and pick one person to share eye contact with. Continue to talk with that person while you calm down. Deliver a message to that person. As you begin to feel the nervousness decrease, you can move your eyes to someone else and stay with that next person for a while.

## Show the Audience What to Pay Attention To

Nervous energy is helpful, if you choose to use it. If you let it control you, the listeners won't pay close attention to your message, and they will pay close attention to you. Which do you prefer? You need to focus on getting your ideas to the listeners. If you're thinking about them, you won't be thinking about yourself; as a result, your attention and the audience's attention can be on your message.

## The Least You Need to Know

➤ Respect the importance of being nervous. Don't misinterpret it as a negative response to being a presenter; welcome it!

➤ Use breathing, eye contact, and your speaking pattern to manage your nervousness.

➤ Practice in the setting you'll be presenting in so that you can take control of your surroundings and build confidence from knowing the surroundings.

➤ Don't begin until you're ready to begin.

# Chapter 16

# Food Before the Presentation?

## In This Chapter

➤ Why you should eat before you make a presentation

➤ What foods and drinks help you gain energy

➤ What foods and beverages to avoid to minimize embarrassing problems

➤ What to offer the listeners to eat or drink

Food is an issue many presenters ignore. They grab a doughnut or a cola before the presentation. Or they drink their coffee and forget about breakfast because they don't have time—and arrive at their morning presentation hungry and with only nervous energy to sustain them.

Or they are at a meeting where the dinner served is hot and heavy; for example, roast beef, mashed potatoes, bread, and chocolate cake. The listeners are so full by the time of the presentation that they can't stay awake.

As a presenter, you should probably think about when and what to eat and drink. Your choices of food and beverage can have an impact on how well you concentrate on your message and on how well you deliver it.

And although you often don't have to worry about the food served before or during your presentation, if you're going to be speaking at a large meeting, food will probably be offered. If you have an opportunity to help choose the food served to the listeners before or during the presentation, try to get food that helps rather than hinders your listeners as they try to stay alert.

# When to Eat and Drink

You should always eat at some point before you make a presentation, but try to arrange your schedule so that you can eat about an hour or so before you begin. You need to eat so that you have energy. Time the meal so that the digestion process doesn't drain your energy.

### Consider This

Remember when you were a child and went swimming all day in the summer? Remember that if you ate lunch at the swimming pool, you had to sit out of the pool for an hour so that you wouldn't have stomach cramps and drown? In reality, you were probably only really subject to cramps and drowning if you ate a lot of hamburgers and hot dogs and then jumped in the pool and swam vigorously. Digestion doesn't happen for just the hour after you eat and then end. It continues on for many hours. In fact, the demand on your body from digestion is probably greater *after* that first hour than during that first hour after you eat.

But the "Don't eat and swim or you'll drown" message is an easy one to remember. Use the guideline as you organize your day when you're going to present. Don't plan to have a big meal just before you present. But don't forget to eat at some point so that you have energy!

If you eat a light meal about an hour before you have to present, you won't feel full and will have lots of energy. However, if you eat a big or heavy meal just before you present, your body will be spending a lot of energy processing the meal, and you won't have as much energy available for the presentation. Schedule your day so that you benefit from the right meal at the right time.

Should you have breakfast? This is not the place to have the breakfast versus no breakfast argument. And when you're making a presentation, you probably don't need to try and change your normal behavior and add another element of newness. But if you eat a light breakfast of fruit and maybe some toast or a small muffin, you should have enough energy to be effective as a presenter without being logged down by food.

Most people hit a point of low energy around 10:00 a.m and sometimes again at 3:00 p.m. If you are unlucky enough to have to present around either of these times, remember that you might be working with a low level of energy, and your audience might be listening with a low level of energy. Pay attention to these presentations and plan your eating habits on those days a bit more carefully. Have a snack of juice or fruit about an hour before the presentation, for example.

**Handy Hint**
If your presentation is scheduled around a meal, consider eating just a small portion of whatever is being served. If you want to eat after the presentation, speak to the catering group and ask them to put a meal aside for you.

## What to Eat and Drink

What you want to eat and drink depends on what gives you energy and makes you feel good. Some people want to have some fruit and some tea. Others want coffee or a glass of water with a light snack.

There are no rules for what a presenter should eat—or should not eat—but you should consider what your normal eating patterns are and how you react to food so that you make good choices. You want to eat food that makes you feel energetic and drink a beverage that will lubricate your throat.

When you select food for your meal or snack before a presentation, choose something you like that you know won't contribute to drying your mouth and throat. Choose something that will provide energy but won't require your body to give a lot of energy to digesting it.

**Handy Hint**
If you have a scratchy throat, drink some tea with lemon and honey. Or drink some hot water with lemon and honey. These choices are classic for dry or scratchy throats.

For example, some people eat a sandwich an hour or so before they speak so that they are full but not over-full. They avoid cookies and cakes because sweets are often heavy on the stomach. But some people have a cookie because they react well to the quick burst of energy from the sugar, and with only a cookie, they don't feel weighed down with food.

Some people avoid chips and crackers because they're salty, and others choose crackers because they're light and filling.

If you have a cold, avoid cold medicine unless you really can't speak without it. Cold medicine dries your mouth and throat, making it difficult to use your voice effectively. Try an herbal tea that has ginger or mullein in it. Speak to your local health food store and see if they can recommend an herbal mixture that controls the cold symptoms without making you drowsy or parched.

If you are nervous, sip water and perhaps eat some low-fat, low-sodium crackers. If they're low-fat, they probably won't make your stomach more nervous because they won't "sit on your stomach," a reaction many people have to high-fat foods. And if they're low-sodium, they won't make your throat dry.

# What *Not* to Eat or Drink

There are really no rules about what to eat, but there are lots of rules about what to avoid. Some people have strong stomachs and are energetic no matter what they eat. These people can eat whatever they want, whenever they want, before they make a presentation.

For those of us who have to be a bit more careful, the danger list is predictable. Avoid:

➤ Caffeine

➤ Challenging food—food that is spicy or hard to digest

➤ Alcohol

➤ Carbonated drinks

You have to deal with the outcome of your eating habits, and you know those eating habits better than anyone else. Part of making an effective presentation is to concentrate on delivering a clear message. If what you've had to eat or drink interferes with one presentation, you need to avoid those foods or drinks before future presentations.

## Caffeine Can Get You Jumping!

Caffeine is an energy source, so why would you want to avoid it before a presentation? You might find that a cup of coffee is perfect just before a presentation, but you also might find that coffee makes you jumpy. When caffeine is making you jumpy, you can't harness that energy and use it to be a more effective presenter. You just have to deal with the jumpiness.

So minimize the amount of caffeine you drink before the presentation. And remember that coffee is a diuretic. Coffee drains water from your body. So if you have a tendency to have a dry mouth, avoid coffee.

Tea can be very soothing, but tea also can cause difficulties because some kinds are acidic, contributing to dry mouth. Select your tea carefully so that the tea soothes and doesn't dry you out.

# Delicious But Destructive

Challenging food is any food that can upset your stomach or weigh you down. Challenging food includes beans, green peppers, chili peppers, onions, garlic, and spicy foods. Challenging food also can be any food that is high in fat.

Just think about the challenge you could face if you had a big plate of nachos with jalapeno peppers just before your presentation. They're heavy, for starters, but if you have any tendency at all to react badly to beans or jalapeno peppers, you'll have set yourself up for an uncomfortable presentation.

## Consider This

One speaker who was traveling got in late the night before a major presentation scheduled for 8:00 a.m. He checked into the hotel, got organized, and went out for a quick meal at a local Mexican restaurant. He ordered bean enchiladas with green sauce, and snacked on the chips and salsa on the table as he waited for the main meal to arrive.

The salsa was spicy and very good, and more came with the enchiladas. He covered the enchiladas with the green sauce and started eating, not realizing that he had been eating tomatillo salsa, a spicy food, but not the same as a salsa made from hot peppers. The salsa served with the enchiladas was made of jalapeno and habanero peppers.

Although he noticed that the meal was unusually spicy, he thought it was pretty good. But he reacted half-way through his meal, with gasps and hiccoughing.

He didn't finish his meal and the hiccoughing took hours to diminish. By the next morning, the beans and peppers had unsettled his stomach, and the hiccoughing recurred periodically. What a challenge to make a presentation at 8:00 a.m. after that kind of evening meal!

Of course, if you have a strong stomach, you can do whatever you want. Everyone is different, and what you're used to will probably work just fine. But make sure you think about it and choose wisely.

Onions and garlic do not cause stomach difficulties for a lot of people, but they can cause bad breath. If you plan to speak with the listeners after the presentation, consider avoiding the onions and garlic in whatever you eat before the presentation. And even if you're not planning to spend time with the listeners, think ahead as to whether your garlicky breath might bother you during your presentation.

Spicy foods include many ethnic foods—the foods in Chinese restaurants with red stars or chili pepper symbols next to them on the menu, Mexican chile, or Thai food. If you can eat them and feel energetic, they're good choices. If you can eat them but your stomach has trouble with the spiciness, avoid them before a presentation.

## A Sociable Drink, a Tongue-Twisted Presentation

Alcohol is always a challenge for a speaker. Generally, don't have a drink before you present. Alcohol can dry your mouth and dull your skills. You might find talking throughout an evening of drinking quite easy, but talking isn't quite the same as presenting to a group and appearing professional, credible, and enthusiastic.

It's just not professional to twist your words or slur them!

Some speakers enjoy a glass of wine with the audience before the presentation. They spend at least an hour drinking a small glass of it as the audience assembles and socializes. If you're drinking a small glass of wine and you're spending about an hour on the one, you can probably have that one drink.

But remember the rules of drinking and driving. You don't drink before you drive because you want to be fully alert when driving. Isn't a presentation as important as driving home? Shouldn't you strive to be fully alert and ready to respond to any unusual event or question during the presentation, just as you want to be when driving home later?

The key rule of drinking is that it takes at least an hour for the body to absorb the alcohol from one beer, one small glass of wine, or one drink with an ounce of liquor in it. Although the time of absorption differs according to the drinker's body weight, the one-per-hour guideline is a good base from which to start.

## Bubbles Make You Burp

Carbonated drinks can almost be as dangerous as alcoholic drinks. Carbonation can create an upset stomach. Carbonation can make you burp. If you have any tendency to react to carbonation, avoid sodas before your presentation.

One advantage of presenting today is that people in corporations are increasingly respectful of health concerns and personal preferences. Spring water is usually readily available, and a presenter who prefers a glass of water or iced tea to a glass of wine or a soda seems pretty normal. It's usually pretty easy to control the drink choices.

And of course, some corporations no longer offer coffee, tea, or any other snack foods and beverages during meetings because of cost cutting. These are relatively easy meetings to handle unless you need a glass of water before you present. You have no choices to make!

# What to Do During the Pre-Presentation Meal

You might have to attend a breakfast, lunch, or dinner as part of your presentation. If so, remember that you can use that pre-presentation meal to get useful information from the listeners. You can eat, too, but if you want to avoid the food or eat very lightly, concentrate on talking with the listeners so that during your presentation you can use what they have told you as examples.

For example, rather than worrying about whether you should eat eggs and bacon, find out what their interests are. Talk to the people around you. Visit the tables in the far corners of the room and introduce yourself. Ask the people in the room what they hope to learn from you. Ask them what their knowledge of the subject matter is. Listen to them talk about their jobs and challenges. Sometimes, one of the conversations will be able to become a perfect anecdote to illustrate one of your points.

If you're at a luncheon and you don't want to eat the meal, ask the people at your table about other speakers who have addressed them. What did they like? What did they learn? What made those speakers particularly effective with this audience?

If someone asks you why you're not eating, respond that you prefer to eat after a presentation. Or you can eat a small portion of your meal and explain that you're full. People rarely challenge you if you say you're full because they don't want to offend someone who might be on a special diet for health reasons.

If you're at a dinner, use the meal time to find out what's going on in the organization. Ask people about what they're working on and what is of interest to them in the topic you're presenting.

And as you work through the meal, and you will be working, figure out who's friendly. Identify some people who are responsive and communicate interest in your topic. These are the people with whom you will want to establish eye contact during the early portion of the presentation. These are the people who will smile back at you and make you feel welcome at the beginning of your presentation. As you begin to feel welcome, you will lose any nervousness.

# What You Want Your Listeners to Eat and Drink

What your listeners eat and drink can have an enormous impact on how well your presentation is received. There's nothing more discouraging than delivering effectively a well structured presentation and realizing that the listeners are falling asleep.

All too often, the listeners can't stay awake no matter how well you present because they have had too much to eat or drink.

One presenter found out how hard it can be to keep an audience's attention. She was speaking at a luncheon meeting of a professional association. The audience was made up of about 40 senior managers specializing in risk management. The meetings were always held at an extremely popular local Italian restaurant. Held from noon until 3:30 each time, the meetings opened with a cocktail hour, followed by lunch, followed by a presentation from an outside speaker.

The room set aside for the meeting was small and overheated. The dangers? Drinks, food, the slowest hours of the day, and a crowded, overheated room. By the time the presenter stood up to discuss the risk management issues at her company, most of the audience had consumed two drinks each, enormous servings of brasciola—a stuffed meat entree ideal for cold winter nights but not for mid-day business meetings requiring alert listeners— and a chocolate mousse cake.

She didn't have a chance. The listeners drifted in and out of the presentation, nodding heads were the norm, and oddly enough, there were no questions.

If you have an opportunity to help select the food for a meeting where you'll be present- ing, suggest light meal choices. Suggest having sandwiches or a light entree and see if the desserts can be reserved for the afternoon break.

If you don't have the opportunity to help select the food, and you rarely will, offer the listeners a break before you begin speaking. Create as part of the presentation an activity where the listeners have to do something—such as write on flipcharts, move their seats, or stand up.

# Eat and Drink Conservatively

Ultimately, what you eat and when you eat it might be the least important concern you have. But it's worth thinking about it, even briefly, to ensure you don't sabotage your own presentation. Don't make the error of eating or drinking things that give you dry mouth, sticky lips, or bad breath.

## Food Sometimes Lingers—Visibly

Sometimes what you eat is fine for your stomach and keeps you energetic, but it sticks to your teeth or falls on your clothing. There are certain predictable foods to watch out for, such as spinach, popcorn, and ice cream. If a meal precedes your presentation, make sure you check yourself in a mirror before the presentation begins.

Some foods stick in corners of your teeth, and presenters with green-edged teeth are somehow not quite as credible as others. Other foods stick to your teeth and make talking awkward. Popcorn is notorious for getting stuck in between teeth. Sticky food, and food that melts, such as ice cream, drips on your clothing. Of course, so does coffee, which somehow manages to drip on white shirts and pale ties just before you start your presentation.

If you will be eating before you present, and particularly if your presentation is an important one, or if you have a habit of dropping food, check yourself in a mirror to make sure you don't have any of your meal or snack lingering visibly on your teeth, face, or clothing.

And if for any reason you find remains of your food on your clothing and it won't come off easily, make sure your presentation is high-energy. Keep those listeners involved in what you're saying, and then the spot won't become an object of fascination for them.

Bored listeners seek excitement, even if it's just trying to figure out what's on your lapel.

And always consider that it might be worth modifying your normal food patterns, just in case, just this time.

## The Least You Need to Know

➤ Food and drink can create problems for a presenter, so pick food and drink carefully and don't eat a big meal just before you make a presentation.

➤ Caffeine, spicy foods, heavy and high-fat foods, alcohol, and carbonated beverages are typically the sources of stomach pain, burping, and other physical discomforts that presenters want to avoid.

➤ If you are asked for your suggestions for the food and beverages to be served during the meeting at which you will be presenting, suggest light foods. Suggest that alcohol be reserved for after the meeting.

➤ Check yourself in a mirror before you present to make sure you don't have any food stuck to your teeth, in between your teeth, or on your clothing.

# Chapter 17

# Prepare and Practice, Practice, Practice

## In This Chapter

➤ How to prepare for a presentation so that you don't have to memorize it

➤ An easy process for remembering the words you want to say

➤ Practicing your presentation to make it interesting and fresh

You probably have a busy job, an active social life, and a lot of commitments you keep hoping to meet. So it's probably not your preference to have to find time in your busy schedule to prepare your presentation well in advance and to practice it enough so that you know how to deliver it effectively.

But unless you are an excellent presenter and are experienced in dealing with unexpected events, you need to prepare the presentation carefully and practice it.

You don't want to memorize it, but you do want to make sure you present your ideas clearly and in a style that is interesting to the listeners.

## Consider This

If you doubt the need to practice and be fully prepared, consider the fate of the retail executive who prepared his sales presentation, asked his staff to prepare the visual aids, and left on a business trip, returning an hour before the evening presentation he was scheduled to make to a group of buyers. He quickly grabbed his materials, which were sitting where he had asked his staff to leave them, got to the presentation room, and spoke with the buyers.

They chatted about concerns, issues, trends. They all had light beverages and hors d'oeuvres. The executive excused himself just before the presentation was to begin and quickly reviewed his notes and the visual aids. He checked to ensure the machinery was working and the chairs comfortably positioned for everyone to see and hear him.

The presentation began, and he discovered as he proceeded that there were typographical errors on the presentation, items that should have been on the visual aids were missing, notes he had made on the draft were part of the visual aids. He also realized as he was speaking that there were points that should have been earlier in the presentation, and others that should have been withheld until the listeners were already persuaded to purchase the new product launch.

This executive didn't under-value his listeners, but he was experienced. He trusted his staff, and he had always been able to trust that his staff would produce the right visual aids. But he didn't know that several had been out with flu. They didn't know he wouldn't review everything before using it.

He was able to manage the visual aids problem by skipping those that were seriously flawed and talking through the issues, engaging the listeners with his energy. But he wasn't able to resequence the major thoughts. The presentation was disjointed.

And he'll never know whether he got the level of buy-in possible. He probably did begin to appreciate, however, the importance of practicing, even though his basic presentation skills were excellent.

# Prepare

*You have to prepare.* You have to identify the messages you're sending and the sequence in which you'll present the information. You have to decide how much detail to include. And you have to prepare appropriate visual aids.

Also for any major presentation, you'll want to prepare your personal support materials, such as a script or notes. Even if you don't plan on reading the script to the audience, or if you don't plan on using any notes, you'll want to prepare them to help you remember the messages and key points in sequence.

Some people believe that having a script is easier than having just notes and then having to find the right words as the audience watches. Realistically, however, making a presentation effectively with a script is significantly more challenging than making a presentation directly to the audience, when you can choose words to meet the audience's needs and to respond to their interests.

So decide what you'll need to get prepared. There will usually be one of three circumstances. Sometimes, you'll be using a script, because the words you'll be saying must be carefully designed and controlled. This situation occurs when you're speaking about a topic that is sensitive and requires careful wording or when you'll be using a *TelePrompTer*.

The second situation is when you'll be speaking from notes. This type of presentation is usually longer than 15 minutes and requires that you have facts available. Having notes helps you keep the facts handy while it keeps you focused on covering the material in the sequence you've planned.

The third situation occurs when you'll be presenting material with which you are very familiar, the presentation isn't very long, and the visual aids contain all or most of the facts you'll need to remember.

These three situations cover most of the presentations you'll give, the ones you know about in advance so that you can be prepared. The situations as described assume you'll be using visual aids, but of course, you won't always use visual aids. Most speakers who aren't using visual aids do bring notes, so use the guidelines for preparing for the second situation for a "no visual aids" presentation.

**Beware**

Most script readers are wooden, boring, and speak in a monotone. They don't sound spontaneous and don't pause in natural places. So if you use a script, practice so that the words are familiar to you. Practice so that you know where to put the emphasis and where to pause.

**Definition**

A **TelePrompTer** is a device that speakers use at major conferences. The speaker stands behind a lectern, and a TelePrompTer is placed on each side of the speaker. The image from the computer is projected onto glass squares. The speaker reads from the image on the glass. Because there is one square on the left and one on the right, the speaker turns her head from side to side, appearing to be giving eye contact to the audience.

# The First Situation: You Have a Script

If you're going to use a script, you'll go through the following steps before the presentation:

➤ Prepare the script.

➤ Read the script.

➤ Prepare the visual aids with message titles.

➤ Revise the script to improve its sequence.

➤ Resequence the visual aids as appropriate.

Each of these steps is discussed in the sections that follow.

## Prepare the Script

If you're using a script, you'll have to write a script. But write the script so that it sounds conversational, not part of a formal essay.

First, decide what your message is and select the key support messages. Outline the information so that you have an effective sequence and all the necessary relationships among facts are clear and easy to follow.

Second, draft a script as if you are talking the material through. Don't worry about grammar or wording or sentence structure. Write the words as if you are speaking them, using the outline to guide the sequence and to ensure you include all the facts as planned.

Third, review the script to make sure it is complete.

**Beware**
Don't memorize the speech. Get familiar with it. Memorized speeches are boring. Speakers who have memorized a speech focus on what they've memorized, not on the listeners. Listeners like to be paid attention to.

## Read the Script

After you have the script prepared, read it out loud numerous times. Read it loudly. Read it slowly. Read it rapidly.

Learn the flow of the logic. As you are reading, you will become familiar with the flow of the logic you've established with the outline. You'll also begin to be aware of points that are in the wrong place and facts you'll need to move to other places in the presentation. Don't move them yet, though.

Get familiar with the words. Part of the reading and re-reading process is getting to know the words you want to use when you make the presentation. If you've drafted the script as if it is a conversation and not as a formal essay, you'll have chosen words that are specific to you and which you know will make the points clearly. Each time you read the script, you'll keep learning more of the sounds of the script as you want to present it.

Read the speech often enough so that you become familiar with its sequence, its facts, and its words. Just don't read it so often that you memorize it. You're trying to make the flow of the speech easy to deal with. You're making the words comfortable for speaking. You're not memorizing.

## Prepare the Visual Aids with Message Titles

After you've read the script a few times, prepare the visual aids, using message titles. Choose the visual aids so that they help the listeners remember what you're saying, understand something they need to see to comprehend it, and recognize that you've changed messages or topics.

Put the visual aids in sequence, and then each time you read the script, look at the accompanying visual aids, too.

## Revise the Script to Improve Its Sequence

Just before the presentation, maybe one or two days in advance depending on how much time you've devoted to preparation, redraft the script. Modify the script by moving the facts to where you now believe they belong. Add words you think you'll need. Eliminate words and information you consider to be excessive, based on the readings you've done.

Mark the key concepts and themes. Identify with underlining or bold text the key messages you need to send. Mark the significant facts that make your message clear and believable. These are the main messages you'll want to pay attention to, so you'll want to know where they are.

Next, mark the grammatical units. Highlight the major units of grammar. For example, mark the script with a highlighter or pen to show where the subjects and verbs are. Mark the prepositional phrases so that you know where they begin and where they end. You won't want to do this for every script throughout your career, but you will benefit from learning how to make the words in phrases stay connected as you speak.

Finally, mark the verbs. Underline the verbs so that you know which ones are most important. The ones you underline are the ones you'll stress. If you stress the verbs by saying them louder or by making sure they're very clear, it's easier for the listeners to hear exactly what you want them to hear. Remember, too, to make sure the verbs are interesting. The following shows you how to mark your notes.

Sales decreased each quarter

Marketing <u>will modify</u> the campaign

Finance <u>will analyze</u> sales data

Reps <u>will review</u> call lists

Environment was a factor

Winter storms—18

Unusual spring holidays schedule

## Resequence the Visual Aids as Appropriate

After you've modified the script to match what you've learned in a better sequence, re-sequence the visual aids to match the new order. Make sure you have the right visual aids and that the message titles are still the right message titles. Add any visual aids you need to add. And always eliminate any that have become irrelevant.

# The Second Situation: You Will Speak From Notes

If you can use notes instead of a script, start with the same basic steps:

➤ Prepare a script

➤ Read the script

➤ Prepare the visual aids with message titles

➤ Distill an outline from the script, revising the original sequence as appropriate

➤ Prepare the notes

➤ Resequence the visual aids as appropriate

Let's look at these individually too.

## Prepare a Script

Create an outline that highlights your major and supporting messages. Place the facts where they are clear and relevant. Eliminate information you don't need. Create the examples you need.

Write the script from the outline. Choose words—the words you would say in a perfect world where you wouldn't be nervous. Be conversational. Add stories and examples of points you're trying to make. Capture the way you normally speak, not the way you normally write.

# Read the Script

Read the drafted presentation out loud frequently. Read it in all sorts of ways: rapidly, slowly, in a sing-song voice, with great exaggeration of key points.

You're trying to learn the flow of the logic and get familiar with the words. You want to practice wrapping your mouth around the words in the sequence you would like to use.

# Prepare the Visual Aids with Message Titles

As you become familiar with the flow of the script as you want to deliver it, prepare the visual aids with message titles. Use enough visuals to make the information clear to the audience.

# Distill an Outline from the Script, Revising the Original Sequence

Just before your presentation, maybe a day or two in advance, revise the sequence of your presentation. Rethink the outline you originally created. Think about how you felt pronouncing words and saying the examples. Resequence the presentation so that the flow of ideas is logical and easy to remember.

# Prepare the Notes

Prepare notes so that you have all the key messages and facts in sequence. Include the nouns and verbs, all of the subjects, verbs, and direct objects that anchor your messages and facts. Don't include the adjectives and adverbs. You want the notes to be easy to read and to contain only the major elements and important words. You'll add the adverbs and adjectives when you speak, based on the responses of the audience.

When you prepare the notes, create them in columns so that the print you see is about three-and-one-half to four inches wide. Use upper- and lowercase letters, and use a "serif" typeface. A mix of upper- and lowercase letters in a serif print is easier to read than all uppercase letters in a sans serif type.

> **Handy Hint**
> Write the important numbers and words in the notes, even if they're going to be on the visual aids. Better to have them twice than to have something disappear and be unable to remember it!

**Consider This:**

Columns help you read notes and scripts more easily when you are presenting:

➤ Use upper and lowercase letters

➤ Use mix of upper- and lowercase letters

➤ Use serif type

➤ Avoid all capital letters

➤ Avoid sans serif type

If you can, use boldface type to make sure each of the letters is easy to read. And print the notes in a size large enough to read easily. The following two figures show different ways to make notes. The first is easier to read.

*Serif print with upper- and lower-case letters is easier to read.*

> Sales decreased each quarter
> 　　Marketing will modify campaign
> 　　Finance will analyze sales data
> 　　Reps will review call lists
>
> Environment was factor
> 　　Winter storms – 18
> 　　Unusual spring holidays schedule

*Non-serif print, especially "all caps," is difficult to read.*

> **SALES DECREASED EACH QUARTER**
> 　　**MARKETING WILL MODIFY CAMPAIGN**
> 　　**FINANCE WILL ANALYZE SALES DATA**
> 　　**REPS WILL REVIEW CALL LISTS**
>
> **ENVIRONMENT WAS FACTOR**
> 　　**WINTER STORMS – 18**
> 　　**UNUSUAL SPRING HOLIDAYS SCHEDULE**

## Resequence the Visual Aids as Appropriate

At this point, check the visual aids and make sure they are in the right sequence, based on your modified outline. Add any you need, and eliminate any that don't contribute directly to the presentation.

# The Third Situation: You Will Speak with Only Visual Aids

You might find it useful to put small copies of the visual aids next to the speaking notes.

➤ Prepare a script

➤ Read the script

➤ Prepare the visual aids with message titles

➤ Mark special notes on visual aids frames

➤ Resequence the visual aids as appropriate

## Prepare a Script

If you'll be using only visual aids to make your presentation, you'll still need to prepare an outline and then a script. Make sure the outline is sequenced effectively to deliver and support the main message. Make sure the script is conversational.

**Handy Hint**
Read the message titles only, in sequence. Is the logic of your presentation clear? If you weren't there to talk the listeners through the logic, and all they had was the visual aids, would the major points be easy to understand? If not, add visual aids as needed and modify the message titles to provide a high level overview of your message and supporting logic.

## Read the Script

Read the script out loud frequently to learn the flow of the logic and get familiar with the words you want to use. Read it frequently enough to be comfortable with the flow and words, but don't memorize it.

## Prepare the Visual Aids with Message Titles

After you have a working script, prepare the visual aids, making sure the message titles follow the logic of the presentation.

## Mark Special Notes on Visual Aids Frames

Write notes about key facts or messages on the frames of the visual aids. If you're not using frames, or if you're using slides, which don't accommodate frames, create notes even if you don't plan to use them.

## Resequence the Visual Aids If/As Appropriate

Just before your presentation, one or two days before you'll talk, make sure the sequence is appropriate and add or eliminate any visual aids as needed.

# Practice!

If you're using the preparation method as described here, you'll be practicing even before you're ready for your final "practice" session or dress rehearsal.

## Read the Message Titles of Visual Aids Out Loud

Just before the presentation, read the message titles of the visual aids out loud to make sure they flow, to make sure you're comfortable with the sequence, and to make sure you can say all the words comfortably.

Reading the message titles out loud helps you remember the sequence of the messages and submessages.

When you're reading the message titles, make sure you say the verbs clearly and with emphasis.

## Use Pictures or Stuffed Animals

If you can't practice in the room where you'll be presenting, use pictures in your home or office. Speak to them as if they are people. Or line up your children's stuffed animals and speak to them as if they are your audience.

**Beware**
If you are nervous about a presentation, do not practice in front of a mirror! You'll just become more aware of everything you do and of how you do it. Your job is to focus on the messages and the audience, not on yourself.

## Avoid Mirrors

It is often wise not to speak to a mirror because you can become very focused on how you look and not on how you sound. You should always check your appearance in a mirror just before you present, but avoid practicing to the mirror.

## Stretch Vowels and Punch Verbs

As you practice, play with how you speak. Say the vowels for a long time, stretching them. Say the verbs very loudly. Say the verbs with a high voice. Say the verbs with a low voice. Play with the words and the sounds.

If you want people to understand what you're saying, they have to hear the vowel sounds, so if you practice spending a lot of time on each vowel sound, you'll probably pronounce each one clearly during the actual presentation.

If you want to have a speaking pattern that is lively and interesting, make sure the verbs are the words the listeners hear. Verbs are the energy source of language, and they carry a lot of the meaning. Make sure you say them with energy.

## Use Video

If you have access to a video camera, practice your presentation and have someone videotape it.

Watch the videotape and listen carefully. Try to hear if your messages are clear and if the presentation is easy to understand. Use it to listen to your pronounciation and pace. Are they appropriate? Interesting? Clear?

**Beware**
Use the video practice several days or even a week or more before the actual presentation. If you see yourself on video-tape too near the presentation, you might become self-conscious about your appearance and about your habits of gesturing and talking.

## Effective Speakers Prepare and Practice

Most speakers who respect their audiences spend time preparing and time practicing. You won't always be able to prepare a script, but you should try. You won't always be able to practice thoroughly, but you should practice some.

At minimum, make sure you have a well-sequenced, Message-based℠ outline or notes with appropriate visual aids. Make sure each visual aid has a message title.

You can always review those message titles to keep yourself focused on the key messages and the flow you've established that will make your message clear.

## The Least You Need to Know

➤ Prepare a conversational script, even if you're not going to use a script during the presentation.

➤ Always have message titles on the visual aids so that you can use them to practice the presentation.

➤ Mark the verbs in your script or notes. You'll want to pronounce verbs clearly and carefully to ensure the energy they create gets across to the audience.

SON, GIVE ME ONE OF THOSE PRACTICE QUESTIONS.

"ARE YOU SOME KIND OF IDIOT?"

# Getting Buy-In

When you prepare for presentations, make sure you are including everything you're supposed to include and presenting ideas in ways that make it easy for listeners to believe and find credible.

It is easy to prepare a presentation that makes a great deal of sense to you but omits information that someone will need or includes information that someone will find offensive. It also is easy to present information you find straightforward and relevant and discover that the listeners don't understand it or don't see its relevance.

So part of preparing a presentation is checking with key people to make sure the presentation will work. You need to review with key people what you'll be saying, how you'll be saying it, and what you intend to cover and not cover. Use the following questions to pre-think who your key listeners will be.

---

### Identifying Key Listeners—And Asking for Assistance

1. Who are your key listeners, the ones who really care about the topic you're presenting?

   _____

   _____

2. Who will be listening to your presentation who understands the topic you're presenting? Can this person give you some time to review the messages and facts you're presenting so that you are sure you've covered everything logically?

   _____

   _____

3. Who will be listening to your presentation who does not understand the topic you're presenting? Can this person give you some time to review the messages and facts and tell you whether they make sense?

   _____

   _____

---

### Consider This

When one presenter described the upcoming changes to the building's layout, no one really understood what she was saying. She thought her presentation was quite clear, but no one in the audience had any experience with designing building space for corporate work "optimization."

Everyone listened, and few people asked questions. They simply didn't know enough to know what questions they could ask! To the listeners, the presentation focused on engineering and architectural terminology and facts. What they were seeking was an explanation of who was going to sit where and what the space would look like.

Another part of preparing for a presentation is knowing who might cause you difficulties in winning your points so that you can get their buy-in in advance or at least identify their concerns and speak to those concerns during the presentation. If you prepare your presentation by asking decision-makers and influencers for their input on how to be successful with your presentation, you're more likely to be well-prepared for the challenges some of your listeners might throw at you. The following worksheet can help you identify stakeholders in the way things are today. Always know who holds a stake in the satus quo.

---

## How Is Your Idea Flawed?

1.  Who is least likely to like your idea?

    _____

    _____

    1A.  What will this person or these people dislike about your idea?

        _____

        _____

2.  Who is affected by your idea?

    _____

    _____

    2A.  Assume that your idea will hurt everyone who is affected. How will they be hurt?

        _____

        _____

    2B.  What arguments will these people make to prove your idea is not a good one?

        _____

        _____

---

# Get Input from Decision-Makers and Influencers

Chapter 6 described how to prepare a presentation and how and why to speak to decision makers and influencers. You should always perform those steps thoroughly.

As Chapter 6 pointed out:

➤ Don't structure your presentation until you know all the information that must be included.

➤ Identify and clarify for yourself the message before you begin to draft the presentation. Figure out what you'll put into the presentation that might need support from others in the audience—plan to pre-sell the influencer.

➤ Work from the assumption that your idea is flawed. Identify all the ways your argument could be faulty so that you can build in the appropriate responses when you structure the presentation.

➤ Prepare the facts and extra visual aids you might need so that you can respond to arguments raised during the question and answer session.

But after you've prepared the presentation, consider returning to a few of those people and asking them to review your presentation. Ask them if it is clear. Ask them if it is addressing the ideas in a way that makes sense to them and that puts the ideas in the right frame.

**Definition**

A **frame** is a perspective or a viewpoint, the spin or slant. For example, business professionals frame situations as opportunities, not as problems. Framing an issue appropriately is difficult, particularly with a sensitive issue. An effective presenter spends time understanding what frame to give the messages and facts she intends to present.

You won't be rehearsing in front of these people, although if you talk someone through your presentation, try out some of the phrasing you plan to use. If the people you consult respond favorably to the phrases or words, you probably have chosen them well.

Don't take a lot of time from these people either, particularly if they plan to attend your presentation, but ask the following questions:

➤ Do they have any examples that might be useful?

➤ Are any of the examples or facts you plan to include sensitive for any of the listeners invited to the presentation?

Use the following worksheet when planning your presentation; it can help you identify sensitivities that might exist about your idea.

## Who Has a Stake in Keeping Things the Way They Are?

1. Who created the way things are today?

   _____

   _____

2. Who has won a promotion because of their contributions to the way things are today?

   _____

   _____

3. Who loses power if things change?

   _____

   _____

4. Who loses access to power if things change?

   _____

   _____

5. Who looks bad if things change or if what they created has to be changed?

   _____

   _____

# Develop Potential Questions and Challenges

Besides consulting some of the potential decision-makers or influencers who are affected by your presentation's ideas, develop a comprehensive list of questions any of the listeners could ask. List all the challenges someone could make.

Consider:

➤ Are there numbers you'll present that someone might not accept as valid?

➤ Are there facts you'll present that someone might not accept as valid?

➤ Are there examples you'll use that someone might not understand or believe?

➤ Are there ideas that are difficult to explain or validate, although they're important?

Use the following worksheet to think about your listeners and how your ideas might affect each one. It will help you to plan your pre-presentation meetings.

**201**

## Develop an Impact Map

List all the people who you expect to attend your presentation:

_____

_____

_____

_____

Label people "3" if they will be significantly affected by the idea you're presenting.

Label people "2" if they might be significantly affected by the idea you're presenting.

Label people "1" if they won't be affected by the idea you're presenting.

Talk to some of the "3"s to see how they will react to your logic and facts. Try to talk to some of the "2"s to see how they will react to your logic and facts.

### Consider This

A presenter who was new to the department, although experienced with the company, was asked to make a presentation to the executive team about ways to restructure. He prepared very carefully because he had a near-passionate belief in the need to restructure the group. The team assignments that had been made were too broad. Teamwork was confusing because too many people from too many functions were involved. The teams were too large, and getting work done took a long time.

So he prepared a presentation, stressing the benefits of limiting team size, and of teams being held accountable for achieving goals in short time frames. He described facts in ways that painted the existing team structure as a disaster.

What he didn't know was that one member of the executive committee attending his presentation had designed the team structure for the department. The team structure had won business awards. On the strength of the team structure, the executive had received significant work assignments and achieved executive status quickly.

The presentation was not a success.

If you are presenting a financial model, will everyone find it easy to understand? If you are discussing a new marketing campaign, will everyone understand why you're suggesting it? If you're discussing a new software program, will everyone know why it's needed and understand the terminology you plan to include?

Think through all the questions someone could ask by playing your own devil's advocate. Try to destroy the logic of the presentation. Create the arguments. Assume the presentation is shallow and poorly developed. Identify all the points of logic and questions you can ask that would prove that your messages and facts are irrelevant, flawed, and inappropriate. This is the list of questions you want to deal with as you review your presentation.

## Consider This

One financial manager was very frustrated about an upcoming presentation. Every time he explained the new financial model he had designed and that his group was using, people said they just didn't understand it. He explained the model repeatedly, but everyone claimed it was not something that made sense to them. He knew that it wasn't enough to just describe the steps of the model and the theories that justified it.

When asked to make a presentation about the financial model to an overseas department, this financial manager became worried. How could he explain the model to people who didn't even speak the language he spoke? So far, he hadn't succeeded in explaining it to people who should have understood it; at least he thought they should have understood it.

He conquered the presentation challenge by outlining the steps of the analysis and then describing the purpose—the message—of each phase of the model. He focused the presentation on the results of each of the steps. He explained how to use the model and the assumptions underlying the model.

He structured the presentation so that the primary message was that the model was useful for certain business decisions. He supported it by explaining the business issues that shaped the decision-making—the assumptions. Then he described the phases of the model. Finally, he reviewed the steps of the model and the calculations and mathematical underpinnings.

The presentation was successful.

# Build Responses into the Presentation

Review your presentation one more time and make sure you've answered every question and challenge with the information built into the presentation. Add any information that will help address potential challenges.

Prepare for the challenges:

➤ For every possible question you don't plan to answer as part of the presentation itself, prepare an answer. Create the charts and graphs needed and bring them to the presentation, just in case you need them. Find the facts and references and bring them to the presentation.

➤ For every challenge someone might pose, develop a persuasive response using the structure described in Chapter 9.

Part of the difficulty of making a presentation is appearing credible. Sometimes, no matter how well you present an idea, the listeners are going to say "no" to it. You might be clear, accurate, and persuasive. You might be energetic and credible, but they're going to say "no."

You have been effective, though, even if you lose your point, if you're perceived as credible. But you will not be thought credible if you can't respond effectively to the challenges a professional makes to your messages, ideas, and facts.

## Consider This

One presenter discovered the hard way the importance of being fully prepared for a presentation and the Q&A session. Part-way through his presentation, the listeners became very excited about the implications of his idea. They wanted to know more about some of the details of his idea that he hadn't really thought through. The speaker panicked. He realized he couldn't answer some of the questions, and in fact, some of the challenges were strong enough to make him challenge his thinking on the idea.

Because he hadn't pre-thought what challenges he might face, he wasn't prepared. He hadn't built into the presentation the facts that would have helped the listeners meet their information needs. And because he hadn't pre-thought how he might be challenged, he didn't expect some of the questions. So rather than deferring answers gracefully, he panicked.

His presentation was not a success.

A credible presenter is prepared for most challenges. No one has all the answers all of the time, and it's perfectly normal to have to tell someone that you don't have an answer to his question. But it's better to be prepared with an answer because you've pre-thought where the difficulties will be.

At minimum, make sure you know in advance what sticky issues could be raised so that you have no surprises, or at least as few as possible! If you've thought of the challenge before the presentation, you'll know how to respond to it when you're in front of the listeners.

Remember, they don't expect you to be perfect, but they do expect you to appear well-informed about the subject you're describing. If you look scared when they ask a question that seems pertinent to the subject, your credibility is going to be diminished.

# The Least You Need to Know

➤ Prepare for the presentation by listing every possible question or challenge anyone could pose.

➤ Bring any charts, graphs, facts, or references to the presentation if they could help you respond effectively to someone's challenge.

➤ Prepare effective, persuasive responses to the arguments someone could raise, particularly if those arguments could make your message seem non-credible.

# Part 5
# How Will I Ever Stand Up There?

*There are many presenters in the business world, and each has his own style. Some presenters pace a lot. Some presenters stand still. Some presenters are highly animated and speak rapidly. Some presenters are intense and speak fairly slowly, emphasizing what they're saying carefully for the listeners.*

*It can be tough to figure out just what makes a presenter effective. How can so many people do so many different things when they present and yet seem to be effective? How can so many people do the same basic things, and yet so many of them are boring?*

*The keys for effectiveness are focus and* energy.

# What Do They Expect?

You've done what you need to do to get ready for the presentation: You've planned the presentation itself carefully to make sure it's Message-based℠ or persuasive, you've prepared the visual aids, you've got the logistics and support put together to make the impression you want to make, and you've practiced the presentation so you are comfortable delivering it.

But you don't really know, even now, what they expect. "They" are the listeners, the audience members who will respond favorably to your message if you deliver it well. What do they want? What do they expect from you? What will they see and hear if you are credible?

Audiences expect you to be "hear-able," "understandable," focused on meeting their needs, energetic, appropriately enthusiastic, focused on the message, and professional. They want you to be clear, interesting, logical, and easy to hear. They want to hear enough information to support your message that they can make a decision and get back to work.

They do not expect you to be a "perfect" speaker. They do not expect you to amaze them with your fluent speaking style, your brilliant use of grammar, and your dazzling sense of words. They want you to communicate a critical message to them in a way that enables them to respond appropriately to that message.

It's the message, not the delivery, that's important. But it's the delivery that will enable them to get the message!

# The Challenge Is Not the Presentation You Wrote

Everything begins with the presentation you prepare. You have to have the content, but that's the easy part. You have to have content that's worth delivering. But most present-ers worry equally about whether they are good "presenters." They have an image of what the perfect presenter looks and sounds like. They try to imitate what they think is a perfect speaker.

There are a lot of theories in business that suggest that perfection is not the goal, and it is not a necessity. You've probably dealt with the rule of "80/20," often called Pareto's law. This "law" has been a major factor in making business decisions for a long time.

**Handy Hint**
Consider the slick speaker who is all show and no substance. Consider the speaker who is lots of substance and no show, who is hard to hear and to understand. Then consider the speaker who has good information presented logically and who clearly cares about the substance and about the audience's ability to hear it and understand it. Deliver well, but deliver substance.

Pareto, a 19th century European scholar, identified a pattern of significance. We use that pattern to communi-cate that 80% of outcome exists from 20% of the effort. For example, 80% of the errors might be due to 20% of the employees. 80% of sales results might be due to the efforts of 20% of the sales force. The 80/20 rule suggests that you need to concentrate your efforts to achieve the maximum return. You don't have to give 100% to gain 100%. You do have to choose what you'll pay attention to and follow through.

Presentation delivery is one of the areas where perfection is not the goal, and in fact, perfection is probably damaging to your effectiveness. You don't need to have 100% perfect word choice or 100% perfect word pronunciation. Your grammar doesn't have to be perfect, and your sequence doesn't have to be perfect. You do, though, need to have a Message-based[SM] logic that the listeners can follow.

You need to recognize the elements of presentation delivery that will give you the 80% return. You'll get an 80% return from how you deliver your carefully sequenced, Message-based[SM] presentation. You'll devote 80% of your presentation preparation to a critical aspect of the presentation, its content. That's necessary to make sure that your present information matters to the listeners. You'll get the maximum benefit by using your delivery skills to get the message to the listeners.

So plan to prepare the presentation carefully, but plan also to put your attention during the delivery on the elements that will benefit you the most—the delivery skills of focus and energy.

# Don't I Need to Aim for Perfection?

There is an interesting issue surrounding perfection in presentations. Perfection is saying grammatically perfect sentences and using clever words and examples. Perfection is a speaker with gestures that fit the words. But perfection can be damaging. The perfect presenter is often not credible. The perfect presenter who speaks clearly with just the right words and just the right pace and just the right example perfectly timed is often the presenter who is not paying attention to the audience. The perfect presenter is often the one who is paying attention to himself and his perfection.

Audiences respond poorly to polished, perfect speakers because they become boring very quickly. After all, who are the best conversationalists at a party? Are they the ones who have practiced their stories repeatedly so that they know how to get the right laugh at just the right moment? Or are they the ones who listen to you and hear what you're saying so that their response is directed to you in the words you need to hear to understand?

Good conversation is the result of listening to and thinking with the other person. Conversation includes errors in word choice, pronunciation, and grammar. Conversation is rarely sequenced effectively, but it includes so much give-and-take that the right ideas become clear, and the style of talking and listening evolves to suit the participants in the conversation.

No presenter can rely on all the give-and-take built into a normal conversation, so the sequence of the ideas is the most important element in preparing for a presentation. Once you know what the sequence of the ideas needs to be and you have ensured that everything you'll say is Message-based℠, you need to use the skills of a good conversationalist.

Remember Pareto and the rule of 80/20. Always prepare the material, but put your efforts where they will count when you make the presentation. Perfection is not the goal. Communication is the goal. Put your emphasis on effectively delivering a well-structured presentation. Don't worry about the words. Do worry about communicating with the audience members one-to-one.

**Consider This**

The CEO of a spin-off company of one of the largest American corporations gave a presentation to a group of consultants about the new company, its technology investments and challenges, and its structures. The consultants listening to the CEO were fascinated by the topic and listened, for a while, intensely. But as the CEO presented, the consultants quickly realized that he had a thick script and that he was reading the script. He wasn't referring to the script to keep himself on track. He was reading it, word-for-word.

The spin-off company was an exciting venture. It was bringing a new technology from Japan to the United States, and its success was highly dependent on the CEO's ability to work globally, think creatively about corporate structure and employee performance, and partner with numerous outside advisors. His presentation was designed to create interest among the consultants in contributing to the work the CEO was committed to doing with his spin-off.

But the consultants in the audience stopped listening. They didn't find the presentation compelling. The content was compelling, but the delivery was dull. The delivery was the CEO reading, not the CEO communicating. The message to the consultants was, "This script has been put together by my communications group, and here is what they said."

The CEO's speaking had nothing about it that suggested he cared about the company or the consultants listening to him. It was a boring speech and a wasted evening for the CEO and for the consultants.

## The Words Are Less Than 10%

Researchers in communication have studied the components of presentation effectiveness for many years. The studies show that less than 10% of the effectiveness of a presentation is due to the words the presenter uses. That means that about 90% of the effectiveness of a presentation is due to the delivery skills of the presenter. Almost all of the impact of a presenter is the result of how someone speaks and uses nonverbal communication.

## Communication Is Verbal, Nonverbal, and Symbolic

Communicate has three channels: verbal, nonverbal, and symbolic. Verbal communication is the words you use. Nonverbal communication is how you use your body and voice. Symbolic communication is how you use the symbols around you, such as clothing. Let's look at each of these in more detail.

## Verbal Communication—Easy to Manage, Easy to Manipulate

Verbal communication is the words you use. Words can be manipulated, and you know how and when to manipulate them. You do it all the time when you want someone to think an error was minor not major, or when you want someone to focus on your solution and not your error.

You should always use effective and appropriate words, but recognize that the words you choose are carrying a small portion of the message itself—less than 10% if the researchers are right.

## Nonverbal Communication—Easy to Manage, Hard to Manipulate

### Consider This

One speaker was working overseas with a group that spoke very little English, although they had moderate skills in listening to English. They could grasp about 20% of what he was saying. The speaker did not speak any of the audience's language. But the presentation was successful largely because the nonverbal communication was powerful enough to carry the message to the audience.

What made this presentation work? The words were almost irrelevant, and the nonverbal communication was colored by cultural differences. But nonverbal communication has enough universal elements that it carried a great deal of the message. Of course, the context of the presentation was known, so the listeners could focus on the probable content issues and vocabulary. The visual aids helped, too. But the key here is that the words themselves were almost nonimportant.

Nonverbal communication is what you do with your body, hands, face, and voice. It's the pacing of the talk, the gesturing, the animation of your face, the emphasis you place on certain words. Nonverbal communication happens when you look at something to your left or at a clock rather than at the person you're conversing with. It's the communication that tells someone what you're interested in or what you care about—or don't care about. You can choose to manage your nonverbal communication and gestures, use animation, and communicate how you feel. You can also manipulate nonverbal communication. Nonverbal communication is difficult to manipulate, but not impossible. Think of nonverbal communication as eyes, voice, and gestures. You can manage your nonverbal communication by using it, but it's hard to use nonverbal communication to show truthfulness when you're not being truthful. It's hard to make nonverbal communication believable when you're not being sincere.

Think about that presenter you saw who stood woodenly and spoke in a monotone. Also think about that presenter's subject matter. The content was probably interesting, but the delivery made it boring, and you probably didn't listen to most of what he said. He could have forced himself to add some gestures, and he could have put some energy into his voice.

Think about the presenter you saw who was wildly energetic and exciting to watch. You watched and watched, but you left the presentation not understanding what he said. This speaker didn't match his content to his nonverbal communication. He was all delivery with little substance.

Now think about the presenter you saw who was sincere and enthusiastic, and who had to keep pausing to find appropriate examples for the audience. Remember how easy it was to remember his key points after the presentation ended?

These examples of nonverbal communication suggest that you can choose to use nonverbal communication to deliver a message effectively and sincerely. Chapters 20 and 21 will help you learn how to make nonverbal communication easy to use effectively.

## Symbolic Communication—Easy to Manage, Easy to Manipulate

Symbolic communication is important, and Chapter 14 reviewed some of the choices you have to make as a presenter. Symbolic communication is easy to manipulate. You can always put on the "right" suit or the "right" tie and send the "right" message.

Symbolic communication is something presenters must manage, and we usually manage it by making a choice that enables the audience to listen to us and not to get distracted by our symbolic choices. Of course, sometimes we make symbolic choices with the intent of having the audience pay attention to them. Those instances have something to do with establishing ourselves as being something special or unusual for the listeners.

**Consider This**

Why might you choose to send messages with symbolic choices?

A presenter might choose to wear a uniform, although a business suit would be equally appropriate for the situation. But the uniform might remind the listeners of the speaker's background and credibility.

Or a presenter might wear a hat, as one woman did during a presentation to over a thousand listeners, 97% of whom were men. Her hat was a clear statement about her femininity in a predominantly male profession.

An executive might choose to wear a manufacturing plant uniform or a construction site hardhat to show her closeness to the listeners at the plant or on the construction site.

## Use Verbal, Nonverbal, and Symbolic Communication to Present Effectively

Your challenge is to present your message so that the listeners hear and understand you. What they expect is to understand your message and the supporting detail. What they expect is to be engaged by your ideas and by you. They expect you to be enthusiastic about your subject matter.

They don't expect you to behave flamboyantly unless you usually behave flamboyantly. They don't expect you to speak each word perfectly and each sentence with the grammar you'd use when writing.

They expect that you will work to get the message across to them clearly so that they can decide whether the message matters enough to act on it or believe it.

The audience expects you to be focused and energetic.

## Be Focused

What is focus? You are focused when you:

➤ Make the message clear and keep the information relevant.

➤ Keep the listeners thinking about the message and the details so that they understand that the message matters to you and to them.

So how you structure the presentation influences "focus." But so does eye contact, a key skill in delivering presentations effectively. Chapter 20 will help you understand how to provide focus through eye contact.

# Be Energetic and Appropriately Enthusiastic

What is energetic? Think of the presenters you have watched during your career. Some were energetic, and some were dull. The energetic presenters didn't jump around and use wild gestures. They generated a sense of energy. You listened to them and got the feeling that they cared about the information they were sharing and the facts they were presenting.

When you communicate energy, people listen. And people who have to listen to you present want you to be energetic. They want to see that you care about your subject. They want to hear your enthusiasm and sincerity. They want to know from the way you present that you are involved with them as people. They want to know that you care about the subject, not the word choice and grammar.

Don't think that word choice and grammar are completely irrelevant. You need to develop language skills that enable you to have a lot of words from which to choose when you present. And your sentences should have reasonable grammar underlying them. You certainly don't want to make repeated grammatical errors to the extent that an audience remembers the grammatical errors and not the subject.

**Handy Hint**

It's always worthwhile to improve your language skills. But during a presentation, language skills are almost always less important than a delivery style that provides focus and energy. Language skills are an important factor only if your language skills are so poor that they become something the listeners pay attention to.

They'll know you have energy if you focus yourself and use your voice to make understandable statements. They also expect you to be enthusiastic. They expect the pace of your voice to be lively. Lively doesn't mean fast, and it doesn't mean smooth. It means that you speak with a pace that has variations in it, with enough volume that the listeners can easily hear you.

How often have you sat in a presentation turning an ear toward the speaker, hoping to be able to hear what she was saying? Speakers who have energy make sure the words travel to the listeners and make sure the words are the right words for each listener. They make sure the examples are just right for the moment. Energetic speakers don't worry about using particular words they drafted into the speech. They worry about using the words the listeners will understand and respond to.

# Be Focused on the Message

Your listeners also expect to have an easy time knowing what message you're sending. They enter the presentation expecting to hear what you want them to know, think, or do as a result of the presentation.

They expect to be able to follow your logic without having to work hard at it. They expect you to use visual aids that will help them understand your comments, but they don't expect the visual aids to be the presentation itself.

So your task is to use your delivery skills to make it easy for each listener to get the message you're delivering.

**Beware!**
Remember, *you* are the presentation. How you deliver your message and the supporting details will often determine whether the listeners will know, think, or do what you want them to know, think, or do. Always structure the presentation logically, and then spend your delivery being effective at delivering, not worrying about the words themselves and whether they're perfect. Pay attention to the listeners!

# Be Professional

Each audience you present to expects you to be a professional.

Professionals are well-informed in their field of expertise. So the audience will expect you to know what you're talking about, or at least to act as if you know what you're talking about.

Professionals listen carefully to others so that they can share ideas and perhaps modify ideas as new information becomes available. So your audience will expect you to listen carefully to their questions and concerns and to respond appropriately. They'll expect you to integrate their comments if those comments help strengthen the message and information available.

Professionals take responsibility for the information they are sharing and make sure people can understand it. So your audience will expect you to repeat information as needed to help them understand what you're saying. They'll expect you to have examples and data to make your points clear.

Professionals care about what they're communicating. So your audience will expect you to be sincere and straightforward with them about the message, the details, and the questions discussed.

Your listeners expect you to be professional and interesting. They do not expect you to say the perfect word at the perfect moment of your presentation.

Think about the five critical questions you can ask yourself as you present. These questions are shown in the following checklist.

---

**Pre-think Your Presentation Style and Monitor it Throughout the Presentation**

Yes  No

❑  ❑  Can they hear me because I am using my voice well enough to make it easy for the sound to carry to each listener, even the ones in the back?

❑  ❑  Can they understand me because I am pronouncing my words completely and carefully without slowing down the pace of my speaking to an unnatural slowness?

❑  ❑  Can they follow the logic of the message and ideas I'm presenting so that the message makes sense and is relevant to them?

❑  ❑  Will they be able to use this information to decide whether to know, think, or do what I'm asking of them?

❑  ❑  Can they see that I am energetic, enthusiastic, and sincere about the ideas because I am communicating with sincere eye contact and gestures that are appropriate to me and the topic?

---

# The Least You Need to Know

➤ Put your effort where it matters—on effective preparation of the presentation (before the day of the presentation) so that you can concentrate during the presentation on how you provide focus and energy.

➤ Use all three channels of communication effectively so that your words capture the message, your nonverbal communication shows your focus and energy, and your symbolic communication sends the appropriate messages about your credibility.

➤ Concentrate during a presentation on the audience. Listen to them. Pay attention to their nonverbal communication so that you can adapt your presentation and examples to suit them.

# Effective Presenters Focus

Focus. You've seen presenters who focus and those who don't focus. You know the difference because you are engaged by those who focus, and you are bored by those who don't. But what is focus? What are you responding to?

Think for a moment about that presentation you attended a few months ago. It was about a new analytical tool your finance group was about to implement. The new tool was going to help your company improve the quality of its decision-making. So it's an important tool, and it was a very important presentation.

But remember how the presenter didn't always make sense? Remember how you noticed after a few moments that the speaker kept looking at your hair? At the clock? Remember how he seemed to be looking at everyone all the time, scanning the audience as if he had lost something?

And do you remember when the presenter got confused and lost his train of thought, having to stop, review his notes, and painfully get back on track? And do you remember that he had to walk all the way across the room to get back to his notes—giving you lots of time to notice that he looked uncomfortable and nervous, particularly now that he had to go get his notes.

The presenter was not focusing. The presenter was not sending you a message that you, the listener, were the most important factor of the presentation. He was not helping you through the presentation ideas.

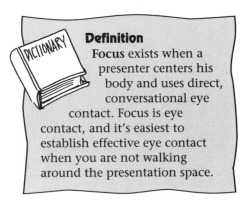

**Definition**
**Focus** exists when a presenter centers his body and uses direct, conversational eye contact. Focus is eye contact, and it's easiest to establish effective eye contact when you are not walking around the presentation space.

He also was confusing himself because he kept looking at so many people and things, and when he stopped looking was when he had to stop presenting and get himself reorganized and refocused.

Establishing and maintaining focus is important: During a presentation, the listeners should feel that they are the important element of the conversation. They should feel as if they are having a personal, one-to-one conversation with you, the presenter. They should be participating in a conversation during which you, the presenter, are guiding them through facts and explanations that make the message clear.

Most of the listeners' contributions will be through their nonverbal responses and occasional questions, but the presentation is most effective when it is a give-and-take conversation. Some of the give-and-take, of course, is going to be nonverbal—through eye contact and imperceptible nodding and acknowledgment.

So focus is a result of effective eye contact, and you need to make it easy for yourself to establish and maintain that eye contact.

**Definition**
**Stance** is posture; how you stand.

## Stance Permits Focus

The first element of focus that you have to conquer is stance. With an effective stance, you can begin to be an effective presenter. With an effective stance, you can begin to use your nervous energy and appear confident and enthusiastic, even if you're not.

## Centering

The goal is to stand tall by centering your body weight. You want to center your weight so that you feel anchored but not heavy.

Try this:

1. Stand so that your feet are flat on the floor about a foot apart. Aim for the same width as the width between your armpits.

2. Make your feet parallel. You might feel pigeon-toed, but you shouldn't look pigeon-toed.

3. Rock slowly and gently from side to side until you can feel how to stand so that your weight is over the center of your feet and not on the sides of your feet.

4. Rock slowly and gently back and forth until you can feel that your weight is centered between the front of the arches and the balls of your feet.

5. Bend your knees a few times to make sure you are not standing stiffly with the knee joints hyperextended.

6. After you have established this position, lift your shoulders, not your arms, and then let your hands fall gently to your sides. Relax your hands.

You are now reasonably well centered. Guard against letting your neck get tense. Avoid stiffening your neck.

You should be feeling certain things:

➤ You feel as if you are tilted a little bit forward.

➤ You can twist and turn your body as a unit, smoothly, without moving your feet.

➤ You feel as if you could easily move forward and walk briskly.

The goal of centering is establishing and maintaining good posture. Many of us were taught to stand as if someone were pulling a string up our spines. But this creates tension and stiffness and often means your head and shoulders are misaligned. By learning to center, you can stand tall with relaxed shoulders and a head that is truly centered over your body.

The key to focus is centering, so center your body weight and stand tall. As you bcome a confident presenter, you will not want to stand in this one position for the whole presentation. Use the process to learn how to center. Moving around is not a bad idea, but if moving around makes maintaining eye contact difficult, don't move around.

**Consider This**

If you want to work with centering, locate an expert on the Alexander Technique. These people can help you learn how to use your body comfortably and naturally. The Alexander Technique helps you use your voice well, too. The technique shows you how to align your body, allowing you to use your body and voice effectively.

Actors often study the Alexander Technique to learn how to use their bodies. By working with the technique, they learn how to make their bodies communicate wholeness and strength. They also learn how to distort the "correct" use of the body and voice to communicate distress, fear, age, and so on.

If this technique can be distorted to communicate the things you don't want to communicate as a presenter, it can be used to communicate what you do want to communicate—credibility, professionalism, confidence—when presenting.

Two excellent resources for exploring the Alexander Technique are Sarah Barker's *The Alexander Technique: Learning To Use Your Body For Total Energy*, Bantam Books, 1991, and Judith Leibowitz's and Bill Connington's *The Alexander Technique: The World-famous Method for Enhancing Posture, Stamina, Health, and Well-being, and for Relieving Pain and Tension*, Harper & Row, 1990.

## Staying Mobile and Still

After you are centered, you can move your upper body smoothly without moving your feet. You might wonder why this is an advantage, but think about your nervousness. If you are nervous, you're going to want to move around. And if you move around, you are going to show your listeners that you are nervous. People who move around, particularly with little movements and steps, look nervous.

Why not anchor your feet firmly, stand tall, use your upper body to communicate energy—and leave your feet planted until you calm down? Centering helps, and staying in one place, at least at the beginning while you get your nervousness under control, also helps.

## "No Motion" Can Provide Focus

One of the advantages of standing still, of "no motion," is that you can create focus. You can look at individuals in the audience without having to watch where you're putting your feet.

Just think about all the places your feet can get into trouble: the cords to the slide machine, the cart that is holding the overhead projector, the electric outlets in the floor that someone forgot to close. You can either look at individuals in the audience, or you can watch your feet, or you can fall over the obstacles.

If you were the listener, which choice would you want the speaker to make?

# There's Ultimately Only One Rule

Eye contact provides focus, and stance permits you to establish and maintain eye contact. That leads to the rule, the one rule you cannot break when you are presenting: Do not talk unless you have eye contact.

## What Is Eye Contact?

The presenter who scans is not establishing eye contact. The presenter who sees each person in the audience one-by-one is establishing eye contact.

Eye contact is looking directly at one person, seeing that person, and conversing with her. Eye contact means you are fully aware of what the person looks like and what response that person is giving you at any one point.

Consider also smiling while making eye contact. The smile can lock the listener in, keep him attentive, and result in the listener feeling even greater contact than otherwise.

## Go Slowly and Steadily

Effective eye contact means staying visually with each person, one at a time, for the time it takes to communicate a complete thought—a sentence, a paragraph, a specific but brief point. When you change eye contact from one person to another, the change should be slow. And while you maintain the eye contact, the contact should be steady, with minimal blinking.

**Handy Hint**

Blinking increases when you are nervous, so if you are aware that you are blinking a lot, try to stay with one person for a long period of time and concentrate on that person and his responses to your comments. Breathe deeply and slowly to calm down. You'll know when the blinking slows down.

Everyone blinks, and some of us naturally blink more frequently than others. You can work to slow down excessive blinking if you choose to, but don't pay attention to blinking. Do pay attention to managing your nervousness by centering, staying in one place, and using your breathing to manage your voice.

## Be Sincere

You want eye contact to be sincere, which means you have to maintain eye contact long enough to be aware of the person's responses, and so that the person is aware that you have made eye contact with him.

You're establishing personal contact so that you can have a conversation with him. You aren't trying to stare down the listener and win points. You are trying to make sure you are responsive to his reactions to your ideas.

## Do Not Stare

Eye contact is not necessarily staring. If you feel as if your eyes are narrowing their focus, you are probably staring. If you have no peripheral vision, you are undoubtedly staring. If you have a sense of looking down a tunnel, you are staring.

But if you keep your peripheral vision active, your eyes will soften their focus, and you will be maintaining eye contact that is appropriate without staring.

If you are concerned that you are staring, make yourself aware of the side wall, or put a hand up so that you can see it with your peripheral vision. Don't turn your head, just get that part of your vision to be working again.

**Beware!**

Some people don't like to have eye contact with a presenter. Someone might be shy, or come from a culture that does not value personal eye contact. Perhaps someone just doesn't like eye contact, with you or anyone else. If you see that someone is uncomfortable when you maintain eye contact with him, don't maintain eye contact with him.

# So How Do You Not Talk Unless You Have Eye Contact?

So if the goal is to establish slow, steady, sincere eye contact, what happens if something goes wrong? What if you need to change an overhead transparency? What if you need to work with the slide machine or give the listeners handouts? What if you get distracted and need to refer to your notes to get back on track?

Do not talk unless you have eye contact!

If something needs your attention, stop talking. Do whatever you have to do to make the visual aids work, to prepare your thoughts, or to return to your notes. Stop even if you just have to think about what you're saying for a moment. When you are ready to begin again, look at one person to reestablish eye contact, and begin again. The listeners realize you have paused, and they will wait.

> **Handy Hint**
> Many presenters, particularly ones who are nervous, talk rapidly and never pause. But listeners like to have a presenter pause. It allows them to think about what's being said. When you stop talking, they get to think and relax for a moment. So if you have to stop maintaining eye contact and therefore must stop talking, consider it a gift to the listeners.

## Using Notes

One of the biggest challenges presenters face is using notes effectively. If you have prepared for your presentation and are familiar with the information you're covering, the notes should be supporting you. Just remember, you do not talk unless you have eye contact! So if you need to refer to your notes, stop talking. Break eye contact. Read your notes and get your thoughts together. When you're ready, look up and establish eye contact with one person, and have a conversation with her.

## What If I Don't Know the Content Very Well?

Sometimes, you might be making a presentation for which you're unprepared. The request was last minute. The person who was supposed to present is out ill. Your schedule has been so hectic that you've been unable to prepare properly.

The rule will help you survive the presentation: Do not talk unless you have eye contact. Be methodical:

➤ Put your notes together.

➤ Prepare the opening statements well enough that you can make them without having to pause.

**Handy Hint**

If you are using a lectern for your notes or script, follow the rule. When you need to read the notes or script, break eye contact, prepare your thoughts, reestablish eye contact and keep going.

➤ When you need your notes, stop talking.

➤ Read your notes and prepare your statement.

➤ Reestablish eye contact and have a conversation with someone in the audience.

If you follow the rule, you can handle almost anything that happens and look comfortable and prepared. Just don't mention to the audience that something has gone wrong. Break eye contact. Deal with the problem or need. Reestablish eye contact and keep going.

Unless you announce to the listeners that you are uncomfortable about something you're doing, they will rarely know. Establish and maintain eye contact, and you focus on them and the message while they focus on you and the message.

The key is eye contact, which provides focus. The support skill is stance, which allows you to establish eye contact without worrying about your feet.

# Wait a Minute, I Have to Stand Still?

You might be thinking that standing still is not going to suit you. You might be thinking, too, that you've seen a lot of powerful presenters move around a lot. And you are right!

The purpose of standing still is to enable you to establish and maintain eye contact effectively. The main element of focus is eye contact, so you want to do everything you can to make sure eye contact is making you appear energetic, confident, and professional.

**Handy Hint**

If you are making a presentation that is 20 minutes or shorter and are nervous about presenting, stand still and put your energy into the eye contact and delivery of your presentation. But if your presentation is longer than about 20 minutes, you'll want to move.

A lot of people can use eye contact well when they move. These people move with a purpose, they don't wander around aimlessly. They don't make unnecessary ministeps or switch their weight from foot-to-foot. They know how to establish and maintain eye contact, and they also move purposefully, demonstrating with their motion that they are confident and energetic.

If you like to move around, go ahead, as long as you establish and maintain eye contact and don't break the rule.

Remember, there is only one rule, and that is to stop talking unless you have eye contact. There is no rule that says you have to stay in one place all the time.

If you're nervous, make sure you stand still and put all your energy into the eye contact and delivery. When you calm down and get control over what you're doing, motion will be something you can handle without communicating your nervousness or creating nervousness.

# Wait a Minute, I Can't Scan the Audience?

Many people have been taught to scan the audience. Some have learned that if they're nervous, look at the clock in the back of the room, or look at people's noses or foreheads. Unfortunately, if you scan the audience or look at the clock or look at people's noses or foreheads, they'll become aware of your focus and follow it.

Of course, you might want people to look at the clock and not you. You might find it amusing to get someone worried about what he left on the tip of his nose, or what's on his forehead. But if you want people to focus on you and what you're saying, you'll need to look each person in the eye.

Realistically, unless you are working in a culture that does not equate eye contact with trustworthiness, you're going to have to establish eye-to-eye contact, not eye-to-nose or eye-to-forehead contact.

Even worse if you have been avoiding eye contact: scanning is dangerous. If you scan the audience, you're going to get confused. As you scan, you take in lots of visual information, and your brain has to process that information. It has to figure out that you're looking at brown wallpaper and then at the ceiling that is white and made of cork and then at the floor that is covered with a grey and pink carpet and then at the other wall that has windows and grey drapes.

If you scan, you cannot focus your mind. If you scan, you are going to get so much information that your mind is going to shut down and deal with the information. And that means you're going to get lost in your presentation and have to start all over again after you refocus.

So don't scan the audience. Focus. Establish good posture and make eye contact with one person at a time. Keep the eye contact direct, steady, and sincere. Change from person to person slowly.

Establish your eye contact pattern before you begin speaking. Look at the person in a back corner first. Hold for a while; five to ten seconds. Get your peripheral vision working. Switch gently to the person in the other back corner. Hold for a while and make sure you're breathing properly. Switch to someone in a front corner and hold the eye contact. Switch slowly to someone in the other front corner. Try someone in the middle. This pacing can be maintained throughout the presentation. It makes you look confident, comfortable, and focused.

# The Least You Need to Know

➤ Focus is eye contact.

➤ Make eye contact with one person at a time, and establish a personal conversation with each one.

➤ Use centering to position yourself to maintain eye contact. It's easier to stand still and maintain eye contact than it is to move around and maintain eye contact.

➤ Don't scan the audience.

# Chapter 21

# Effective Presenters Use Energy

> **In This Chapter**
>
> ➤ Energy is crucial to holding the listeners' attention
>
> ➤ Voice is key to being heard
>
> ➤ Pacing helps the audience maintain interest
>
> ➤ Gestures support the message being delivered
>
> ➤ Facial animation shows the listeners you're interested in the topic

Think about the presentation you attended last month, the one you had to listen to because you're a user of the system being re-designed. The systems group has been working on the re-design for six months now, following intensive interviews with you and other users.

The systems design group made a two-hour presentation to all the users to review what they've done so far, what modules will be available, and how you can expect to change the way you do your job. They wanted to get some input on the documentation you'll be using because they have a history of writing user documentation that is not user-friendly.

So for two hours, you listened as best you could. You tried to figure out what the group was telling you. You tried to stay awake. The presenters had colorful overhead transparencies, and they seemed to know what they were talking about, but they spoke slowly, carefully, and quietly. Each of the presenters spent a lot of time reading the contents of each transparency to you. One of the things that really annoyed you, too, was that most of the people presenting spent most of the time changing the transparencies and staring at the screen while they talked.

If you had to describe the overall style of presentation, the word "wooden" would come to mind. Although, to give the systems group credit, the presentation probably made sense, if you had been able to pay attention long enough.

The fatal flaw of this presentation was lack of *energy*.

# Voice Power

**Definition**
  Energy is the sense of power a speaker communicates when she uses a full voice, not a loud voice. Energy exists when a presenter's gestures and expressions match the topic and suit the presenter. Energy is not loudness and extreme animation. Presenters who use their voices well tend to have energy, whether they are "stand still" presenters or "moving" presenters.

**Definition**
  A full voice is the result of deep breathing. If you breathe deeply, your voice gains resonance, and each sound you make has power behind it to carry to the listeners. Even if you don't have a great voice, you can use your voice fully.

Think about effective presenters you've listened to. Probably very few of them had wonderful voices, trained voices like actors often have. Very few of them would have spoken smoothly, without errors, with perfect words, and with no pauses.

In fact, most of the effective presenters you've listened to have been business people just like you. They've had to stop and think about which words to use. They've had to use their notes. They've used incorrect words or grammar from time to time. And many of them probably had at least one element of poor voice quality: scratchy, screechy, too high, too low and raspy, heavy accent, or poor enunciation.

What made them effective was that they used the voice they had. They spoke with a full voice so that the sound carried to you and you didn't have to work hard to hear them. They managed their accent. They paused often enough that you could think about what they were saying.

Remember, the major source of energy for a presenter is the voice. If you speak with a full voice, you create a sense of energy and commitment. And if you combine good use of your voice with appropriate gestures, you communicate energy, enthusiasm, commitment, comfort with the subject, belief in the message, and just about every other quality you're up there trying to communicate.

If you speak with a full voice, you don't have to shout! Your voice will carry because there is enough air pushing it to ensure it carries to the listeners.

You can have a voice that does the job if you're willing to work on your breathing and pacing.

## Breathe

The key to using your voice well is breathing. Most people breathe shallowly, particularly when under stress. So if you get nervous before you speak, and most of you do, your breathing becomes shallow, and your voice gets tight. Your throat dries out more quickly because you're working harder to get sound out at the right volume level.

To breathe deeply, you need to become aware of your breathing pattern. Try putting your hand lightly below your chest, not on your stomach. Try to breathe so that you are pushing out your hand. Practice breathing deeply in through your nose and out through your mouth—the breathing pattern you learned about in Chapter 15.

If you exercise, you already understand the basics of breathing. If you jog with a companion, for example, you know you can't carry on a conversation and run hard simultaneously. If you try to do both, you have to consciously breathe deeply to continue jogging and talking.

People who sing know how to use their breathing to make their voices work well. If you sing, you know you have to breathe deeply to sing clearly.

Try pushing the air out of your lower chest where the diaphragm sits. See how different it feels from pushing air out from your upper chest? You need this breathing pattern to create a complete sound when you talk.

**Definition**
The **diaphragm** is in your lower chest and acts like an air valve. It rises and falls to let air in and push air out.

To get a sense of your diaphragm and deep breathing, lie flat on the floor and push the small of your back into the floor. Keep your knees bent. Put your hands lightly on your lower rib cage. Try to breathe so that your hands move when you breathe. Breathe deeply and get a sense of what it feels like to have your hands moved by your breathing.

## Shape the Words

When you make a presentation, shape the words. You'll want to pronounce each of the sounds completely. In fact, you'll probably get a sense that your mouth is moving a lot more than when you speak quite normally without paying attention to "full" voice and clarity. This is a good sign!

As you breathe deeply, you'll have lots of air available to shape, and the sounds you make will be easier to hear. Conveniently, this quality is "volume" rather than "loudness." You don't want to scream because screaming pushes the sound out of your upper chest.

Screaming hurts, and it makes your voice sound awful. Aim for volume, which you get from breathing deeply and shaping the sound as you push the air out.

# Pronunciation and Vowels

Pronounce words carefully, but don't dramatically alter your normal speaking pattern. Make sure each of the sounds comes out, but don't slow down and ar-ti-cu-late.

## Pronounce Vowels Completely

Vowels are very important. The only way we can tell the difference between the words pen, pan, and pin, is if we hear the speaker pronounce the vowel sound in the word completely. If that speaker has an accent, hearing the vowel is even more important. We have to have the time to hear what the speaker says and interpret it, while the speaker keeps talking.

Realistically, we tend to lose a lot of the words a presenter says unless we can hear the sounds, recognize the words being said, understand the concepts being communicated, and remain current with the words as they're spoken. So if presenters will speak the words so that we can figure out exactly which one has been said, we'll listen more effectively. The figure below will help you remember to pronounce vowels clearly.

*Pronounce vowels carefully and completely.*

Pronounce vowels completely and fully. Spend time shaping the sound. Don't distort them, just make sure you say them. The comment, "I'm suggesting we invest in a major upgrade to all our desktops" all too often comes out, "I'm suggesting weev stina may jerr upgratoo are disktops." Unfortunately, what we hear doesn't help us know exactly what the speaker says.

Try saying this sentence so that the listeners receive all the sounds. Make sure each vowel gets pronounced clearly and completely. Spend a fraction of a second more on each one, and make sure your mouth "wraps around" the sound.

One of the advantages of speaking the vowels clearly is that you gain the tiny bit of time you need to also speak the consonants more clearly, without sounding as if you've just won an elocution contest. No one wants someone to over-stress clear pronunciation. Listeners do tend to appreciate it, though, when they can easily hear sounds you say and quickly identify the words they represent.

## Consonants Help, Too

Once you can use your breathing to provide the air needed to shape the vowels, you can start pronouncing the consonants carefully, too. It helps if listeners can easily tell the difference between a "d" and a "t." But remember, the vowels are the key to knowing the difference between words. The vowels use the air you're breathing, and the consonants cut off the air.

**Handy Hint**

Managing an accent is a big challenge, and most of us in business today have to manage an accent to enable others to understand. If you pronounce the vowels fully and completely, you give each listener a chance to really hear the words you're saying right as you say them.

Even if the pronunciation of a vowel isn't quite the same as a textbook might define as correct, if the listener can recognize the vowels, the listener can probably figure out which word is being said. Accent management is a lot easier than accent reduction.

# Pacing and Patterns

Your speaking patterns are probably just fine for the presentations you make. You probably sound sincere and speak clearly. There are some patterns, though, that you'll want to monitor. You'll want to use a natural pace, and you'll want to make sure that words you normally emphasize are worth emphasizing.

## Don't Slow Down

Pacing should be lively. You don't have to slow down to be clear, although you do need to make sure each vowel sound is complete and that the listeners can hear you.

So keep the pace of your presentation natural. Use the pace you would normally use if talking to someone one-to-one. Just make sure you pronounce each vowel fully, and the pace will adjust the little bit needed to accommodate the pronunciation.

## Emphasize Verbs

When you speak, remember that the verb is the most powerful element of the language. Make sure you say each verb clearly and completely. Consider saying verbs a little louder. Give them some stress. Don't stress all of them, or your speaking pattern will sound very odd. But figure out in advance which verbs are key to the message you're sending, and try to emphasize them during the presentation.

When you practice your presentation, practice saying verbs in interesting ways so that you have lots of variations to select from as you speak. For example, you can be loud, use a different tone, or say the verb a bit more slowly than you've said other words.

## Gestures

As you speak, you'll need to use some gestures. Unfortunately, most business presenters get the sense that their hands weigh a hundred pounds each when they are standing in front of an audience. But you'll need to work with those weights, and you'll need to send the right messages with your gestures.

The easiest guideline to remember is to use gestures you normally use, just make them visible, simple, and as needed, broader.

Gestures support the voice. By using gestures the speaker improves the volume, speed, and tone of her voice. So gestures aren't just a visual tactic, they affect how the voice is received. Gestures animate the body and face. They change the way the body and face behave, making for a more interesting speaker.

Gestures also shape the phrasing of content. When a speaker gestures, she naturally groups the words in naturally-sounding groupings, making the words flow more naturally.

One way to use gestures easily is when speaking a list or an ordinal sequence. When saying first, second, third…the speaker can easily gesture with one, two, and three fingers, either on one hand or grasping the fingers with the other hand, leading to natural gesturing.

## Spontaneity Wins

Don't plan the gestures you'll use. Be spontaneous!

Presenters often rehearse the gestures they want to use, particularly if they tend to use few gestures. But planned gestures are the least energetic choice you can make.

Gestures work with the voice to make you appear energetic. Gestures support what you're saying, not by making pictures but by showing your energy level. Gestures help you show how committed you are to the message you're sending.

## Consider This

One speaker who was preparing for a major presentation to a group of about 1,000 was very concerned as to whether his gestures would be appropriate. He wanted the listeners to see how enthusiastic he was about his message. He wanted them to see him as an energetic, well-prepared professional.

But he kept planning his gestures. As he practiced, he looked wooden and unnatural. Worse, he periodically used a gesture that looked obscene. He was demonstrating how a product worked, and the hand gesture was very inappropriate. The gesture was accurate for the demonstration, but demonstrated other things quite well, too.

The presenter insisted, however, on planning his gestures. He wanted to control the presentation to guarantee success—not something that you can really do.

During the presentation, as you can imagine, he used the gesture to demonstrate the product. The audience went totally silent, and he had a lot of trouble getting their attention back. He did succeed, and overall, his presentation was well received. But people remember that gesture! And when they went silent, he almost lost them.

Unfortunately, some people use a lot of gestures quite naturally, and others use very few. Realistically, everyone gestures. Everyone has some level of gesturing that is normal and appropriate to their speaking style and personality.

If you normally use a lot of gestures, simplify them, but use them. If you normally use few gestures, make sure the audience can see them, and you might want to exaggerate them a bit. But don't pre-plan them.

**Consider This**

When you are speaking to an audience, many cultures are often represented. Be sensitive to the gestures you use so that you do not use a gesture that will be misinterpreted. For example, the "peace" sign in the United States is read quite differently in the United Kingdom. To the British, the peace sign is an obscene gesture. In the United States, we circle our thumb and forefinger to say, okay, but in Brazil, that is an obscene gesture. And in the United States, we use our hands to wave some to come toward us, but some people from some African cultures might think we were calling them dogs.

You can't memorize all the gestures people use around the world, but you can use your eye contact to pay attention to reactions you get. If something you're doing seems to be bothering someone in the audience, stop doing it. While you're having a one-on-one conversation with each person in the audience, you can easily remain aware of the reactions of that individual and of others sitting nearby.

If you do identify a gesture that seems to bother someone, after the presentation, ask that person what the gesture means. Learn from the people you present to, and over time, you'll know how to modify your gesture choices to be appropriate.

## Use the Window

To keep gestures visible, you need to work within the window of vision you share with your audience. You're maintaining eye contact, and they will do the same. So the window is as wide as your face, plus about eight inches on either side. It is as high as your face, down to about your chest.

Keep your gestures within the window. If you normally gesture, but you gesture low, by your side, raise your arms so that the gesture occur within the window. The following figure shows the gesture "window."

When you're nervous, you'll have a tendency to pull your arms in and hold them close to your body. When you present, that position signals nervousness and perhaps fear. So move your arms away from your body. Try to gesture with the whole arm so that your elbows are not tightly held near your body. Even if you're nervous, you can modify how you use your arms so that you don't send the message that you're nervous.

*Use the window to keep your listeners focused on your face.*

## Simplify and Broaden

If you tend to gesture a lot, make each gesture simpler. And if you do gesture a lot, you probably make a lot of small motions with your hands. So broaden the gestures to move the whole arm and use the gestures less rapidly. And make sure your gestures are in the window.

If you need to broaden your gestures, increase the distance between your elbows and lift your arms a bit. If you need to use less broad gestures, think about keeping your arms and hands closer to your body so that you don't stretch your arms and hands out directly to your sides. Keep them within the window, and use the whole window.

## Look Alive!

Someone once called a well-known executive an in-person audiotape. Have you ever seen one of these speakers? They talk at us, and they have no facial expression at all. They talk, but the audience can't tell if they care about the content.

You need to be appropriately expressive with your face. You don't want to smile broadly when the topic is serious, and you don't want to look serious when you're trying to get the listeners excited about something.

The easiest way to use facial animation is to share eye contact sincerely with one person at a time, listen to each message you're conveying so that you think about the words and what they mean, and pronounce words completely, moving your mouth as needed to do so.

If you share eye contact with individuals who are listening to you, you will begin to be expressive because you will be having a conversation with the audience, one person at a time. No one converses without some animation. Your level of facial expressiveness might be minimal, but you do have a level of expressiveness.

The challenge is to make sure you're paying close attention to what you're saying. Focus on the one person you're talking with so that you can hear the words you're saying. Pay close attention to how that listener is responding.

## Pronounce Words Clearly and Animation Will Follow

As you speak, pronounce each word clearly and completely. And as you breathe and use your voice energetically, you'll find that your speaking pattern creates facial expressiveness.

However, you also have to pay attention to what you're actually saying! If you hear what you say and mean each word, you'll have an appropriate level of expressiveness.

If you're using a script, or if you have memorized the presentation despite all recommendations to avoid memorizing, recognize that it will be very, very difficult to have appropriate facial animation. You'll be paying such close attention to your reading or to your memory that you won't be listening to your words and paying attention to your audience.

It is very challenging to read a script or deliver a memorized speech and have facial animation. Readers and memorizers tend to have unnatural expressions, intonation, pacing, and vocal patterns. In fact, readers and memorizers are often very dull and boring, even though their words are accurate.

## The Least You Need to Know

➤ You communicate you have energy when you use your voice well.

➤ You can use your voice well only if you breathe deeply and listen to what you're saying so that you communicate that you mean what you say.

➤ If you breathe deeply, use the breath to pronounce your vowels completely, and stress your verbs, you'll create appropriate and interesting pacing for speaking.

➤ Use gestures to support what you're saying and look energetic, but don't pre-plan gestures; keep them simple, broad, and in the window.

➤ You'll have appropriate facial animation if you listen to what you're saying, and share eye contact with people one-to-one.

# Chapter 22

# Using Visual Aids and Machinery

## In This Chapter

➤ Use the machinery well so that it doesn't make you look silly

➤ Use pointing to support your message

➤ Position yourself to be able to orchestrate what's going on

➤ Don't let the machinery take over

If you're going to use focus and energy so that you appear enthusiastic, confident, well-informed, and professional, you'll have to make sure that you effectively use the visual aids you've prepared. If you can't locate the one you're looking for, or behave as if you've never seen it before, you'll look disorganized and uninformed.

If the machinery causes difficulties, or if you trip over electric cords, or if you can't find markers when you need them, you won't establish or maintain a professional image.

Machinery can help you or hurt you, so respect it. Use focus and energy so that you remain the focal point of the presentation, and use the machinery only to project the visual aids and support your message.

Consider what the listeners remembered when a presenter wrote on a flipchart during a presentation, as the flipchart continued to shrink because it had telescoping legs that were not firmly twisted into a locked position.

**Beware!**
The thing to remember with visual aids machinery is that the machinery will either fail or do something peculiar when you least expect it—so be prepared!

Or consider the difficulties the presenter faced when his major visual aid, an expensive, lengthy videotape of the new plant's production line, was destroyed by the video machine.

And then there was the presenter whose slide presentation on the computer played as a slide show rather than a presenter-driven set of visual aids. It was pretty difficult to give the presentation when the slides changed by themselves! The presenter hadn't set up the slides to be a slide show, but apparently someone had reviewed the presentation and reset it.

# Guidelines for Mastering Visual Aids Machinery

To use visual aids well, you need to make sure they are a source of support, not the presentation itself. The focus and energy come from you, not from machines and images. Although the images can help the listeners remember and understand what you're saying, those images can't sell a message or close a deal. You are the one who must sell that message!

With visual aids:

➤ Do not talk unless you have eye contact!

You've already learned in Chapter 20 why and how not to talk unless you have eye contact. It remains the one underlying rule for presenting effectively in business settings.

➤ Provide a message title.

You also know from reading Chapter 11 how to provide a message title for each visual aid.

➤ Give an overview of the visual aid without directly repeating the message title.

Don't just read the message titles to the listeners. Explain what the visual aid shows before you discuss the details presented.

➤ Do not read a visual aid to the listeners.

They can read it for themselves. If the words on the visual aids are sufficient for sending the message, you don't need to make a presentation. If you need to make the presentation, it's because you want to make sure the message is clear. It's because you have to pick special words and specific examples for the listeners, each based on how they respond to your presentation. One presenter learned the easy way how much an audience appreciates a presenter who pays more attention to the audience and the message than to the visual aids and the machinery. This presenter had an audience of about 100 sales people. She was introducing a new product, and she knew the sales people were displeased with the product's packaging.

As she presented the product, the sales strategy, the sales plan, and the incentives plan, she shared eye contact with as many of the sales people in the audience as possible. She realized as she began to describe the incentives plan that the group thought it was far too limited. She also realized that they must not have understood the plan or they would have been pleased with it. So she paused for a moment, thought of a different way to explain one of the unusual aspects of the incentive plan, and then described that aspect a second time.

The audience easily could recognize that she had made a significant pause in the flow of her presentation. They could hear her voice shift to a different tone as she thought through and described the special aspect of the incentives plan that they hadn't understood.

By the time she ended her presentation, the audience was ready to do the sales work needed to gain the incentives she had described. She had been very credible because she had helped the audience hear and understand the major points of her presentation.

She didn't worry about having a visual aid for each new point—she simply talked to the listeners. She didn't follow her plan once she realized that the audience needed more explanation, not just the planned visuals.

> **Handy Hint**
> A successful presentation is supported by the visual aids. Visual aids do not communicate messages clearly and sincerely; people do.

## Overhead Transparencies

Overhead transparency machines are common, easy to use, and potentially problematic for you. You know to check the room in advance and make sure that the machine is set up to give large, clear images with minimal keystoning. But also check to make sure there are no cords to trip on and that there are extra bulbs in case the current bulb blows out. Locate the buttons for on/off, too.

Typically, you'll have to walk to the machine to switch transparencies and then walk away to permit everyone to see the screen. The machine's projection arm almost always blocks someone's view.

## Consider This

There is probably a mandate that requires manufacturers to redesign visual aids machinery that already works well. The goal seems to be to confuse the user.

One presenter with years of experience was making a presentation at a new hotel in his city. When he arrived, he set up his presentation, and he planned to use overhead transparencies. But he couldn't find the on/off switch for the machine. He looked and looked. He felt the underside of the machine, and he checked all the places he'd found buttons before: in the middle, in an opening on the side of the machine, on the side, on the front, on the top. But he couldn't locate the button.

He called the visual aids group at the hotel and asked for their assistance, wondering what they would do to turn on the machine. The button was a tiny white button on the top-right corner of the machine. It was about a half an inch long and a quarter inch wide. It simply didn't look like a button!

Other buttons for overhead transparency machines can be enormous red buttons—ones that look like you're not supposed to touch them because they are red, for danger. Others have been placed next to the bulb switch that allows you to brighten the light. Unfortunately, you also can find it difficult to use the correct switch when you need it because you keep pressing the bulb switch instead.

## Beware!

A presenter who touched the screen found out that the screen, when touched, can ripple for a long time, making the images unfocused. Another presenter learned that some screens fall down when touched.

When you walk to the machine, walk directly and confidently toward it. Change the transparencies by holding the new transparency in one hand and grasping the old one. Place the new one over the old one, and pull the old one off the machine (out from underneath the new one). Turn around and walk directly and confidently back toward where you want to stand. Don't back off! Don't retreat!

If you need to point to something on the visual aid, place a flat-sided pencil or a pen on the transparency. Use the pen or pencil as a pointer. Avoid going to the screen and touching it. If you go near the screen, you'll be lit by the projected light and look odd. If you touch the screen, it will move and make the image hard to read.

Remember, do not talk unless you have eye contact. If you have to sort through the transparencies to find one you've decided to use sooner than planned, just don't talk while you do the sorting. If you need to read notes you've written on the frame of a transparency, don't talk while you read the notes.

## Slides

Slides are relatively easy to manage because after you've placed them in the tray and reviewed them to make sure they all project correctly, you're ready to go as long as you don't have to change the order in which they appear and as long as the machine works correctly.

You can stand in a place where you can see and easily read the slides without blocking the audience's view of them. You also can use a wireless remote control, which eliminates one cord that you won't have to trip over. But check the remote control and make sure it works properly!

As with overheads, it is best to avoid going near the screen. If you need to point, avoid the wooden pointers. Consider putting an arrow right on the slide when you create it to point out a significant point of interest.

Some people use the laser pointers that shine arrows onto the screen. Watch how your audience responds. To many audiences, any pointer, whether wooden or laser, calls to mind junior high school classrooms. That's probably not the image you want to create. If your audience is comfortable with the pointer you use, it probably doesn't matter if you use it.

## Computer Slides

If you are using slides that are computer-generated through a projection machine, make sure the computer and the projector are correctly linked and check to be sure that the slides are readable. Often, the

> **Handy Hint**
> Use cardboard frames or flip-frames with overhead transparencies. The frames make it easier to pick up one transparency, particularly when there is a lot of static electricity. The frames also provide a place for notes, making it possible to deal with one less item, the notes.

> **Handy Hint**
> When you use a remote control, with or without a wire, hold it in your hand or place it on a nearby, reachable table or lectern. Do not twist and turn it or swing it around! Nervous presenters play with whatever's in their hands, and the playing communicates the nervousness. It also can make the slides change when you don't want them to change.

> **Beware!**
> Make sure you turn off the screen saver so that it doesn't interrupt your presentation, particularly if you have a creative screen saver.

computer slide image is wavy at the edges, so if the slides have a lot of information on them, or if the images are of thin lines, the visual aids will be difficult for the audience to read.

# Flipcharts

Flipcharts are an easy tool to use as long as you check the flipchart and make sure you know how it will try to sabotage your presentation:

> ➤ Does it have telescoping legs? Make sure they are twisted firmly into place so that the flipchart doesn't telescope down as you use it.

> ➤ Does it have a brace to strengthen it? Make sure the brace is still attached and that it works. Often, the the brace is broken, and the flipchart is flimsier than you think. Flimsy flipcharts can fall down or get pushed down when you write on them or if you touch the page to point at an item.

> ➤ Does the flipchart have holders for markers? Make sure they aren't sticking out. Many presenters have been stabbed by those holders. Place the markers where you can reach them, and close the holders.

**Handy Hint**
If you have trouble spelling a word, guess. Don't talk about it unless the listeners mention it. If they mention it, ask them how to spell the word, correct the spelling on the flipchart, and keep going. Don't apologize!

**Definition**
A **lectern** is the box you stand behind so that your notes can sit on its shelf. Some lecterns are large and have controls for the lights and electronic gadgetry in the room. Other lecterns are portable, and others are on wheels, even though they are very heavy and can be difficult to move. Some lecterns are desk-top size.

A **podium** is the structure you stand on. A podium is higher than the floor for the chairs the listeners sit on.

As with the overhead transparencies, stand where you won't block the view of the flipchart.

When you write on the flipchart, write large letters, and write quickly. It is better that you pay attention to the audience than that you write pretty letters.

# Lectern

If you are going to use a lectern, recognize that you must have a lot of focus and energy. The lectern is a barrier, and you must work extra hard to get past the barrier and make a connection with your audience.

As a speaker, you might stand on a podium, but you speak from behind a lectern. If you're on a podium, make sure it is steady. Many podiums are constructed for the meeting you're participating in and then torn down, so they are not necessarily sturdy. They wobble. If you don't stand carefully and firmly, they can wobble with you, creating quite a sight.

## Consider This

One presenter had a tough lesson to learn about podiums. She was wearing high heels, and the podium she was standing on for a presentation had been constructed the night before just for her presentation. It looked sturdy, but it wasn't.

As she began her presentation, she was nervous, and she was shaking a little bit. But she concentrated on her eye contact, and she held still, she thought. She didn't understand that the little bit of motion left was creating a slight wobbling of her feet because of the high heels. And that wobbling was affecting the podium itself. It didn't waver, it just shimmied a little bit.

The motion was barely visible from the audience, but it was noticeable for the presenter who was standing on what seemed to be quicksand. She did not have an easy job concentrating on the listeners and her message.

You'll use a lectern if you have notes or a script. Do everything you can to eliminate the lectern, but if you have to use it, remember to be cautious. Know how it works if it's mechanical—just in case it's a telescoping lectern or has lots of buttons for lights and projectors. Know how sturdy it is, and make sure the listeners can see you over the top of it.

Lecterns create barriers. They bounce the sound of your voice back at you instead of letting it flow directly to the listeners. Lecterns inhibit your gesturing, so you look stiff and not like yourself.

If you are short, lecterns can make you appear less than professional. There's something silly about a speaker whose head barely rises above a huge lectern. You can ask for a box to stand on, just make sure it's a sturdy box. But recognize that even with a box to stand on, you're going to have to work extra hard to use focus and energy and to appear professional.

One corporate executive didn't have extensive speaking experience, and he didn't know how different lecterns could be from hotel site to hotel site. He was

## Handy Hint

If you're going to use a lectern and it has a lot of writing on the front of it, consider using a banner to cover the front. Of course, if the writing is your corporate logo, the company would probably prefer you left it visible. Listeners will read what's on the front of the lectern, so use focus and energy to capture their attention.

short, about 5' 2". The lectern was about 4' 8". Without a box to stand on, all you could see was the tip of his head. And because he wasn't prepared, he almost couldn't get hold of a box to stand on.

If there's a way to speak without using a lectern, try to eliminate the lectern.

Lecterns also can be flimsy and booby-trapped. Portable lecterns often fold up, so if you lean on a portable lectern when speaking, don't be surprised if it folds up on you.

## Consider This

One speaker found out how portable and flimsy some lecterns can be. The lectern in the meeting room was old. It folded for storage, and the top was stored separately. When the base was unfolded, the top fit over it loosely.

Unfortunately, as the speaker launched into the main portion of his presentation, the part that he found exciting, he pounded on the lectern's top. And the lectern came to life! The top flew up, the base folded up and fell sideways, and the speaker's notes went all over the front of the room.

It took several minutes to gather the notes, refocus on the listeners, and complete the presentation. And unfortunately, the logic of the presentation was broken, as was the mood of success and excitement.

Lecterns and other visual aids machinery can behave in unusual ways, and when they do, the presentation usually suffers.

Because lecterns are items companies buy and use for many years, a lot of lecterns are not in great shape. The ledge that should prevent your notes from sliding off might not be there.

Check the lectern you'll be using and use it wisely:

➤ Do not lean on a lectern.

➤ Rest your fingertips lightly on the lectern's ledge so that your hands are available for gesturing.

➤ Don't gesture from your sides, or you'll look like a penguin!

➤ Stand firmly so that you don't sway. The straight up and down sides of the lectern make a little swaying look like a lot of swaying.

You also can try to turn the lectern part of the way toward the audience so that you can rest the notes on the ledge. But with the lectern turned, you can stand next to it, turning to refer to the notes as often as needed. When you do this, you eliminate the barrier without losing access to your notes. Just don't turn the lectern so far that the audience can see the shelves underneath the ledge. Some audiences get distracted very easily, and the shelving is a great distraction for them.

# The Least You Need to Know

➤ When you use an overhead projector, stand so that you don't block the listener's view of the image and walk firmly to and from the machine when you need to change transparencies.

➤ When you use slides, position yourself so that you can easily see and read the slides.

➤ Write quickly with large letters if you're using a flipchart. Keep the listeners focused on the message and content, not on the art of writing.

➤ If you use a lectern, make it work for you. Don't lean on it. Gesture more than usual so that you look energetic. Use your eye contact particularly well so that you can make a visual connection with the audience. Don't let the lectern-as-barrier win.

I'M GLAD YOU ALL COULD MAKE IT TODAY...

# Presenting with Technology

In today's business world, you're going to be using a lot of technology to communicate. Some people already use the Internet to make virtually free telephone calls, and some of these people have video-telephones. They can see the person with whom they're speaking.

The technology isn't good enough yet to make it appear as if we're each talking to each other in person. But a lot of the technology is good enough that we're relying on it more and more often.

## Consider This

It's not unusual to have to deal with technology-driven presentations throughout the day. You could easily be based in New York and have a series of presentation challenges throughout any one day or week. For example, you might have an early morning or midmorning video teleconference with the European offices of your company. You'll be working on a second cup of coffee and at your highest level of energy, and the group in Europe will be struggling with their late afternoon energy lag.

Then, you could have to attend another video teleconference presentation in the early evening so that you can work with the office in the Far East. These are particularly tough because you're at the end of your day, and the people in the Far East are just waking up. You're low energy, and they're still trying to get focused for the day.

Your day is often filled with presentations, and increasingly, those presentations are shaped by technology and scheduled to accommodate many time zones and geographic locations.

The evening news is a good example of how sophisticated the technology for presentations has become. When a broadcaster is in her studio, she can speak with people, virtually face-to-face, who are at two or three different locations. Experts on the events of the day can discuss their viewpoints and argue, right in front of us from multiple locations. We get "just-in-time" debates and observations.

But you can also see the limitations on that set up. The picture is great, and the sound is outstanding. But there remains a slight time lag as the image and sound are sent over the wires. That's why you hear the overlapping of talking. That's why the interviewer often has to repeat a question.

The person in the remote location needs a few seconds to receive the broadcaster's comments, so if he doesn't know the broadcaster has spoken, he might continue speaking after only a slight pause. Then, as he continues to speak, he also hears the broadcaster's words. He has to stop to hear them, and so, often, they must be repeated.

The technology used today when presenting poses challenges for everybody. We must use the technology effectively, and you must make sure you respect the reach that technology gives you. It's useful to be able to speak to someone half a world away, but if speaking to them creates a conflict because you didn't understand them or because the technology interfered with or modified the messages you wanted to send, you haven't used technology to create effective business communication.

## Consider This

In most overseas telephone conversations today, there no longer is a noticeable time lag, and the conversations are comfortable. We don't have to wait several seconds to get a response. But the video and audio together still sometimes produce those lags. And the lags on the telephone are not completely gone, depending on how modern the equipment, cables, lines, and so on are at both ends of the conversation.

As technology continues to improve, communicating will get easier and more natural. Just as most overseas telephone calls are now easy to manage because the sound carries so quickly across the vast distances, the video teleconference technology will eventually eliminate the lagging sound. The technology will become less expensive, and more people will get used to using it, so we'll use it more often.

Despite its imperfections today, technology is already a major challenge for the business presenter. It will pose greater challenges the more commonly it is used.

This chapter gives you guidelines for using today's technology effectively. It will not tell you how to handle the many cultural and language barriers technology introduces into a presentation set up. Don't underestimate the cross-cultural challenges technology makes us deal with. Find out as much as you can about the people with whom you'll be communicating. Just as you need to work with influencers and decision-makers, you also need to find out how to work with the people at the various sites.

Remember, too, that cultural differences exist between people from different parts of the United States just as much as they exist between people of different national backgrounds, educational experiences, professional histories, and ethnic backgrounds.

## Beware!

Use technology to listen to your audience as much as you use it to send your messages. Deliver a message clearly and manage the question-and-answer process, and you'll have a high likelihood of helping your listeners know, think, or do what you're asking. If you concentrate on your written speech and read it to them, you won't listen to their needs and you won't be able to use the technology to create conversation and sharing.

# Telephone Conferences

It is common today to give a presentation at a meeting where some of the participants are participating by telephone. These presentations are difficult. So much of a presentation's power is carried by nonverbal communication that the loss of the face-to-face communication can be very damaging.

Many of these telephone conferences are being made across sites. The sites are sometimes different offices in the same city. They are often in different countries, with each country at a different point in the day. Timing is often critical to engaging an audience when their energy and receptivity to new ideas is high. But telephone conferences often put together people who are very different points of their days.

You need to pay attention to the impact of timing on your presentation. How can you schedule the telephone conference so that the majority of people and all of the key people are listening when their energy is at a high level? How can you use energy to keep all the sites listening and interested?

In most presentations, your primary tools are focus and energy. With telephone conferences, you've lost the ability to control focus because there is no eye contact except with those in the room. You can certainly establish eye contact with those in the room, though. That eye contact will help you use the energy skills. Even though the people on the other telephone conference sites won't be aware of your eye contact, if you maintain eye contact with those in the room, you will probably communicate effectively with those at the different sites.

You also can use your energy skills:

➤ Use your voice well so that it is full and easy to listen to.

➤ Speak clearly so that each word is fully pronounced.

➤ Pause enough so that people have a chance to think about what you're saying.

➤ Pronounce the vowels carefully and completely.

When you present to an audience representing multiple cultures and languages, and you don't have all of the nonverbal information you need to be able to listen to the audience's responses and reactions, it's difficult to make sure that the message you want to send actually gets sent. It's appropriate, though, to stop periodically and ask if anyone has any questions.

Just remember to give everyone at all of the sites enough time to think about what questions they have and whether they want to ask them. It takes time to prepare a question and it takes courage to ask it, especially when you can't see the presenter.

**Handy Hint**

If you will be using a telephone conference for your presentation, before the conference call make sure you list the questions the listeners might have. You can stop periodically during your presentation and ask if there are questions. If there are no questions, ask one yourself, choosing them from the list you've prepared.

People will often not ask a question when they participate in a telephone conference. Sometimes it's hard to interrupt the presenter at the other site. And sometimes it's potentially embarrassing to have to ask a question, especially when you can't see how people will react to the question. So if you as the presenter ask a few questions, you might be helping the people at the various telephone sites to get their questions answered without risking their reputations.

## Protocol

If you're giving a presentation during a telephone conference, make sure you send the visual aids to each site well in advance. The remote listeners need to see what you're reviewing with the people who are in the room with you.

You must also make sure all the participants know who is present and talking:

➤ The first time you speak, introduce yourself. Give your name, role, and relationship to the other meeting participants. If everyone knows you, you can give just your name.

➤ Every time you speak again, unless everyone knows your voice or issues, re-state your name. "This is Tom here in Dallas."

➤ As you speak, make sure you speak clearly. Pronounce those vowels completely! Use your breathing to make your voice as full as possible.

➤ If someone has to leave a telephone conference, announce their departure.

➤ Don't shout. But do make sure you are speaking loudly enough to be heard comfortably at the remote sites.

➤ If someone interrupts with a question, make sure that person identifies himself. If not, state clearly who has asked the question, then summarize the question and respond.

Every now and then as you present, stop the presentation and ask the people at the remote sites if they have any questions. You can see the people in the room with you, so you'll know whether they need you to stop. But you can't detect the hesitant listening style of a meeting participant in a remote site. You'll have to ask whether there are questions.

Be careful, too, with facilitating a telephone conference. All too often the facilitator spends so much time providing closure and getting to clarity that people at the remote sites stop listening and participating. The people at the remote sites can only hear what's going on, and if the facilitation process becomes the major element of the meeting for them, they're not going to participate anymore.

Do use a strong facilitator; just make sure that the facilitator spends time bringing in the people at the remote sites. Ask the facilitator to make sure the remote sites have equal talk time.

> **Handy Hint**
> If you are at the remote site of a telephone conference, be aggressive. Interrupt the discussions as often as you need to so that you can stay involved and interested. Don't interrupt rudely, but do interrupt when you have trouble understanding a point the presenter makes or a discussion being held among participants at other sites.
>
> Out of sight, out of mind. So speak up!

## Risks

Telephone conferences carry some basic risks. Above all, they are less personal than presentations with everyone together in the same room.

You won't have eye contact, and eye contact is a means for communicating your confidence and professionalism. You will have lost the major skill for focusing.

The next time you participate in a telephone conference, watch how people use their eyes. They often are looking at the floor or wall and not at anyone else. They're trying to focus on what they're hearing, but they can't watch the person who's speaking. Most of us want to see what we hear. Recognize that if people can't see you speak, they might not hear what you say.

# Video Conferences

Video conferences are the technology that still shows the most growing pains. Video conferences almost always have to deal with the lag between sites. The sound and image must travel, and the travel time still creates a choppiness to the meeting.

When you present at a video conference, you can use focus and energy, but focus won't be as effective. It's just very difficult to make eye contact with someone through a video camera. You can, however, simulate eye contact by focusing on the camera lens. You can pay close attention to how the people at the remote sites are reacting to what you're saying. You can relatively easily figure out that someone at a remote site has questions by watching what they are doing and looking at.

Your use of energy will be critical. You have to speak clearly and carefully. If people listening and watching have a different native language, you'll have to speak more clearly and carefully, but without losing the natural pacing and intonation.

Remember to use verbs well. If you pick them carefully and say them completely, you'll be able to keep the conference interesting.

## Protocol

At the beginning of a video conference, make sure everyone introduces himself, or provide introductions. If someone enters late, it is probably a good idea to interrupt your presentation and make sure everyone knows who the newcomer is.

Make sure the remote sites have copies of the visual aids. Check out the video conference facility well in advance. If you are using a video conference facility that allows you to project images, make sure you know how to use the machinery. Some of the technology is easy to use, and some of it is complicated and doesn't produce a great outcome.

Make sure you know where the people are who run the facility. It is highly likely that the machinery will click itself off or that a remote site will disappear. Know how to get help.

## Risks

The risks of video conferencing arise from the time lag and an innate sense of separation. Video conferences are not comfortable for everyone.

The challenge of communicating with remote sites where multiple cultures are represented is considerable. It's hard to communicate effectively with a diverse population. It's harder to communicate effectively when the diverse population is spread out and the camera and cables are the physical connections.

Yet the value of video teleconferencing is potentially immense:

➤ Video teleconferencing can permit global meetings to occur more frequently and minimize time lost to travel and the costs of the meetings.

➤ Issues can be discussed face-to-face. Although the discussion is still not completely natural, at least you can see the other participants in the discussion. You gain access to a portion of the invaluable nonverbal communication that so greatly determines whether communication is effective.

# TelePrompTers

The TelePrompTer causes a lot of presenters a lot of pain. The TelePrompTer is used when you're making a major presentation to a large group. Your presentation will be scripted, and you'll be reading.

But somehow you have to look and sound natural. And even though you don't really make eye contact with anyone, how you use the TelePrompTer makes it appear as if you're making eye contact, or it makes it appear that your head is wagging like a puppy's tale.

## Guidelines

With a TelePrompTer, make sure you have practiced reading the script aloud, preferably in the setting. Work with the script to ensure the words and phrases flow comfortably and are easy to pronounce.

**Consider This**

One presenter didn't practice her script before using a TelePrompTer in front of an audience of about 500 sales professionals from her company. She was comfortable speaking to large audiences, and she was a good speaker. But she hadn't spent a lot of time on her script, and she ran into trouble.

As she was using the TelePrompTer, the word "infirmary" kept scrolling into view. The speaker traditionally had trouble with the word, "infirmary," often distorting it to become "infirmarary." The constant mispronunciation of the word became a major element of her presentation. The audience listened for it, and they remembered the mispronunciation after the presentation.

Had she prepared for the presentation by reviewing the script and reading it aloud frequently enough to identify difficult words and phrases, she would have been able to substitute another word, such as "health-care facility." This phrase is longer, but she would have been able to pronounce it more easily.

Have the person working the TelePrompTer mark the text so that prepositional phrases appear together on the same line. Have her mark the text so that you know whether you're at the beginning or end of a paragraph. Ask her to mark the words you want to stress, too.

Know your script well enough that the flow of ideas makes sense to you, just in case the TelePrompTer stops working.

# Risks

Using a TelePrompTer can make you read a script rather than talk to the listeners one-by-one. It's particularly hard to remember to communicate a message and not just read when there's a large audience—often sitting in the dark.

But you have to communicate your message, and your audience should not be aware of your script. Listen to what you're saying. Say each word as if it has just occurred to you.

If something does occur to you, break away from the TelePrompTer. Look at a listener, and deliver that thought. Then look back at the TelePrompTer, find your place, and keep going.

As you use the TelePrompTer, minimize the artificiality by:

➤ Moving your head from one side to the other as you read the two "pages" of the TelePrompTer. Move your head slowly and at the end of a sentence or paragraph.

➤ Using gestures so that you are sufficiently animated to appear engaged in creating the content and wording.

➤ Listening to each word and saying it as if you are hearing it for the first time. Show that you know what each word means.

➤ When sharing examples, think about what each example means. Get a picture of the example in your mind and describe it carefully, as if the example is just occurring to you.

> **Handy Hint**
> A good TelePrompTer operator knows how to scroll the text to match your pace. If you decide to ad lib for a few moments, he will know to hold the place so that when you return to the TelePrompTer, you can find exactly where you left off. So practice with the TelePromp-Ter operator who will be working with you at the meeting itself.

> **Handy Hint**
> Focus and energy are important to the audience. If you can't actually see someone in the audience when you go to make eye contact, pretend. Look at a place where someone's eyes should be. Almost everyone in that vicinity will think you've made eye contact with them, and that's a valuable message to send.

# Day-to-Day Technology Challenges

You use technology almost every day when you present ideas using voice mail and e-mail. Although you will probably not give a formal presentation using the telephone or computer, you need to remember that when you send messages via technology, you are making a mini-presentation.

When using day-to-day technology to do business, use it effectively:

➤ Structure your ideas to be Message-based℠ or persuasive.

➤ Focus on what you want the listener or reader to know, think, or do, not on the facts of the situation.

➤ Be concise so that you include everything needed to permit the person you're communicating with to know, think, or do what you want—but don't include anything extra.

➤ For voice mail or e-mail, choose words carefully, paying close attention to which verbs you use.

➤ For voice mail, pronounce words carefully and completely but not artificially slow.

# Prepare for the Technology

Always make sure you prepare for the technology when you prepare your presentation. Figure out all the things that can go wrong, and then plan how you will make them go well.

Consider:

➤ Will there be people who don't speak English as well as you do?

➤ Will there be a time zone difference that could affect how attentive people are?

➤ Will you be able to get the visual aids to the other sites?

➤ What local concerns might interfere with getting the listeners to know, think, or do what you're asking or suggesting?

Decide how to manage these issues, and you'll be less likely to fall victim to the technology. The goal is to use the technology to communicate more effectively.

# The Least You Need to Know

➤ Respect the value and risks of technology—you can reach more people more easily and efficiently, and you can make a lot of errors because so many sites, cultures, languages, and time zones can be represented.

➤ Technology can create a barrier, or you can use focus and energy to get past the barrier.

➤ Technology can minimize participation from people at remote sites, or you can encourage participation.

➤ Get familiar with the technology and with how you will use it.

➤ Practice with the technology.

➤ If you'll be presenting a speech, find ways to make it come alive.

# Chapter 24

# Contingency Planning

## In This Chapter

➤ What humor can do to help or hinder your effectiveness

➤ How hecklers can ruin your presentation, or make themselves look silly while you look good

➤ How you can effectively deliver a last-minute presentation

When you give a presentation, you are still the same person when you stand up to speak to business friends as the one who was sitting down and chatting with those business friends.

And when you give a presentation, you will speak clearly and know your subject, and you will miss words, use awkward grammar, and occasionally mumble. But speaking is a very forgiving behavior. We have so much more than our words to communicate with when we speak that it is often quite simple to get the message out.

Remember, as you learned in Chapter 19, over 90% of the message you're sending is conveyed through your gestures and voice, not through your words. No one speaks perfectly. You have focus and energy to carry your message to the audience, but you need to make sure you provide the right content.

So it helps if you prepare to deal with a few basic challenges that can arise for a presenter:

➤ You need to decide how to deal with the telling of jokes and stories.

➤ You have to think about what you'll do if someone heckles you or creates an ongoing challenge during the presentation.

➤ You need to know what to do when you don't have sufficient time to prepare your presentation.

# Humor

Many business presenters think that they have to be funny to be effective. In fact, workshops on presentation skills often suggest you open a presentation with a joke. Many after-hours business groups that meet to work on presentation skills help people practice making jokes effectively. Books are available from which you can choose jokes for your presentations. The message seems to be that business presenters should use humor in their presentations.

If you are a great joke teller, opening with a joke can be a good way of relaxing the mood of the meeting and showing that you're open. But if you're not a great joke teller, or if you choose the wrong joke, opening with a joke can be the death knell of the presentation.

How do you recognize the death of a joke? The listeners stop moving, communicate their embarrassment, and stop participating. They won't look you in the eye. They move around in their seats uncomfortably. They stare at the hand-outs. They avoid you.

If you're planning to tell a joke, consider:

➤ Is the joke appropriate?

➤ Do you have the patience to wait for the listeners to hear the joke, figure out what's funny, and then laugh?

➤ Will you be able to make the rest of the presentation if they don't respond well to the joke?

If your answer to any of the above questions is "no," don't plan on using humor during your presentation.

Presenters often select a joke but don't realize that the joke is offensive to some of the listeners. One presenter told a series of jokes to a group of a thousand people. That series of jokes cleverly and almost viciously lampooned both United States political parties and all the major political figures of both United States political parties. By the time the speaker began the actual presentation, much of the group was disinterested in the topic and intensely uncomfortable. The speaker had set a tone of criticism, and that tone made it difficult to listen to the ideas he was introducing, describing, adeptly discussing, and offering for consideration.

**Handy Hint**
Always "listen" to your audience. If the listeners are squirming while you tell a joke, they are probably not liking the joke. If the listeners are very quiet, they are probably having trouble accepting the joke. You might have chosen a joke that insults someone, or a joke that touches a subject they find uncomfortable. Stop telling any joke that isn't working. Don't apologize. Stop.

Another presenter, and you've probably seen at least one of these, opened with a joke, and no one laughed. He panicked, and launched quickly into the presentation itself, talking rapidly and eventually getting himself confused. He had to stop, get reoriented to the topic and his thoughts, and then begin again. Throughout the presentation, he communicated discomfort because he had not established a relationship with the audience.

Yet another presenter introduced with a joke that insulted quite a few members of the audience. The joke wasn't intended to be harmful, but it clearly was. The presenter couldn't get the audience to respond. She presented the joke well, and she waited for the audience to "get" it, but people were uncomfortable with that joke.

# Use Humor If You're a Great Comedian

Great comedians work with timing. They understand how to time a joke, how to set up the punch line. They practice how to draw out a story, add pauses, and increase the pace to bring the listeners along with them. Some presenters are good comedians and can tell jokes well. They might not practice as much as the great comedians do, but they do understand pacing, timing, and pauses.

## Consider This

If you watched Johnny Carson, you watched a master comedian. He had a staff of outstanding comedy writers, and they produced hundreds of jokes for each one that actually got used during *The Tonight Show*. Carson rehearsed each joke until he sounded perfectly "off the cuff." He knew how to time the joke, how to wait for the audience's response, and when to do damage control.

One of Carson's greatest skills was damage control. He knew how to move a joke that fell flat into something funny, just by commenting on that flatness of the joke.

If you have Carson's skills at telling jokes, by all means include joke telling as part of your presentation. But if you don't know how to time the joke or recover from a flat joke, consider carefully whether the risk of the joke is worth it.

After all, aren't you there to deliver a message?

If you know how to use pacing, timing, and pauses, you can probably tell a joke, as long as the joke you're telling is appropriate to the audience and doesn't hurt anyone.

# Use Humor Carefully or Risk Offending

If you choose to tell a joke, make sure it doesn't insult any group, unless you fully intend to insult that group. Make sure your wording doesn't belittle someone.

**Handy Hint**
If you plan to tell a joke, make sure you ask several different types of people whether it's funny. Practice a few times so that you know how to deliver each piece clearly and effectively. If anyone you ask suggests the joke might be offensive, don't use it.

One guideline for joke telling and behavior in general is to consider whether you would tell that joke in other situations. Ask yourself the following questions:

➤ Would you tell the joke or anecdote to your mother?

➤ Would you tell the joke or anecdote to your grandmother?

➤ Would you tell the joke or anecdote to a religious leader?

➤ Would you tell the joke or anecdote if it were to be broadcast to the country?

➤ Would you tell the joke or anecdote to everyone in the company cafeteria at lunch time?

Use the following worksheet to think about how humor might or might not fit into your presentation. Ask a lot of questions before you decide whether to use humor in your presentation.

---

## Think Soberly About Humor

1. Why will you use humor?

    _____

    _____

2. What type of people appear in the joke? Do you mention nationalities? Men? Women? All "these people"? Does the humor laugh at someone or a group of people or type of person?

    _____

    _____

3. Does the humor depend on funny pronunciations or misunderstandings?

    _____

    _____

---

4. Who might think the humor is inappropriate?

_____

_____

5. If you plan to use yourself as the target of the humor, will the joke make you appear weak or ineffective?

_____

_____

Humor rarely has a universal definition. What some people find very funny is embarrassing or stupid to others. What many people of one country think is uproariously funny, is stupid or insulting to many of the people of another country. And what was funny 10 years ago is often no longer funny today. The context and sensitivities change.

Think about all the plays that have traveled around the world successfully and all the plays that were considered funny in the country where they began but which failed miserably when they traveled. Most of the plays that tour successfully tap into themes such as patriotism, heroism, and love. Many of the plays that fail are comedies. For example, British comedies are sometimes considered coarse by U.S. audiences. Some eastern European comedies simply don't make sense when translated.

**Beware!**
If you have any doubt as to the acceptability of a joke to a broader or different or more public audience, don't tell the joke!

What was funny in the 1960s and 1970s is often not relevant or understood in the 1990s. For example, comedians whose jokes 20 years ago were about drug use often seem offensive to a society today that is worried about drug abuse. Comedians who used to tell jokes about "My wife…" sound boorish today.

Do you want to risk telling a joke that might be funny to you because of who you are, what your background is, and what you've thought funny in the past? Can you risk sounding offensive, boorish, or out of touch with today's sensitivities? Do you really know what today's sensitivities are? Can anyone keep up with today's many sensitive issues?

Many people who announce speakers at business conferences try to be gracious and humorous when introducing the next speaker, and they often end up insulting someone with a gender comment or other currently inappropriate "joke."

You might not like political correctness, and many people are undoubtedly overly sensitive to political correctness, but is it worth sacrificing the message you need to deliver to fight it?

**Definition**

A **heckler** is someone in the audience who interrupts, harasses, and annoys you. A heckler usually has a specific point he wants to make, and he makes that point in ways that interrupt the flow of your presentation, prevent other listeners from asking questions, and intimidate you.

# Hecklers

A common problem for many presenters is hecklers. If you are speaking on a potentially controversial subject, or if in your preparation you realize some people aren't going to like what you're saying, you'll need to prepare for managing hecklers.

Use the following figure to identify potential hecklers. Try to be prepared for hecklers by knowing who might heckle you and on what subject.

## Who Might Heckle You? Pre-Think the Source of Potential Trouble!

1. List the people who will attend your presentation:

   _____

   _____

2. Which of these people, if any, has a tendency to heckle the speaker at a presentation?

   _____

   _____

3. Which of these people, if any, might be adversely affected by your ideas and recommendations?

   _____

   _____

4. Which of these people, if any, is facing a lot of job stress at the moment?

   _____

   _____

# Treat Each Heckler As If He Is Sincere

Above all, treat each heckler openly and honestly. If someone interrupts you:

➤ Look her straight in the eye.

➤ Listen to what she has to say.

➤ Pause for several seconds and think about what she's challenging.

➤ Communicate your calmness and act comfortable with the challenge she's making.

➤ Respond with a sincere answer.

Hecklers want to get you off your timing. They want to confuse you. They want to prove they know more than you do or that their issue is more important than your presentation. They often cannot hear logic.

The other listeners want to know how you will handle the heckler. They'll want to see how credible you are and how well you know your subject and believe in it. So always treat the heckler as if the complaint is honest! Use focus and energy to communicate your comfort with the situation and subject.

One of the hardest things for any presenter is to deal effectively with hecklers. Unfortunately, many hecklers are emotional about their concerns. They are either angry and they intend to show you their anger or they are illogical because they're so caught up in their issue that they can't listen to you.

Your job is to respond calmly and sincerely. Your job is to think about what they're challenging you on and figure out what business issue might sit underneath the unpleasant things they're saying or shouting. You need to find some tiny element of valid business concern and respond to it.

For example, if a heckler challenged your presentation about the marketing strategy by demanding to know why a product is being introduced, you can comment on the product's target market and show how the strategy supports the product. You can discuss how the strategy will help the target audience recognize the value of the product.

You don't have to defend the existence of the product unless you think that it needs to be defended. But don't defend it at all unless defending it serves a business purpose.

# Use Eye Contact Carefully

When you have to respond to a heckler, make sure you respond to the concern he raises with direct, sincere, straightforward eye contact. However, after he knows you are responding to him and treating him as if his question is a legitimate one, gently turn your eye contact to others in the audience. Slowly move your eyes away, establishing eye contact with people as you do so, until you are not visually anywhere near the heckler.

**267**

If you do this gently and carefully, not by pulling away visually but by gently "floating" away, you will not be looking at him when you finish responding, and you will therefore not be giving him visual permission to continue heckling you.

Some hecklers will continue to heckle you because they really want to heckle you. If this happens, keep using the same technique. It is highly likely that the audience itself will deal with the heckler. Your patience under fire will add up to an audience—minus one—who thinks you are credible.

You can also defer further discussion, saying something like "We're covering the same ground again, so why don't you and I meet privately after my speech?" or "I'd be happy to continue this with you afterward, but I'd like to continue." You can also poll the audience: "I think we've covered this [to the audience]. Should I resume or would you like us to continue on this topic?"

Your job with a heckler is to:

**Beware!**
Don't challenge a heckler! Audiences will protect someone who is "one of them." Let the audience deal with the heckler. Your job is to communicate the message of your presentation. Act patient.

➤ Establish eye contact so that the heckler knows she is "seen."

➤ Respond to the business concern underlying the challenge.

➤ Move your eyes gently away from the heckler so that you don't give her visual permission to start a second heckling process.

Some hecklers will shout you down and the eye contact shift won't work, but use it consistently!

Remember, if you're using eye contact effectively to provide focus, you're already sharing eye contact with people throughout the audience. You've already established a pattern of focus and you're using energy to keep the listeners engaged in the message and supporting ideas. Your management of the heckler will follow the same pattern.

# What If I Don't Have Time to Prepare?

There are many reasons you might not be adequately prepared. Perhaps you didn't know you were going to make a presentation until the last minute. Or perhaps the person who was going to make the presentation is out ill, and you've received the request to replace her. Or perhaps you did everything you could to prepare, but short of creating some notes and visual aids, you've had no time to practice.

There is only one true rule for a presenter, "Do not talk unless you have eye contact." This rule will help you through any situation in which you haven't adequately prepared.

If you are not fully prepared

> ➤ Make sure that at minimum you know the major message and major submessages.

> ➤ Make sure you have a minimal number of visual aids to help the listeners through the content so that they can see things they need to remember or understand.

> ➤ Do not talk unless you have eye contact.

**Handy Hint**

Always remember that you can "act" confident even if you're not. If you act confidently, the listeners will assume you are presenting information you are comfortable with. You also will begin to feel comfortable as you make the presentation. If you act the way you want to feel, you will probably begin to feel the way you want to feel.

Essentially, if you're not prepared, you have to make sure that you are using focus and energy to show the listeners that you are confident making the presentation.

You don't have to be confident, but you *do* have to appear that you are confident!

## The Least You Need to Know

> ➤ Don't use humor unless you can use it well. A bad joke or a joke that sends an unintended message can ruin a well-structured, Message-based℠ presentation.

> ➤ Treat hecklers as if their concerns are sincere. Don't maintain eye contact. In fact, don't give eye contact to anyone in their vicinity once you know where the hecklers are.

> ➤ Use focus and energy to deliver an outstanding presentation, even if you don't have adequate time to prepare. Do not talk unless you have eye contact.

# Part 6
# What Happens After I Present?

*You did it. You made your presentation, and all you need to do now is hear how great an idea it was, right? Well, sometimes that's how it will work, especially if you've done your pre-work effectively.*

*But realistically, there's usually a fair amount of post-work you'll have to do. You'll have to figure out whether you were effective and how to be even more effective the next time. You'll want to follow through with the commitments you've made to people—what information do they still need? What action steps need to be completed?*

*And you'll want to talk to people who aren't quite ready to buy in, but who might be ready if you give them another opportunity.*

# Chapter 25

# Effective Presenters Welcome Questions

## In This Chapter

➤ Understanding how valuable Q&A can be

➤ Preparing to manage the Q&A session

➤ Knowing what to do with a difficult or hostile questioner

Many times presenters are upset that the listeners ask a lot of questions. But the best response to any presentation is a lot of questions. The worst response to a presentation is the silence of the listeners.

Think about a presentation you attended when everyone in the audience stayed past the time set for the end of the meeting and asked questions about the presentation, reviewing details, contributing ideas, asking for more information about the plans and action steps. This was a great presentation!

Then think about the presentation you attended when no one in the audience asked a question. You sat in the audience, and you could feel everyone trying to get out of the meeting quickly. You could see everyone avoiding the speaker's eyes. You could tell that the presentation had fallen flat.

True, sometimes you will be so clear, so effective, and so in tune with what the listeners want to hear that they won't have any questions. You'll have made your message clear, and the listeners will be satisfied.

More often than not, though, you'll make your presentation and your message will be clear, but it also will be of interest to the listeners. They'll want to explore the implications of what you're saying. They'll want examples of how what you're saying will affect them. Or they'll want to know how everything is going to fit together or work.

# Why Do People Ask Questions?

People ask questions for a lot of reasons. The good reasons are that they want to know more about your message. The frustrating reasons are that they didn't understand what you said, or maybe they want to make sure you know that they know a lot about the subject.

There are three situations that occur during the Q&A: no questions, bad questions, or good questions. Use the questions asked to gauge how well you presented the material. If you get no questions, consider whether you made sense. Maybe the listeners don't know what to ask because they're not sure what you said. Or if you get no questions, maybe you were so clear that they can move immediately to make the decision you've asked for.

If you get bad questions, review your presentation to figure out how to improve it next time. Bad questions focus on repetition of what you've said, not to probe but to repeat. If you get good questions, welcome them. And don't worry about not having all the answers. You also can get the answers to people later on.

**Handy Hint**
Questions are one of your best guides to knowing whether you've made a presentation effectively. If the listeners ask questions that force you to repeat details, you probably did not make a clear, well-understood presentation. If the listeners ask you questions that probe, challenge the information, and ask you to help them explore the implications of the message you've delivered, you've made an effective presentation!

If you receive a lot of questions asking for repeated information, use it as a suggestion to be more clear the next time you make a presentation. You might not have structured the presentation to meet the audience's needs, so reconsider how you're setting up your presentation:

➤ Is the message itself clear?

➤ Are the submessages directly related to the main message?

➤ Have you included the details needed to clarify the message and submessages?

➤ Have you provided sufficient visual support to enable the listeners to understand and remember your messages and follow the logic of the messages?

If you get a lot of questions from people who seem to want to make their knowledge or presence known, you have to be patient. Just as you would with a heckler, treat each questioner respectfully, acknowledge each set of comments and questions, and avoid the questioner's eyes except in your initial response to their comments and questions.

Seek good questions. And if you get good questions, welcome them.

## Challenges

A lot of questions will challenge you. People will want to know more about your information, and they will want to make sure your thinking is complete and clear. They'll disagree with you. They'll ask for more information. They'll challenge your thinking and want to know how you got to a conclusion. These are great questions!

### Handy Hint

"Listen" to your audience. You'll be able to "hear" how they're thinking. If you hear silence, you probably didn't win their full attention or establish your credibility. If they are responsive and actively thinking and challenging your thinking, you've engaged them. You can "hear" an audience as it thinks because you can feel the energy they are using. A nonresponsive audience feels absent.

If you have trouble "hearing" your audience, watch their eyes. If their eyes are on you, you're probably doing well. If their eyes are elsewhere all the time, you are not engaging them effectively.

What if someone says, "How can you be so certain the sales cycle will turn with these events?" Recognize that this question is an opportunity to show how you analyzed those events and their effect on the sales cycle.

What if someone says, "If what you're saying is true, what will we do when the next competitor launches their attack?" Here is an opportunity to review your competitor analysis. You have a chance to show how thorough you've been in analyzing the information that contributed to the message you're sending. You get to show that you truly understand all the context, even if you didn't use it during the main presentation.

## Welcome Probing Questions

Some questions will probe your ideas and facts. Probing questions also are a great opportunity to show how much you know and how thoroughly you understand your subject.

So be pleased when a listener asks, "You used a chart early in your presentation that showed us the key barriers to international expansion. Could you review that chart with us and explain how you identified some of those barriers and review the analysis that led you to this issue?" You now get to review the thinking behind your ideas, and the listeners will quickly recognize how much preparation you've done and how well you know your job.

They'll also learn a lot more about your perspective.

## Understand Implications

If the audience starts to challenge the message you've sent and asks what it will mean to them, you've engaged them. They want to know how your message will change their lives and how your message affects the workplace, the market, the product line, and the company.

Remember, someone might say, "Help me understand our alternatives if this scenario plays itself out as you've described." Accept this opportunity. Welcome it. And respond with your analysis of the future. Consider this a great opportunity to show how far your thinking extends.

> **Handy Hint**
> Prepare Message-based℠ or persuasive explanations for questions you anticipate receiving. You want to have logical, focused explanations of the key messages, facts, and principles underlying your presentation.

# How Do I Respond?

Respond to questions as briefly as possible. Respond to the question asked and don't wander too far away from your central message. And try to foster dialogue. It's a lot easier to have a dialogue with listeners than it is to play the "answer man."

When you manage questions and answers, you have to follow certain steps:

> **Handy Hint**
> Pause. Remember that pausing gives everybody a chance to think. Presenters who pause appear confident because they are not intimidated into speaking quickly to fill the silence. Speakers who don't pause sound afraid of the audience. Even if you're afraid, pause, and then you won't communicate your fear.

➤ Listen to the person asking the question by sharing eye contact and listening to exactly what the person is saying.

➤ Do not try to respond immediately—pause!

➤ If you're going to repeat the question or paraphrase it, do so after you pause.

➤ If you're going to answer the question, respond.

➤ If you're going to defer the response, explain why.

# To Repeat or Not to Repeat

One challenge you'll face in any presentation is deciding whether to repeat the question you've been asked.

The best way to decide how to deal with the actual question is to consider the size of the audience, the loudness of the questioner, and the clarity of the question.

If you've listened carefully to the questioner and shared eye contact all the time, you'll have told the questioner that you value the question. You'll also be able to figure out whether the question is:

> ➤ Clear and everyone has heard it

> ➤ Clear and few have heard it

> ➤ Unclear and everyone has heard it

> ➤ Unclear and few have heard it

If the audience is small, the room small or medium-sized, the questioner is reasonably loud, and the question asked seems pretty clear, you should not repeat the question. Make sure you pay close attention to the other listeners—after you've listened carefully to the question and while you are pausing briefly after the questioner has stopped talking. If the other listeners look confused, they didn't hear the question or they didn't understand it. If the listeners look comfortable and there have been no significant changes in their behaviors as listeners, they probably heard and understood the question.

**Handy Hint**
If the question is hostile, reframe the question as you clarify it so that the question appears positive. "So this is cost-cutting to the bare bones?" is a hostile question. You can soften the hostility by saying, "You seem to be looking at cost cutting as a nonstrategic activity. Is your concern whether the program is strategically intended and designed?" Respond to the positive question.

If you have heard and understood the question, but it is unlikely the whole audience heard and understood it, you'll want to repeat the question or paraphrase it. Generally, if the audience is large, if the room is medium-sized or large, or if the questioner is in the front of the room and speaking somewhat softly, you'll want to repeat or paraphrase the question.

If the questioner is reasonably loud but the question requires clarification, you'll want to repeat the question by clarifying it. You'll want to share eye contact with the questioner and confirm what she has asked. "Let me see if I understand your question. Are you trying to get a deeper understanding of the MRP software?" "You seem to be trying to examine the underlying logic of the inventory valuation method."

You'll need to clarify the question and make sure everyone hears what you clarify regardless of the size of the audience or the size of the room. Otherwise, they won't know why you're answering the question the way you do. As you clarify the question, you'll be "repeating" the question for the rest of the audience.

Sometimes, you will know that much of the audience didn't hear the question, and even if they did, they wouldn't have understood it because you didn't understand it. In this situation, you'll want to clarify the question with the questioner. It won't matter how big the room or audience is. This situation demands clarification before you respond.

## Focus Response and Tie to Themes

After you know what the question is, and after you've paused a bit, respond directly to the question. Answer the question, and avoid repeating your presentation.

> **Handy Hint**
> Remember, pauses help the listeners think and give you a chance to decide how to respond effectively. Pauses make you appear confident. Be brave! Pause!

Tie your response to your message and try to reemphasize your major themes.

If someone challenges your analysis, clarify the point they've challenged by adding the information or explanation needed, and refer to the main message, "So you can see that it's important for us to decide on when to begin implementation of this process."

Answer only the question. The tendency is to answer a question by reviewing all the main points you presented originally. Don't!

## Use Eye Contact to Share Information

As you respond to a question, make sure you maintain eye contact. The focus you've established during your presentation is essential to making the Q&A professional and effective. You don't want to make a great presentation and then act as if you don't want the listeners to be in the room!

There is a considerable tendency by many presenters to make a polished presentation with focus and energy but to then back away from the listeners as the Q&A begins. These presenters stop sharing eye contact and stop using energy. They lose a lot of credibility.

Then again, there are presenters who are polished and professional when presenting, but perhaps a bit too polished, verging on the stiff. But when the Q&A begins, they come to life! They love the dialogue! They become animated and enthusiastic.

Try to establish and maintain appropriate levels of animation and enthusiasm throughout the presentation and the Q&A session by using focus and energy consistently.

# Have Extra Facts and Handouts Prepared

When you prepare your presentation, you'll be listing all the possible challenges and questions you can imagine anyone might ever ask. If responding to those questions or challenges requires additional visual aids or handouts, make sure you bring them with you.

Don't use extra information just because you have it, but do come prepared with extra information just because you might need it.

# What Do I Do with Difficult Questioners?

You might have some difficult questioners. Some people ask tough questions, and some people who ask questions are mean about the questions and challenges.

Just as you would manage a heckler by respecting the challenge, respect the difficult questioner.

If someone in the audience is being difficult, whether through repeated tough questioning or through hostile questioning, follow these guidelines:

➤ Look him straight in the eye.

➤ Listen to what he has to say.

➤ Pause for several seconds and think about what he's challenging.

➤ Respond with a sincere answer.

## Clarify and Share Eye Contact

Often, a difficult questioner just wants to be heard. A difficult questioner sometimes has a need to have everyone in the audience know he knows something.

Spend time clarifying the question and reaching agreement on exactly what the questioner is asking. You can often help the questioner look good and minimize the difficulties that could arise from future questions from that person.

For example, sometimes a listener is not well-informed on a topic, but he feels a need to comment on your presentation. This situation is typical of someone new to your team or new to the company who wants to make it known that he is well-informed and valuable. When someone asks a question or poses you a challenge, and you can tell they really don't know what they're asking, reframe the question to make them look good. Modify the question so that it asks a question worth asking and then answer it.

When you make a questioner look good, he will often become a supporter of your ideas.

## Clarify and Minimize Eye Contact

Always use eye contact throughout unless the person has been questioning you repeatedly, in which case, let your eyes gently wander to a separate section of the audience by the time you finish answering the question.

**Handy Hint**

If someone in the audience has special knowledge or experience, ask for her comments on an issue or idea. Demonstrate to the listeners that you welcome their input. In the process, you'll be taking some of the pressure off you. However, if you don't know someone's opinion or attitude toward your presentation, don't ask unless you are fully prepared for whatever comment you get.

## Clarify and Ask for Assistance from Listeners

Remember, too, that in most presentations, you have an entire audience with which to work. These people have been sitting there and listening, and they probably can contribute. Encourage a dialogue. Encourage someone who has special information to respond to a question. Get the whole group involved! Refer to Chapter 24 for ideas on handling hecklers. You can use those skills with any difficult Q&A session.

The more you put the burden on the audience to participate, the more you will engage them. You can clarify questions and information by asking the audience to help you clarify them. You can ask them for information. The more you directly engage the listeners, the more likely you'll win your point. The more the audience thinks about the information and contributes to it, the more likely they'll "know, think, or do" the message you've delivered.

# What Do I Do with Questions I Can't Answer?

Sometimes, you won't know the answer to a question. Other times, you might know the answer to the question but it won't be the right thing to share with the listeners.

## Clarify

If you can't answer a question, make sure you confirm or clarify the question. Spend the time necessary to repeat the question in a way that shows the questioner that you've understood the question. Or spend the time necessary to work with the questioner on exactly what the question is. "You're asking about the budgets for the final quarter."

When you confirm the question, share eye contact with the questioner to make sure the questioner "hears" that you've heard him.

**Handy Hint**

When you can't answer a question, make sure you don't try to start talking to clarify the question just as the questioner completes her question. Give the questioner plenty of time to finish the question. Pause. Then clarify the question.

When you pause between the question and your clarification of the question, you make the listeners aware that you respect the importance of the question. You acknowledge the question and the questioner. You also give yourself a few moments to think about how to deal with the question—whether to clarify and then answer it or whether to clarify and then defer your response.

## Respond and Commit to a Response

Respond gracefully with a brief reason why you can't respond, "I do not have the final quarter budget information yet. We expect to make that available in the next few weeks." Commit to providing a response, "I will send you the information within the next two weeks. You can expect to receive a fax."

Don't forget to follow through!

If you make a commitment to follow through on a request from a listener, make sure you follow through. Even if your only response is that you're still searching for the information requested, make sure you let the listener know you are being responsive. You can lose a lot of support by appearing not to care about what the listeners care about.

## The Least You Need to Know

➤ Welcome questions as signs of your effectiveness.

➤ Evaluate the questions to figure out whether you've structured your presentation well and whether you've been clear and complete.

➤ Make sure the listeners hear and understand questions that are asked, but don't repeat questions that were easy to hear and understand.

➤ Use focus and energy throughout the Q&A process. Avoid changing your style. If you back off and lose focus and energy, you lose credibility. If you get animated and enthusiastic only during the Q&A, you send the message that the presentation itself wasn't of great interest to you. You also suggest to the listeners that you were nervous during the presentation and perhaps lacked confidence.

# Chapter 26

# Effective Presenters Follow Through

> **In This Chapter**
>
> ➤ What do you do after the presentation?
>
> ➤ What is expected of you?

After you make your presentation, you still have a lot of work to do. You will have promised some people more information, and you'll want to speak with people who had concerns. You'll want to contact the listeners who seemed almost ready to buy into your idea.

Remember, you made a presentation to deliver a message. You want the listeners to know, think, or do something. If you have listeners who need more information before they know, think, or do what you want, you need to follow through.

## Consider This

When the audit manager made a presentation to the Audit Committee of the Board of Directors, she recommended a series of follow-up steps be implemented to ensure that the work done by the audit group remained strategic and "value-added." Several of the members of the Audit Committee thought her ideas were excellent, and one of the committee members thought her ideas interesting but perhaps not high priority.

When she finished the presentation, she arranged to call each of the committee members within the three days following her presentation. She called the "almost buyer" first to find out what his concerns were. She used the concerns he described to prepare a mini-follow up presentation for the other committee members.

As she made her follow up telephone calls, she gave a two minute review of her presentation, adding in the answers to the concerns she had explored with the one "almost buyer."

Her last call was to the "almost buyer," and since she had discussed each concern with him, he had become a buyer. Each of the other "believers" was fully supportive anyway, and her telephone follow-up discussions maintained their support.

She was able to implement her recommendations with the full support and sponsorship of each member of the Audit Committee of the Board of Directors.

## Beware!

If you can't get the information to respond quickly to someone's questions, at minimum, let them know the status of the information gathering. Don't let the person with a question keep waiting. You'll lose your credibility, and maybe the support of the person who's waiting for the information.

# Get That Information Out

Respond within 24 hours with the information or materials promised or with an update on your progress and commitment for delivery of the information or material.

If you promised someone an answer to a question and can't get the information quickly, make sure you leave them a message that acknowledges their question and tells them what to expect. For example, you might say, "I know you want to know about the costs estimated for the new ingredients, and I'm waiting for clarification of the preliminary cost figures I've been given. You can expect an answer within the next three days."

## Document Action Plans

If the presentation created action plans for you or anyone else, you need to document those plans and issue them. Again, get those action plans out to the people who participated in the presentation within 24 hours. Action plans should list action steps and the person responsible for each one.

Often, your presentation will convince a lot of people to act on your message. But if you don't confirm the commitments that people make to the message, they will often forget and the commitments give way to the demands of other projects and priorities.

---

**Action Plans for Meeting 3/15/97**

| | |
|---|---|
| Complete plan | Joe Jamison |
| Ship brochures | Jody Jepson |
| Complete analysis | Jimmy Jackson |
| Complete variance report | Judy Jumpers |

---

# Call as Needed

Don't assume that everyone at the presentation will remember your key messages and facts. If you need action, and you didn't get that action by the end of the presentation, follow through. Call the listeners.

## Call the Supporters

Call each person who seemed to support your idea. Call them, get their comments on the idea, and try to get firm commitment.

If any of the believers raise any issues or discuss new aspects of your presentation with you, use their comments with the "almost buyers."

## Call the "Almost Buyers"

> **Handy Hint**
> If you gather new information and comments that can help influence the almost buyers and the non-believers, put together a brief memo, e-mail, or voice mail. Use the Message-based℠ structure or the persuasive structure, and reintroduce your main message supported by the new information or comments. If you can name the believers who helped provide the new information or comments, you gain their influence, too.

For those who seemed almost ready to commit to the ideas you presented, call and discuss their concerns. Listen thoroughly to what they say and clarify what is holding them back from making a commitment. Provide the information they need. If a believer has shared an idea or perspective that is useful in a discussion with the "almost buyer" then:

➤ Introduce the idea or perspective.

➤ Explain which of the believers suggested the idea or perspective.

➤ Use the new information from the believer to influence the almost buyer.

People often can't commit to something when they first hear it. It can take several discussions before they understand it and begin to own it. You need to give the "almost buyers" plenty of opportunity to examine the ideas and talk through what they like about the ideas.

# Contact the Listeners Five Times

If you are presenting a message that might be difficult for people to buy into easily, try to deliver the message five different times:

➤ The first time is when you contact people before the presentation to get their comments and insights.

➤ The second time is when you ask for people's comments on the clarity of the presentation.

➤ The third contact is the presentation itself.

➤ The fourth contact is a follow up phone call.

➤ The fifth contact might be a memo, e-mail, or voice-mail message that updates and clarifies relevant issues or concerns.

# Create Next Steps

If your presentation is going to lead to another presentation, make sure you set up the next event. Announce the follow up presentation or meeting quickly so that everyone understands that the two are linked.

# The Least You Need to Know

➤ Follow through with all commitments. Aim for following up within 24 hours.

➤ At minimum, let people know if there will be a delay in getting information to them versus what you promised. Don't disappear and lose the ground you've gained.

➤ Create an opportunity to recontact everyone who participated in the presentation, starting with the believers and almost buyers.

➤ Use the five-time guidelines. If you are trying to get someone's attention for an idea, try to raise the issue five different times. Generally, it's not until the fourth or fifth contact with a new idea that people can really hear it and consider it fairly.

# Chapter 27

THAT'S WHERE YOU LOST THEM. WHEN YOU CALLED THEM "MINDLESS DRONES".

# Reviewing the Presentation to Improve the Next One

## In This Chapter

➤ Rethink what you did. What could you have done differently?

➤ Examine the presentation. Was the structure right? Were the visual aids useful?

➤ Think about the delivery. Did you use focus and energy effectively?

➤ How did the Q&A go?

After you make a presentation, review what you've done to learn what works well and what doesn't. Use the experience to improve future presentations!

## Logistics

Think about the room set up and whether it worked for you. The purpose of making sure the logistics are right is to make sure the presentation is smooth. You don't want to spend lots of time getting set up and moving the machinery to the correct position. You don't want to lose time trying to get organized and comfortable in the room.

Think first about what you did well.

---

**What were the two or three things you did very well with the logistics?**

1. _____

   _____

2. _____

   _____

3. _____

   _____

---

Then think about what you could have done differently that would have made your presentation stronger, clearer, more persuasive, more interesting, or just easier to deliver.

What will you do differently?

**Checklist for Logistics**

❏ Was the room set up right so that you could easily share eye contact with the audience members and they could see and hear you?

❏ Were the tables set effectively so that the listeners were comfortable and could be responsive to you?

❏ Did the machinery work correctly?

❏ Did you work with the machinery in that specific room before the presentation to make sure that you knew how to use it and what could go wrong?

❏ Did you have a list of needed phone numbers in case something stopped working?

❏ Were the handouts effective?

❏ Were there enough handouts?

❏ Was there enough information on the handouts?

❏ Did people take the handouts with them or leave them behind? If they left them behind, they weren't considered valuable.

# Structure

How you organized your presentation will have made an enormous difference in your success or failure. So, think about what you did well with organization.

---

**What were the two or three things you did very well with the structure of your presentation?**

　　1. _____

　　　 _____

　　2. _____

　　　 _____

　　3. _____

　　　 _____

---

Then, review how well the visual aids worked. How did they help?

---

**What were the two or three things you did very well with the design and preparation of the visual aids?**

　　1. _____

　　　 _____

　　2. _____

　　　 _____

　　3. _____

　　　 _____

---

Finally, think through the entire presentation and how it felt as you talked. If you can, ask for some comments from people who heard the presentation. Just make sure you ask for their comments privately so that they will be candid.

What will you do differently?

**Checklist for Presentation Structure**

❏ Did the Q&A process show you any gaps in the information you presented?

❏ Did the listeners know, think, or do what you wanted them to?

❏ Was the presentation easy to deliver, or did you find yourself having to create awkward transitions from one idea to the next?

❏ Did the visual aids help the presentation or cause confusion?

❏ Were the message titles on the visual aids the right ones, based on the questions and comments during or after the presentation?

# Delivery

Think about what you did well as a presenter. How enthusiastic did you feel? How focused were you? Did you use your nervous energy?

**What were the two or three things you did very well with the delivery of your presentation? What did you do best to establish focus and communicate your energy?**

1. _____

_____

2. _____

_____

3. _____

_____

Then think through in as much detail as you can what you can work on for the next presentation.

**Checklist for Delivery—Focus and Energy**

❏ Were you centered?

❏ Was your movement from position to position done for a reason or because you were nervous?

❏ Did you maintain eye contact with one person at a time?

❏ Did you use your contact to "hear" how the listener was responding so that you could adjust your pacing, volume, style, or examples?

❏ Did you find yourself choosing words carefully for that one listener as you shared eye contact?

❏ Did you use gestures that were "in the window" so that you emphasized ideas?

❏ Did you use spontaneous gestures?

❏ Did you use your breathing to manage your nervousness?

❏ Did you breathe deeply?

❏ Was your voice clear?

❏ Was the pace of your speaking interesting and lively?

❏ Did you speak loudly enough to be heard in the back row?

❏ Were you hearing the words you said so that you'd sound interesting and enthusiastic about the topic?

❏ Did you pronounce words, especially vowels, carefully and completely so that your pace and clarity were maintained?

What will you do differently?

# Q&A

Think also about what you did well with the Q&A session. Were the questions the ones you wanted to deal with or were they requests for repeat information?

> **What were the two or three things you did very well to manage the Q&A session?**
>
> 1. _____
>    _____
> 2. _____
>    _____
> 3. _____
>    _____

Consider also what you learned about the presentation or the subject matter.

> **What two or three things did you learn from the questions you were asked?**
>
> 1. _____
>    _____
> 2. _____
>    _____
> 3. _____
>    _____

What kinds of things do you need to do differently at your next presentation?

**Checklist for Q&A**

❑ Did you clarify questions as needed to make sure you understood what you were responding to?

❑ Did you clarify questions with the questioner to help the other listeners hear and understand the questions?

❑ Did you respond to the question only?

❑ Did you use your responses to reemphasize your message and theme without repeating your presentation?

❑ Did you use focus and energy to show your interest in the Q&A process?

❑ As appropriate, did you encourage the listeners to talk with you and each other?

What will you do differently?

All of these questions will help you continue to improve as a presenter.

# The Least You Need to Know

After each presentation, examine what you did so that you can learn from the experience and improve your future presentations:

➤ Rethink the logistics set up so that you know the next time how to set up the room, the tables, the machinery, and the handouts to make your presentation easy to hear and understand.

➤ Rethink how to use the Message-based[SM] structure or the persuasive structure to be logical, complete, and focused.

➤ Rethink how to use focus and energy: Were you standing "centered" so that you felt confident and looked confident? Were you using eye contact to establish a dialogue with your listeners, or were you scanning? Were you using your voice well? Could you have used breathing better? Did you use your stance and breathing to manage your nervousness?

➤ Rethink how the Q&A went to be more effective at clarifying questions and managing difficult questioners.

# Glossary

**brainstorming**   Brainstorming means listing every thought that could possibly be related to the issue. No matter how silly or seemingly illogical, list the questions, challenges, risks, and costs. Don't eliminate anything from the list. Be as crazy as you can be to be sure you think of all the possibilities. Identify every potential area of impact of your idea so that you know how your brilliant idea might be squashed.

**business presentation**   A business presentation is a conversation. If the business presentation is effective, the listeners know, think, or do what you wanted them to know, think, or do. At a minimum, they have understood what you wanted and refused after giving you a fair hearing.

**context**   Context is the background of the message. It is the reason you are making a presentation. It helps the listeners understand why they are listening to you.

**critical listener**   The critical listener is the one whose needs govern the choices you make as you prepare the presentation. The critical listener is the person who will make the decision about what to do with your ideas. This person will determine whether what you want to have the listeners know, think, or do gets known, thought, or done.

**deliverable**   A deliverable is something tangible that you produce. It can be a report, a product sample, or a written procedure. A deliverable is always something that can physically be given to someone else.

**diaphragm**   The diaphragm is in your lower chest and acts like an air valve. It rises and falls to let air in and push air out.

**energy**   Energy is the sense of power a speaker communicates when she uses a full voice, not a loud voice. Energy exists when a presenter's gestures and expressions match the topic and suit the presenter. Energy is not loudness and extreme animation. Presenters who use their voices well tend to have energy whether they are "stand still" presenters or "moving" presenters.

**5Ws**   The 5Ws are Who, What, When, Where, and Why. Journalists usually provide this information in the first paragraph of a news story.

**flipchart**   A flipchart is an easel that holds a pad of newsprint. It's easy to write ideas on a flipchart and then "flip" the paper over the top of the easel and start on a new page. The flipchart pages are often gathered after a meeting and someone types the information on them.

**focus**   Focus exists when a presenter centers his body and uses focused, direct, conversational eye contact. Focus is eye contact, and it's easiest to establish effective eye contact when you are not walking around the presentation space.

**framing**   A "frame" is a perspective or a viewpoint. It's the spin or slant you put on a fact or issue. For example, business professionals tend to frame situations as opportunities, not as problems. Framing an issue appropriately is difficult, particularly with a sensitive issue. Many business challenges have to be resolved in ways that don't damage someone's reputation. Sometimes those challenges have to be resolved in ways that don't prevent someone else from achieving their goals. An effective presenter spends time understanding what frame to give the messages and facts she intends to present.

**group, large**   You're speaking to a large group when the number of listeners exceeds 35. Some people consider 35 a large group; some consider 50 a large group; others consider over 100 a large group. If you get a sense that it is difficult to see each person in the audience as a separate person, that group is probably "large" for you.

**group, small**   For most people, a small group has anywhere from one to 35 listeners. Consider your audience "small" if you could easily sit down and hold a casual discussion without having to raise your voice.

**handouts**   Handouts are copies of the visual aids. Sometimes handouts include an outline of the presentation and additional information such as more detailed charts/ tables. Some speakers also provide copies of the script they work from, if there is one.

**heckler**   A heckler is someone in the audience who interrupts, harasses, and annoys you. A heckler usually has a specific concern he wants to make, and he makes that point in ways that interrupt the flow of your presentation, prevent other listeners from asking questions, and intimidate you.

**hidden agenda**   A hidden agenda is a purpose someone has that he doesn't let anyone know about. Hidden agendas are dangerous for presenters because people who have them tend to argue about points that don't seem significant; they often seem irrelevant. But if the presenter knows about a hidden agenda, the arguments make a great deal of sense. And if the presenter knows about someone's hidden agenda, the presenter can respond more directly to answer the concern and keep the presentation on target.

**influencers**   Influencers are people the critical listener trusts. These are the people the critical listener believes have his best interests at heart. Influencers might not have the titles, although they often do, but they tend to have a good relationship with the critical listener. They're the ones he goes to lunch with, "just to chat."

**keystoning**   Keystoning is the distortion of the image from a projector onto a screen so that the top section of the image is wider than the bottom section of the image.

**lectern**   A lectern is the stand you put your notes on. Lecterns are often huge, wooden furniture with lights for the notes and buttons for controlling the visual aids machinery. Sometimes they are lightweight and portable and can easily collapse if you lean on them. Others are half-height and sit on tables.

**Message—Message-based**[SM]   A message is something you need the listeners to know, think, or do. It is not a fact. It is a move to action, or a move to make someone believe something is true. It can be a move to make an audience believe something has a certain level or type of significance.

**message title**   A message title is a brief sentence that summarizes the message the visual aid is sending. "Sales have been decreasing since 2nd quarter." "Fewer children are attending preschools in the Northeast." "Use five steps to submit claims." The message title answers the question, "What must the listeners know, think, or do about the information presented in the visual aid?"

**ownership**   Ownership is when people feel they've helped create an idea so that they partially own that idea. People who help create an idea tend to support it.

**Pareto**   Pareto, a European scholar of the 19th century, identified a pattern of significance. We use that pattern to communicate that 80% of the outcome exists from 20% of the effort. For example, 80% of the errors might be due to 20% of the employees or 80% of sales results might be due to the efforts of 20% of the sales force. The 80/20 rule suggests that we need to concentrate our efforts to achieve the maximum return. We don't have to give 100% to gain 100%. We do have to choose what we'll pay attention to and follow through.

**podium**   A podium is the wooden structure you stand on top of. Podiums can be solid or flimsy and they can permit you to stand still or they can make your every minor movement look like big motion to the listeners. Podiums help you stand above the listeners so that it is easier for a large group to see you.

**presentation, formal**   A formal presentation is often like a performance. A presenter or presenters stand in front of the listeners, and the quality of delivery is very important. The presenter must be clear and dynamic, and the presentation should be carefully structured. Q&A is often held until the end of a formal presentation.

**presentation, informal**   An informal presentation is more like a discussion than a performance. It is rarely made to large groups. Presentations made as part of a meeting are often informal.

**presentation, telling/informative**   A telling presentation is an informative presentation. You need the listeners to know something, but you don't need the listeners to respond with action.

**presentation, selling/persuasive**   A selling presentation is a persuasive presentation. You need the listeners to do something. You need the listeners to respond with action or with a change in their attitudes or beliefs.

**question and answer, or Q&A**   Q&A is the portion of the presentation, usually at the end, when listeners ask questions and the presenter must respond. It's not unusual to have Q&A throughout a presentation, though. Q&A can be difficult to manage unless a presenter welcomes the questions as an opportunity to make the presentation suit the audience.

**roadmap**   The roadmap is the sequence of topics you will explain to support the message; it is the facts, grouped by topic. Each topic will have its own message, so that each time you begin to explain a new topic, or a new fact that is part of that topic, you will explain to the listeners what they should know, think, or do about that topic or fact.

**stance**   Stance is posture, how you stand.

**success**   The success of a presentation is not measured by whether you win your point. It is measured by whether the listeners thoroughly understand your point and give it a fair hearing.

**TelePrompTer**   The TelePrompTer is a device you often see speakers using at major conferences. Usually the speaker is behind a lectern, and there are boxes holding rods with glass squares in front of and on either side of the speaker. The boxes are computers, and the image from the computer is projected onto the glass squares. The speaker can see the script on the glass squares and reads it to the audience. Because there is one square on the left and one on the right, the speaker turns her head from side to side, appearing to be giving eye contact to the audience.

**voice, full**   A full voice is the result of deep breathing. If you breathe deeply rather than shallowly, your voice gains resonance, and each sound you make has power behind it to carry to the listeners. Even if you don't have a great voice, you can use your voice fully.

# Index

## W-Z

# When You're Smart Enough to Know That You Don't Know It All

For all the ups and downs you're sure to encounter in life, The Complete Idiot's Guides give you down-to-earth answers and practical solutions.

# Lifestyle

**The Complete Idiot's Guide to Learning French on Your Own**
ISBN: 0-02-861043-1 ▪ $16.95

**The Complete Idiot's Guide to Dating**
ISBN: 0-02-861052-0 ▪ $14.95

**The Complete Idiot's Guide to Hiking and Camping**
ISBN: 0-02-861100-4 ▪ $16.95

**The Complete Idiot's Guide to Cooking Basics**
ISBN: 1-56761-523-6 ▪ $16.99

**The Complete Idiot's Guide to Learning Spanish on Your Own**
ISBN: 0-02-861040-7 ▪ $16.95

**The Complete Idiot's Guide to Gambling Like a Pro**
ISBN: 0-02-861102-0 ▪ $16.95

**The Complete Idiot's Guide to Choosing, Training, and Raising a Dog**
ISBN: 0-02-861098-9 ▪ $16.95

You can handle it!

**The Complete Idiot's Guide to Trouble-Free Car Care**
ISBN: 0-02-861041-5 ▪ $16.95

**The Complete Idiot's Guide to the Perfect Wedding**
ISBN: 1-56761-532-5 ▪ $16.99

**The Complete Idiot's Guide to Getting and Keeping Your Perfect Body**
ISBN: 0-286105122 ▪ $16.99

**The Complete Idiot's Guide to First Aid Basics**
ISBN: 0-02-861099-7 ▪ $16.95

**The Complete Idiot's Guide to the Perfect Vacation**
ISBN: 1-56761-531-7 ▪ $14.99

**The Complete Idiot's Guide to Trouble-Free Home Repair**
ISBN: 0-02-861042-3 ▪ $16.95

**The Complete Idiot's Guide to Getting into College**
ISBN: 1-56761-508-2 ▪ $14.95

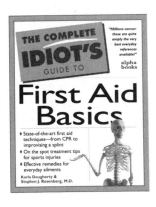